THE
ONLY
AVERAGE
GUY

JOHN FILION

THE

ONLY

AVERAGE

GUY

INSIDE THE UNCOMMON WORLD

OF ROB FORD

RANDOM HOUSE CANADA

PUBLISHED BY RANDOM HOUSE CANADA

Copyright © 2015 John Filion

www.penguinrandomhouse.ca

Random House Canada and colophon are registered trademarks.

Library and Archives Canada Cataloguing in Publication

Filion, John,
The only average guy : inside the uncommon world of Rob Ford / John Filion.

Includes index.
Issued in print and electronic formats.

ISBN 978-0-345-81599-6
eBook ISBN 978-0-345-81601-6

1. Ford, Rob, 1969–. 2. Mayors—Ontario—Toronto—Biography.
3. Toronto (Ont.)—Politics and government—21st century. I. Title.

FC3097.26.F67F55 2015   971.3'54105092   C2015-906253-5

Book design by CS Richardson

Cover image: *Fresh Eyes / Arrivals.ca* by Che Kothari, Devon Ostrom and Kate Fraser+
Commissioned by the Arts and Culture Program of the
Toronto 2015 Pan /Parapan Am Games

Printed and bound in the United States of America

10 9 8 7 6 5 4 3 2 1

Penguin
Random House
RANDOM HOUSE CANADA

To my late Aunt DeeBoo (Geraldine Gribbin)
for encouraging my interest in politics and writing
from the time I was old enough to read

CONTENTS

ROB AND ME

On the morning of my grade eight graduation, as families headed home from church for a traditional Sunday breakfast before the afternoon ceremony, I spotted Duncan O'Neill alone on a bench, a brown lunch bag at his side. Duncan had joined our class towards the end of the year, a big kid two years too old for the grade. He wasn't part of anybody's world, accepted by neither the popular kids who weren't so smart nor the smart kids who weren't so popular.

"A boy in my class is sitting over there by himself," I said to my mother.

"Ask if he wants to come to our house for breakfast," she responded right away.

Duncan was happy to join us. He said many times how much he liked the bacon and eggs, each time quickly adding that his mother sometimes made him a breakfast just like this.

I barely knew Duncan and never saw him again after that day. Why he had popped into my thoughts was a mystery until I recognized the similarity to another big kid who didn't fit in when he arrived at Toronto city council, late in 2000. This one was often loud and aggressive, but I thought I recognized in him a shy, awkward kid who seemed painfully alone.

If Rob Ford had been my grade eight classmate and my

mother had seen him sitting without a friend, she would have said, "Ask if he wants to come to our house for breakfast." Rob would have happily joined us. He would have said many times how much he liked the bacon and eggs, each time quickly adding that his mother sometimes made him a breakfast just like this.

Rob Ford didn't know my mother. But when she died, in 2007, he drove from Etobicoke to North York on a Friday night. He entered the funeral home quietly and, after paying his respects, left the same way.

—

I do not doubt reports of Rob Ford's monstrously bad behaviour. Nor would I deny that a beast lurks within, released by alcohol and drugs. My friends often ridiculed and demonized Ford at the same time, as if you couldn't heap enough scorn on a creature like him. My observation that Rob had many sides to him, and that there must be reasons for the way he was, only irritated them. They saw him as stupid and dangerous, an ignorant buffoon. They wanted him to be simply that. They were uncomfortable with my empathy for the man. Maybe they thought it eroded my belief that Rob Ford was unfit to be mayor. It didn't. I was the city councillor who thought up the motions that took away Ford's powers as mayor of Toronto—and made sure they passed a council vote—in November 2013. I took no pleasure in it— quite the opposite—but believed it had to be done.

For two months afterwards, when I passed Ford in the hall, he met my "Hey Rob" with a menacing glare. Then, during the January 2014 council meeting, I watched with apprehension as Rob slid from his seat and walked deliberately towards mine. He was holding a sheet of paper, which he thrust in front of me. Rob's expression, unreadable at first, became a half smile.

The paper was a football pool, with a spot for me to fill in my picks. He wanted me to play again. "Don't get me wrong," he said, making it clear that our football friendship wouldn't protect me from political payback. "I'm taking you out in the next election. I'm going to smoke you."

—

The football pool was a holdover from the ten years when we sat two seats apart on Toronto council, before Rob became mayor. He represented the mostly working-class area of north Etobicoke, I the more affluent North York community of Willowdale. When newly elected first-time councillors arrive at the beginning of each term, most are barely visible for the first few months. Not so with Rob Ford. He invited immediate comparisons to the late comedian Chris Farley, whose earnest buffoonery produced one misadventure after another. When Ford exploded from his seat to denounce his spendthrift colleagues, I had a front-row view. Proximity to Ford so rattled one councillor that he changed seats. I was always more curious than anything else. What was beneath all that anger?

Between outbursts, Rob sat silently, seemingly detached from everything and everyone around him. "We need to find a way to relate to this guy," Councillor Joe Mihevc suggested one day. My seatmate since 1999, Joe was the sort who fostered relationships with nearby councillors. The big guy to our left was hard to reach. But we'd noticed Rob's obsession with football, and so we started a pool and invited him to join us. Rob never realized that Joe and I knew nothing about the game because, against all odds, our random picks consistently beat his more informed choices.

When he paid us our winnings, we'd tell him we were donating his money to left-wing causes. He loved that kind of boyish pushing and shoving, and gave the same back the few times he won. One year, he clobbered us in the Super Bowl pool and never let us forget it. He would happily endure weeks of losses for a single day of victory.

Apart from council meetings and a few lunches, Rob and I spent little time together. But I was his football pool buddy, which was not a small thing in his life, I came to realize. After he was elected mayor in 2010, and council divided itself into hostile factions, our football bets ended. Bumping into him at a function more than a year into his mayoralty, I bemoaned the loss of disposable income from my winnings.

The day after, my executive assistant told me, "The mayor's office is calling, he wants your football picks." Another staff member stopped me: "The mayor's staff is e-mailing. They need your picks." Taking a washroom break, I encountered a senior Ford staffer at the next urinal. "Councillor," he said, "would you *please* get in your football picks. The mayor is making us crazy."

Late in 2013, after I'd initiated the removal of his powers, the Ford brothers were watching football in the "mancave" at Deco, the family label business, when Doug needled Rob for not retaliating against me. "I kicked him out of the football pool," Rob replied, as if that made us even. After he invited me back the following January, the bets were accompanied by an unusual amount of bravado, mostly about what he was going to do to me in the next municipal election. "I'm giving you a heads-up. You fucked with me, now I'm coming after you. I've got a guy who's going to take you out." It was as if I had embarrassed him in front of the other kids and he needed to show them he could get right up and push *me* down.

In the fifteen years I've known Rob Ford, most of our conversations have started with football or hockey and branched out from there. The topics were limited and discussions tended to be short and to the point. But they showed a man struggling to do the best he could. During Sunday morning calls to sort out the pool picks, we'd talk about the challenges of fatherhood, or his plans to become mayor. Later, as he suffered through addiction, his mood could swing wildly. When I made the mistake of once joking that I could have tricked him by altering the point spread for that week's games, his face turned red and he became cold and menacing.

"You fuck with me, bro, you won't do it twice. I'll be knocking on your door."

Then, when I least expected it, he'd show warmth. As we waited for the elevator one day, I told him I was insulted he hadn't included me in the Top 10 list of councillors he wanted defeated in the October 2014 election. "That's because I've already got my best guy against you," he said. As Rob wound himself up, his brother came along, not realizing I was the instigator.

"Okay, Rob," Doug Ford admonished, in a rare moment of playing the peacemaker.

"Buddy, I'm taking you out like a cheap date," Rob continued to rant at me.

"Rob, okay, okaaay!" Doug tried again.

Something in the exchange triggered a different Rob. He suddenly grew concerned that I'd be unemployed if his candidate defeated me. "You don't need to worry," Rob said reassuringly. "You won't have trouble finding a job. You're a smart guy, an educated guy. You'll be on the radio or write a book or something."

—

Rob Ford showed the world many faces, all real but none really him. He is a jumble of contradictions: attention seeker and shy loner; bully and kind-hearted friend; a savvy politician who can't comprehend much of what happens around him; the self-proclaimed "best mayor this city has ever had" and the guy with such low self-esteem that he'll stare at the floor to avoid eye contact.

But the Rob Ford I know best is none of these. At some point, the ten-year-old inside him made friends with my ten-year-old self. We were the sort of friends who didn't visit one another after school but looked for each other at recess.

"He has a special relationship with you," his brother Doug told me several times. "I don't fucking understand it."

Neither did I. Not until it struck me how few people tried to connect with the person beneath the protective layers.

"I think Rob doesn't have any friends, and you're probably one of the closest friends he has," Nick Kouvalis, his former campaign manager and chief of staff, told me. "You can talk football, with a little side wager. You can have lunch with him maybe. He doesn't have anyone like that. He has people who will do things with him—but they want something from him. They want his money. They want his connections. They *want something* from him."

On his forty-fifth birthday, Rob was in rehab, so I made him a collection of music from the year he was born. The song list began with "Gimme Shelter" and ended optimistically with "Here Comes the Sun." When Rob phoned to say thanks, he spoke so warmly it took me a few seconds to recognize who it was.

Several times, I tried to persuade Rob to let *that* Rob Ford speak with me for this book. He apologetically offered multiple reasons for saying no. His political supporters who "hated" me wouldn't like it; he had to wait till after the election; since big US networks and screenwriters wanted his story, there was no way he could give it to *me*. And the biggest reason: "Dougie says not to."

—

Rob Ford appears simple but is easily the most complicated person I've ever known. Every time I thought I had him mostly figured out, he'd surprise me again. Then I began seeing the patterns within the contradictions, the predictable amid the inexplicable. I wondered about the childhood that produced such a troubled adult. As my football buddy became international news, I was astounded at the lack of effort spent explaining Rob Ford's behaviour rather than merely chronicling it. Since abandoning journalism for politics more than thirty years ago, I hadn't written much of anything. But I decided that Rob Ford's story needed to be told, and it didn't look as though anybody else was going to tell it.

In August 2014, on the final day of his last council meeting as mayor, I went over to Rob to talk football and elections, trying to stay within his comfort zone. But he was in the mood for real conversation.

Documents had been released a day earlier depicting him as a sometimes drunken football coach who mistreated his players. That contradicted how Rob saw himself: a caring coach who expressed it by teaching his players how to win, tolerating neither weakness nor failure.

"It hurt me deeply," he said of the published reports, touching his chest, more sad than angry. "I was bawling to my brother." He seemed barely interested in a new poll showing he had moved back into second place in the mayor's race, a near-impossible feat for any politician with even half his misdeeds.

I asked him what quality in him explained his continued popularity among at least a third of the population. "I think it's because they see you as an average guy," I suggested, wanting his reaction to a term he had often used to describe himself.

"You *think*," he said sternly, like a teacher knowing I could do better. "*You don't think*."

Uncharacteristically, Rob looked me straight in the eye. "An average guy," he repeated. "There is no such thing as an average guy."

1. THE FAMILY PROBLEM

"He's got a problem. He's got a weight problem."
Diane Ford, speaking about her son Rob

The mayor of Canada's largest city was in his office, already wishing he was somebody else, when his chief of staff burst into the room bearing more bad news. "Your mother and sister are on CP24."

Rob Ford grabbed the TV remote control from his desk and flipped on a large wall-mounted screen. The looming presence of his mother filled the room. His mood, already dark, worsened instantly.

"Crap!" Ford shouted.

Diane Ford sat rigid and sideways on her cream-coloured living room couch, the well-presented matriarch of a family with a well-scripted story of political ambition built on selfless and relentless service to the common man. Beside her was Rob's sister, Kathy. One look at her revealed that Rob wasn't the only wounded member of this family.

"I love him to death," Kathy began. "I will support him to his dying day. As my dad always said: 'United we stand, divided we fall.' And we have lived by that as a family."

"Put your teeth in!" her brother shouted at the screen on the wall. "Why aren't your teeth in?"

Without so much as a heads-up to the mayor, Diane and Kathy had invited a local television station into the family home for a live interview. All about Robbie.

"Robbie is not a drug addict," Kathy continued. "I know because I am a former addict—or an addict, if you would want to say. And as an alcoholic—if you want to consider binge drinking once every three months and you get totally plastered—which he just makes himself, makes a *fool* out of himself—and I've even asked him to leave my apartment one time I saw him—fine!"

"That's it! That's enough!" Ford yelled at the screen. "Get them off!"

"All the good that he has done—that's all been overlooked," lamented Diane. "And it's so *hurtful* to the family and *so hurtful* to me as a mother. People want to say that . . . he's ignoring his job at city hall. He isn't! Every single weekend he's at *every* parade. I'd say, 'When are you coming for dinner?' 'Oh, I can't. I can't, Mom.' He's *so busy!*"

Across from Diane, perched on a hard-backed chair, was Stephen LeDrew, chosen for this interview because he was "fair," Kathy told him. Sporting a speckled burgundy bow tie that matched his glasses, LeDrew was the picture of ingratiating inquisitiveness. Smiling. Prompting. Enabling.

It is November 7, 2013. It's been one week since Toronto police announced they'd recovered a video of Rob Ford smoking crack cocaine, six days since the family decided to stand by its story that Rob had no serious drug problem, and two days after Ford's surprise admission that he had indeed smoked crack cocaine, "probably in one of my drunken stupors." A few hours before the interview, a video had emerged of Rob Ford in a drunken rage, behaving like a lethal eight-year-old, punching the air, vowing to kill someone in a ring, stripped to his underwear. Half a year later, another video would surface of the mayor smoking crack, this time with Kathy, in her basement.

LeDrew fed the mayor's mother and sister questions with built-in answers: "Let me ask you the question that a lot of people have been asking. You said that he's not a drug addict."

"No," responded Kathy. "Absolutely not. He couldn't function if he was. He couldn't have accomplished the things he has." She turned again to why her youngest brother wasn't an alcoholic either. "And Robbie doesn't drink *one*. When Robbie drinks, I think he just goes full tilt."

"That's stupid! What did you say that for?" Ford yelled at them.

LeDrew turned to Mom. "You told me on the telephone this afternoon that that's not part of your family culture."

"No. Absolutely not!" Kathy interjected.

"They weren't raised that way at all," said Diane.

But talk of their upbringing sent Kathy heading down some dimly lit corridor. "No, and [Rob] being the youngest and watching all the rest of us grow up and, you know, I'm not saying we were bad or anything, but I'm just saying . . ."

Diane gave Kathy a look that slammed the door shut.

"Okay Mom," Kathy said.

"Idiots!" screamed Rob Ford. "They're sinking me! Get her off!"

LeDrew asked about the family meeting the previous Friday, in this same room where these Fords had gathered for decades to brush aside anything obstructing their path. External threats were the easiest to deal with. Boom! But this was a family whose members stared daily into the face of trouble, just by looking across the dinner table. The two eldest of the four children, Kathy and Randy, were inveterate hellraisers. The middle son, Doug, was gifted but explosive. The youngest, Robbie, appeared undistinguished on all fronts until it was discovered, later in life, that he possessed an inexplicable messianic gift. From out of nowhere, he roused the rabble and paraded them behind the family flag all the way to the mayor's office. A glimmer of self-awareness could have told the Fords where this victory was bound to lead. But even now, as her son's condition became more desperate, Diane Ford wasn't conceding anything.

"He talked, we listened," she told LeDrew. "I talked, they listened. And we *all* had our say. And it was a real outpouring of feelings. There was nothing put on. There were no lies. It was just how we felt about each other, what our expectations—what *my* expectations—are for the family. And you know, we all walked away with a very good feeling. We walked away with a very good understanding of what we—what *I*—expect of Rob."

Ford shifted to an office couch, unable to do anything but watch and listen as his mother directed the conversation about him.

"She never stops!" he shouted about her. "Where are your teeth?" he yelled at his sister. "Why don't they just shut up?" he screamed at anyone who would listen.

Mom was still talking.

"I did say, 'Rob, you've got to maybe smarten up a little bit, get back on line. I know you can do it. I know you *are* doing it. But now you *have to*, you do have to.'" She paused ever so slightly before finishing the thought. "He does have a problem."

Kathy seemed puzzled. "Mom," she interrupted, "you wouldn't have said 'a little bit.'"

LeDrew laughed. Diane too, but in a way that signalled she was not amused.

"Kathy, it's my turn," she reprimanded her eldest child, fifty-three years old at the time of the interview. Mom smiled, Kathy shrank.

"It's your turn absolutely. You've got the floor!" LeDrew extended a welcoming arm towards Diane. "So you said he has a problem."

Across the city, people awaited a mother's desperate plea to her youngest son to head to rehab. It didn't come.

"He's got a problem," Diane began again. "He's got a weight problem."

"Yeah," agreed LeDrew.

"He's got a huge weight problem. And he knows that. And I think that is the *first* thing you have to attack."

"That's enough! Get off!" Rob Ford yelled at the television. "It's over! Get off!"

"He said, 'I definitely want to change,'" his mother continued. "And by changing, you have to change your whole demeanour and everything else will fall into place, because you *aren't* all of the things you're being accused of. And so I said: 'Okay, here's what you do. . . . Five steps: Get yourself a driver. Then, after that, you do something about your weight. And thirdly . . .' What was the other thing I told him?"

"About the car . . ." Kathy tried.

"You mean the alcohol detector?" suggested LeDrew.

"Yeah, an alcohol detector in the car, and that will prove you can't drive your car if you're drinking," Diane confirmed. "And, um—one, two, three, four, five."

"Come on, Steve," urged Kathy. Neither she nor Diane remembered the rest of the family's five-point plan for Rob, and Kathy hoped LeDrew could recall it from the run-through they'd had earlier that afternoon.

"There's the drinking and the weight," the interviewer tried. "And, um, there was something about the company he's keeping."

"Oh, absolutely, absolutely," Diane said. "And just, like, carry on. He said, 'Mom, I've already got the plan.'" Just in time, Diane remembered step five. "Oh, and yes, see a counsellor. Do get help."

"For what?" asked Kathy.

"For anything," said Diane.

"Just, just for that release," Kathy supposed.

"He could go to a psychologist," Diane said. "Just go, just get help. And they will help you through any—any problem that you've got."

"Idiots," shouted Ford. "Shut up. Get off!"

"There's nothing wrong with him seeking help from a counsellor for whatever he needs," LeDrew offered.

"No. No. He will stay here," Diane said, "because knowing Rob, if Rob goes away, and he's not, you know, so bad that he stumbles . . ."

"What's he going away for?" Kathy asked, prompting another silent reprimand from Diane, followed by another "Sorry, Mom."

"People don't understand," continued Diane. "'Take a break, take a break. Oh, you've got to step down. Oh, you've got to get help. Oh, you've got to do this, you've got to do that.' That's not Rob. If he was really, really in dire straits, [if] he needed help, I would be the first one. I would be putting him in my car and taking him."

"It's over! Get off!" Rob Ford yelled at the screen.

"I feel like I have to defend him," Kathy said.

"He's, he's been *attacked*," said Diane.

"Well, yeah," said LeDrew. "But as a sister and a mom, you're defending him. And that's one of the reasons we wanted to chat with you . . . to understand the kind of family that he has."

Kathy ended with a plea: "Let's keep city hall going and let him do what he's good at doing, and that's running the city."

"Not away in some rehab," Diane said.

When the interview ended, Rob Ford summoned his senior staff. They listened while he tried to calm himself with a rant, while they pretended not to be disturbed by this demolition derby of a family.

—

For those who tried to make sense of the Fords, the interview was a revelation. Clearly, Rob wasn't the first Ford to confront an inconvenient truth with a flurry of denials, declared with complete certainty.

I began asking myself the same questions about Diane that I'd wondered about Rob and Doug. Did she actually believe everything she said? Did she really not know her son had a life-threatening problem with drugs and alcohol? Did she believe the denial before it passed her lips, or only the instant afterwards? I thought about everything I knew about Doug Ford Sr., and whether he and his wife were drawn together by their kindred brains, so their combined DNA could create big blond children who thought just like them.

The Ford family's self-appointed spokesman, the middle brother, Doug, learned about the interview just as LeDrew was about to go live. Unable to stop it, he'd watched too.

"I was pissed," he told me later. "I like Stephen LeDrew, [but] you can't trust anyone in the media. That was a low blow. Leave my family alone!"

"Let's get Doug over," LeDrew had suggested to Kathy earlier in the day, but she had nixed that idea. "Oh, God no. Doug needs time to chill out and just cool down. Because *he's hot!*"

I'd been told by a family friend that Doug was so disturbed by Kathy's own drug use that they hadn't spoken in years. Had he been there, Doug would certainly have bumped her off the show. "I have zero tolerance for heavy drugs," he told me in a later interview. "I'm not talking pot, I'm talking heavy drugs. I have zero tolerance. Pills, uppers, downers, all-arounders, all that crap: zero tolerance. I despise it!"

There was real anger in his voice.

"I despise the abuse of alcohol," he continued. "Alcohol in moderation is fine. But alcohol is one of the worst drugs, in my opinion, one of the worst in society. There's a lot of heavier, harder drugs that are bad, but it's widespread alcohol that has created more problems in families, in divorces, in fighting, in stupidity, in everything. Makes you go crazy if you abuse it."

By all accounts, Doug Ford hasn't touched anything stronger than a Diet Coke for many years. But he had seen the explosive rage that too much booze provoked in some families.

By the time LeDrew's interview with Kathy and Diane had ended, Doug was seething. "My sister shouldn't have been out there," he told me. "She's had issues in her life. My mom, for an eighty-year-old, she held her own. She's a mom. Like any of us, you'd stick up for your kids. 'Cause you always see the *good* in your kids, you don't see anything else. And a lot of parents— some, not all—are naive. They just see what their kids do in a good light. There are certain things, even when you're younger, you never tell your parents."

—

Watching live from his home in Windsor, Ontario, Nick Kouvalis was also thinking about Diane Ford and the meeting she'd presided over in that same room in the family home in November 2012—almost exactly a year earlier. As the architect of Rob Ford's 2010 victory and the guiding hand during his first few months as mayor, Kouvalis had stayed in touch with the Fords after he left the mayor's office, and he still had pull with the family. Through his many contacts, Kouvalis had heard that Rob was slipping into a life of serious drug abuse and drinking. Thinking there was a chance to stop the self-destructive slide, Kouvalis contacted Diane Ford and asked for a meeting so he could tell the family what he'd heard.

It was already a bleak day for the family. The day before, November 26, 2012, a judge had found the mayor guilty of conflict of interest and ordered him removed from office. Ford would eventually win an appeal of the decision, but in the meantime there was talk of a by-election, and there was rampant speculation that Doug might run in Rob's place. Kouvalis had asked for the meeting before the decision came down and, uncharacteristically, he wasn't interested in talking politics.

Diane and Nick sat opposite one another in large, comfortable chairs in the formal living room on the main floor. Diane's spot immediately became the head of the table, and brothers Randy and Doug sat on either side of her. Rob was edgy and pacing around the house, popping into the living room but refusing to take a seat.

"This is stupid. I don't know what we're here for," Rob told them all. "I don't have to do this."

Randy and Doug both told him to sit down. He wouldn't. He already wanted to leave.

Diane invited Nick to begin.

"Diane, I wanted to come here today to tell you what I'm hearing, and my concern for Rob," said Kouvalis (who gave me a detailed account of the meeting in a lengthy interview). Kouvalis told the family that he'd heard from many reliable sources that Rob was taking hard drugs, that he was drinking heavily and driving drunk, and that he was hanging out with low-lifes connected to dangerous gangs. He wasn't just an embarrassment to the family; he was becoming a danger to himself. "I'm telling you I've heard these things from so many people. It's got to stop! You need to fix this! This man is going to die if it continues this way."

When Kouvalis had finished, the room went silent for a moment. Then Diane issued a sigh, long and hard, followed by her pronouncement: "I don't believe it."

Kouvalis turned to Doug. "Doug, tell her. Tell her what you know."

And Doug confirmed that he'd heard the same stories about his little brother, also from credible sources.

"Oh, stop," Kouvalis remembers Diane telling her son. "All you care about is being the mayor yourself. This is all about you guys plotting against Robbie."

Doug laughed uncomfortably and shook his head.

Kouvalis turned again to Doug, urging him to behave like a caring brother and force Rob into rehab by publicly calling him out. "All you need to do is say, 'My brother has addiction problems and we're doing our best to get him the help he needs.'"

Doug responded by saying, "I can't do that. I love my brother. I'm loyal to him," Kouvalis told me. "I think he wanted to," he said , "but he just didn't see how he could, without it embarrassing the family and himself." And defying his mother.

"No," Diane declared. "Absolutely not. Robbie's not a drug addict."

Kouvalis, not one to give up easily, tried a different appeal. "I'm worried about your business. Your clients won't stick around if it comes out that he's doing drugs and hanging out with gangbangers."

Now the Fords were getting angry, said Kouvalis. At him.

He aimed his last shot directly at the family's decision maker. What would Diane's friends think about *her*, he wondered aloud, if all of the sordid details about her son's life became public?

Diane Ford got up, walked over to Kouvalis, and made it clear she wanted him to leave. "Don't come back," she told him. "I don't want to hear from you again."

"My goal was to try to get the family to do an intervention, and I failed," Kouvalis told me later. "I was worried about him killing someone drinking and driving. Or getting killed in a fight where somebody pulls a knife or a gun on him."

The family's inability to acknowledge a failing or to change direction would cost them dearly. For a year and a half after this meeting, the Fords continued their denials, until two new recordings made it impossible to continue on that course. By then, Rob Ford's mayoralty was all but lost, the Ford brand irreparably damaged.

2. TRAILBLAZERS

"We were there just blazing a new trail."
—Doug Ford Jr. on the family's move to Etobicoke in the 1950s

During his darkest, drunkest moments, when everything was bleary and blurry, the spotlight he craved became a bare interrogation bulb he turned on himself. Rob Ford spoke in soliloquy, a tragic hero without Shakespearean eloquence.

About you, Dad.

Just raw emotion, not easy to make out, delivered in rants and screams. Rob seemed not to notice if anyone else was in the room. These moments happened in his office at city hall, at nightclubs and bars, in a late night call from his father's grave. The cemetery was around the corner from the family home, where his mother and oldest brother still lived, close to his sister Kathy's house, near Doug's too, and not far from the discomforts of his own home. From this deeply sad place, Rob reached out to people he knew would take his call: his office staff.

Some felt as if they were eavesdropping on Rob's sad speeches; others strained to hear more. They listened for clues to what drove him into a job he seemed to hate. The rants confirmed what they already suspected: Rob ran for mayor because

he thought that's what his dad wanted from him, that if he suc-
ceeded, he would finally earn his father's respect and approval.
And still he couldn't feel it.

At these times, Rob spoke in aching fragments and disjointed
sentences. "I wanted it for you, Dad." "I miss you." "Nobody
respects me."

—

"My dad," Doug Ford told several councillors one day during a
slow part of a council meeting, "he was as rough as they got."

Douglas Bruce Ford was born February 27, 1933, at the
height of the Great Depression. Even among the poor and struggling, he was disadvantaged. His father, Ernest Ford, had come
to Canada from England in 1902, at age eleven. Alone. After his
mother had died, his relatives had sent him to "an institution
known for taking in children who were either truants, disorderly
or orphans, for the purpose of being sent to Canada," according
to Ancestry.ca. The genealogy website says Ernest was shipped
in steerage class, with thirty-two other children. Ernest later
claimed to have been born in Canada.

Douglas Bruce, the youngest of nine Ford siblings, was only
three months old when Ernest died. A new generation of Fords
would need to fend for themselves.

"Through the Depression, they'd live on top of stores in the
east end and his mother had to make ends meet," Doug Jr. told
me. "And in the middle of the night they'd move to another place
'cause they couldn't afford rent." Doug figured that, during his
father's childhood, the large, strong-willed woman the grandkids
called "Big Nana" was forced to move her family a dozen times.

Hard work started at an early age. Doug Ford Sr. delivered
newspapers, not for pocket money like other kids but to help
support his mother. While still an adolescent, he began working
his way through a variety of jobs before finding his niche as a

salesman. "Every job I went into, I was always the Salesman of the Month," he told John Parker years later. The two served together as members of the Ontario legislature for four years. "You know why, John?" Parker stopped the story he was telling me to imitate Doug, rapping his knuckles on the table. "Because I had to be!"

"He didn't have anything," Doug Jr. said. "He had a grade eight education. He made it from scratch. And he had a rough time growing up. He'd say, 'You guys don't have a *clue* how it is to not have money. You don't have *a clue how it is* to work when you're twelve years old in the bowling alley to give your mom a couple of cents.'

"He always said he was an east-ender," Doug Jr. said of his father. "My mother was from the west end, and he used to call her a west-end elite—and my mom *is* a little bit of an elitist."

—

It was a hot summer's day at Sunnyside pool when Diane Campbell and Doug Ford spotted each other for the first time. Doug Ford told me the story in his office one day. As with most of his sit-down interviews, Doug started this one off cautiously, warning me that he had only a few minutes and then using up most of that with political messaging. But once he got going, Doug enjoyed the storytelling and would keep on going, even when his staff reminded him he needed to be somewhere else.

"He was a lifeguard, a big strapping blond-haired guy." She was blond too, and statuesque. They were both the type who knew what they wanted and how to get it.

"On their first date my dad said, 'Do you want a lift home?' They walked outside and all these fancy cars were there. My mom was excited. She said, 'Where are you parked?' And he said, 'Over there.' She walked over and in between the two cars there was a Triumph motorcycle. He said, 'Hop on.'

"'My father won't let me get on a motorcycle,' she said. 'Don't worry about it, hop on,' he replied.

"Well, back in those days they had the dirt roads and they used to oil the dirt roads to keep the dust down," Doug Jr. continued. "Well, you know where this is going. They wiped out. They went one way and the bike went the other and my mom told me, 'Dad jumped up, didn't even look over at me, and ran over to his bike.'" Doug Jr. laughed.

Diane Campbell's parents, who lived in an upper middle-class neighbourhood near Wilson and Bathurst, were decidedly unimpressed with this motorcycle-riding dropout from the wrong part of town.

"You shouldn't be going out with him. He's not from an established family," her father objected, never imagining that, fifteen years later, he would be working for Doug's company.

"I'm going out with him whether you like it or not," Diane told her parents.

That made Doug Sr. more determined than ever to make himself into someone others would look up to and admire.

—

Diane Campbell married Doug Ford on September 1, 1956.

They moved into a two-storey apartment building at 404 Wilson Avenue, just west of Bathurst Street, near where Diane grew up, in what was then the township of North York. Another young couple, Ted and Pat Herriott, lived next door. Their one-bedroom apartments were the type young marrieds lived in comfortably, for a time, while the men worked for promotions and the women waited to start a family.

"They were happily married kids," Ted told me, sitting in the kitchen of his home in a small town north of Toronto. He recalled that Doug didn't say much, unless the topic was politics, business, or football. Diane, the eldest of three sisters, was "a typical young lady, full of vim and vigour." Pat Herriott remembered her as sociable and pleasant. "She was always happy and laughing. I can't remember ever seeing her in a bad mood."

Ted said that Diane "idolized" her father, Clare Campbell—and that her husband and her father were a lot alike. Each was hard-working, old-fashioned, firm, opinionated, and strongly of the belief that there was one correct way to view everything: his way.

Ted, who would work with Campbell for a few years, recalled that his "human relationship skills were nil. He just couldn't communicate very well with people." After reaching a conclusion, Campbell expected others to adopt it without question. "Clare had more thought process than Doug, though. His [opinions] were based on logic. Doug's were just based on gut feel. And once he'd get his mind made up on something, he'd go through a brick wall for it."

Diane was a natural charmer, with social skills that complemented a strong will. But at a time when the women traded recipes while the men talked politics, she deferred to her husband. "He was a large, well-built man," Ted recalled. "Strong, a good worker, got things done, and she could count on him to look after her."

Back then, Diane worked as a secretary and bookkeeper at Jus' Squeezed, an orange juice company that became known for introducing lemon and lime juice in plastic squeeze containers. Pat Herriott was secretary to the general manager at Dominion Textiles. Like many fifties wives, Diane and Pat saw their jobs as temporary, not as the way they would mark their place in the world. That would be based on their success as homemakers.

"Doug was the head of the household," observed Ted Herriott. "Diane ran the house for him. She was the general manager of the house, you might call it."

—

Ted and Doug quickly realized how much they had in common. They took one another to see the poorer parts of town where each had grown up, swapping stories of family struggles during the Depression. "We respected each other for where we came from," Ted told me. "That's where you learn your grit."

Both were in sales with the Canadian branches of American companies: Doug with Swift Meats, Ted with Avery Labels. Not long after the Fords moved in next door, Ted's company was looking for a new salesman. Impressed that Doug was always up and off to work before anyone else, Ted recommended him for the job at Avery.

Doug displayed a remarkable sales tenacity, promising the moon if that's what it took to land new business. He was unconventional by most people's standards. "We had a pressman working for us, Rollie Pearson," Ted recalled. "Once every week or two Doug would say to him, 'Want to have a little rumble?' Those two guys would go out in the back and they'd get each other in holds and really use their strength. It would last a good half-hour, and then it would be over and they'd go for a drink. That was their way of showing camaraderie."

Doug, who played football for several years with the East York Argos, a farm team of the Toronto Argonauts, was less playful with opposing team members who heckled him from the sidelines. Doug would challenge them to come on over. "I just waited for one of them to run over, huffing and puffing," Doug told Ted. "I'd give him a couple of shots, and that would be the end of it."

"Did anyone tell you about the gambling?" Ted asked me. "He was always looking for a good craps game." Doug once boasted to Ted that he knew the odds better than the other players, and based on the wads of money he'd display the next morning, Ted figured it was true. "But he'd always take some of it to his mother. He was always very good to his mother. He looked after her."

—

Herriott remembered the 1950s as a time when you needed neither status nor an education to make something of yourself. "If you organized yourself properly and had goals, you'd go out and make them come to life. Doug and I had that same ambition."

For breadwinners of that era, the first measure of success was earning enough to buy a house. In 1957, after the birth of their first son, Ted and Pat packed up for Rexdale, a section of northern Etobicoke where, more than a half century later, the youngest of Doug and Diane's as yet unborn sons would become a tragic figure. The Fords followed the Herriotts west, buying a grey bungalow on the southwest corner of the West Way and Fulford Place.

The men worked together and the couples remained close, taking dancing lessons on Friday nights or going out for dinner at La Chaumière, the city's first French restaurant. Doug and Ted would have a few beers. Diane and Pat liked to share a bottle of Black Tower white wine. When it came to music, they all preferred the big band sound to the new rock 'n' roll.

Doug Ford "enjoyed a good hat," Ted remembered. The two friends shopped together for Sammy Taft fedoras. When hats went out of style, Doug kept wearing his, a fashion statement his eldest son, Randy, would adopt.

Did Pat and Diane speak about the future?

"That didn't seem to be a subject people talked about back in the fifties," Pat answered. "I think all we'd be talking about was what you're doing in the kitchen, or what the kids are doing." While she and Diane were in the kitchen, the men sat in the living room and talked about starting their own company. "We were both *hungry*," said Ted. "We wanted to be *successes*. It was a time of opportunity, but you needed to know how to seize it."

Towards the end of 1961, Herriott turned down an offer to head up Avery's California operation. He decided it was time to strike out on his own, and he invited Doug to join him as a

partner. First they needed a name. Together they came up with Deco, good branding for a label company and a way of incorporating the initials of both of their first names—Douglas and Edwin—with "co" for *company*.

—

Deco Adhesive Products Limited was registered on February 23, 1962. The Herriotts and the Fords set up shop in a small office at 3077 Bathurst Street, near Lawrence Avenue, a few miles south of the apartment building where they'd first lived. In 1964 they opened a small printing plant, just in time to produce Beatles buttons for the band's two sold-out Labour Day concerts at Maple Leaf Gardens. Pat and Diane both helped with the new company, balancing that effort with the duties of motherhood. Doug handled most of the sales, wooing clients from competitors, while Ted concentrated mostly on office organization. Both men worked long hours and tackled whatever needed doing.

By 1965, just as the hard work started to pay off, the partners disagreed over how best to grow the business. Herriott wanted to stick with adhesive products; Ford insisted they branch out into labels and tags. Talking it out didn't work, nor did a visit to the company lawyer, Alan Eagleson, later of National Hockey League Players' Association fame and infamy. At the end of that meeting, each partner got his own lawyer.

Their 1962 agreement had a shotgun clause. To dissolve the partnership, both men would make simultaneous offers for the company and the higher bidder would buy out the other partner. Both wanted the business, but Doug made the higher bid: $35,000 to Ted's $30,000. It was enough money for the Herriotts to buy a new house and for Ted to start a successful advertising business. Deco now belonged to Doug Ford alone.

The two families didn't stay in touch. As time passed, the Herriotts heard stories that the Fords claimed to have started the company by themselves, out of the family basement in Etobicoke. At first, Ted and Pat laughed it off. Then, as the story was retold over many years, it started to bother them.

Almost fifty years after his relationship with the Ford family ended, Ted still struggled to understand why he and his wife were written out of the Ford story. Why would his old friend Doug Ford, whose business success nobody doubted, conceal Ted's key role in the creation of Deco? And why would his wife and children perpetuate the myth that he was the sole proprietor?

"People don't know what we went through to get that business going," Ted told me. "We used to go on some pretty long trips together, where we would drive all night and sleep in the car. We accomplished a lot together. When Dougie and I were close, we didn't need a big song and dance about who we were in order to impress one another. Had I been in their shoes—the boys' shoes, the mother's shoes—when [Deco] had their fiftieth anniversary, I would have invited all my clients out to meet the guy who started the business with my father. They chose to do something else."

"Yeah, they got the road paved," Pat said. She was referring to the Ford brothers' pressure on city bureaucrats to repair the road in front of the Deco office at 28 Greensboro Drive, so that visitors to their 2012 anniversary celebration would be met with a smooth surface.

Pat tuned in to Diane Ford's interview with Stephen LeDrew, mostly out of curiosity, to see how Diane's looks had held up. "She was a striking woman, and I thought, 'She doesn't photograph well.'" Seeing Kathy reminded her of the times she and Diane had spent together as the young mothers of small children: Pat with two sons, Diane with Kathy and Randy. Pat didn't remember ever seeing Diane discipline her rambunctious children when they misbehaved while playing with her kids. "Diane would laugh at everything they did. They'd get into some kind of scraps and I never saw them get a little slap on the behind. It was just,

'Oh, don't do that.' Giggle, giggle, giggle. If I noticed that with the first two—we never laid eyes on Doug and Rob—that must have been how the family grew up. They had no discipline."

I asked Ted if he attended Doug Ford's funeral in 2006. "No," he said. "I was torn that day. I remember this vividly. I wanted to go, but then I thought I didn't want it to be interpreted in the wrong light. I didn't want to go through something awkward. I just felt uneasy."

—

In Etobicoke, Doug and Diane Ford began building a family and constructing an identity. Their first child, Kathryn Diane Ford, was born in July 1960. Randall Douglas arrived in 1962, and Douglas Bruce on November 20, 1964. Doug Jr. remembers their first Etobicoke home being so far removed from the city that he went on pony rides at a nearby farm. "So we were there just blazing a new trail," he told me.

In 1970, a year after Rob was born, Deco's success allowed his father to buy 15 Weston Wood Road, then a one-acre apple orchard at the end of a cul-de-sac running off Royal York Road. Soon construction began on a custom home. "I distinctly remember moving in," Doug Jr. said, "and having no furniture during the transition. Myself, my older brother Randy, and my dad, we slept on a mattress in an empty room. I remember the room. It was exciting. I was seven. It was January 1972."

From the outside, the sprawling bungalow fit right into the upscale suburban neighbourhood. Inside, a spiral staircase led down to a spacious family room that opened onto an enormous yard with a swimming pool. The backyard seemed removed from everything around it, the perfect spot for private gatherings of every size and description—business socials, fundraising events, graduation parties, political gatherings. By the 1980s, if you wanted to be seen with somebody important in Etobicoke—or to become someone important yourself—you coveted an invitation to the Fords' backyard.

"My mother would always be the one that'd do the entertaining," Doug told me. "My dad would always be the shy one. But when it got started, he'd be holding court with everyone and be the life of the party. Our house was always the open house. My parents always invited everyone in. Everyone stayed there. Anyone. They always helped people out. Always." According to Doug, there is no home in Canada that has hosted more events or more people.

Doug Sr. eventually became a Rotarian and served on the boards of local institutions and charities. The trappings of success even included a yacht. But he never entirely lost that feeling of being on the outside looking in. With disdain.

"There are certain yacht clubs where they walk around with their nose in the air and their pinkie in the air, drinking the champagne," Doug said. "He couldn't stand those guys. 'They're phony as a two-dollar bill,' he'd always say. 'These guys don't have a pot to piss in and a window to throw it out. They're as fake as they come.'"

—

Robert Bruce Ford—"Robbie"—was the last of the couple's four children, weighing in at just over nine pounds when he was born at Humber Memorial Hospital on May 28, 1969. He was "an afterthought," his mother told him during a 2013 Mother's Day appearance on her sons' Sunday radio show. On air, Rob asked Diane about things mother and son had clearly never discussed.

> *Rob:* You had Kathy [in] 1960, you had Randy in 1962, and then you had Dougie in 1964. So you must have had this planned—two [years], two, two. And I don't know what happened. Five years later you decided to have me in 1969.

Diane: Yeah.

Rob: What was going on there, Ma?

Diane: I guess it was an afterthought.

Rob: Wow!

Diane: You were supposed to be a girl.

Rob: I was supposed to be a girl?

Diane: Yeah.

Rob: Wow.

Diane: I had a girl first and then two boys and then it was going to be another girl.

Rob: Wow.

Diane: Wow.

—

At Deco, where he worked long hours, Doug Sr. ruled the roost. Home was no different. He was such an imposing figure, his boys wanted to copy everything he did. They repeated his quirky sayings, mimicked his aggressive behaviour, emulated his work ethic, adopted his doctrinaire beliefs, and followed him into business and politics, espousing the same core values he relentlessly preached. He'd only stopped playing football when his arm got broken in 1959. The boys couldn't wait until they too could play Dad's favourite sport.

"My dad signed us up for *everything*. And he was always there coaching beside us and helping out," Doug told me. "I played football in high school. Loved it. I was pretty good— better than Rob." He chuckled. "I played running back in my junior years, then I moved up the line as I got a little larger in my senior years. Played offensive guard and defensive tackle"—the positions his dad had played. "And if they had to gain a few yards, I'd step back and be the fullback."

Dad's sport, like everything else, didn't come as easily to Rob, although the bulk that prompted some kids to make fun of him helped him push back against incoming tacklers. He played centre on his high school's junior team, which he co-captained the year it won the Etobicoke championship. He wore that team jacket for years. But as part of a family for which life was a constant battle for supremacy, a modest success still made you a loser. If someone in your family was bigger, smarter, tougher— better at anything—they could remind you of that superiority seven days a week. A hundred percent of the time. Or, as the Fords preferred it, a hundred and ten percent.

David Price, a close friend of Doug Ford's from grade nine until 2015, when he violated a Ford family code by speaking publicly about them, told the *National Post* that Rob developed "an inferiority complex" because he was part of only one high school championship team. "Doug and I won two football championships, and he was forever living that one down. Rob won once when he was a junior and never when he was a senior. He got to the finals four times, never won." Doug's superior football bragging rights "didn't sit well with [Rob] at all."

No matter what level of success Rob and Doug achieved, in childhood or later in life, it seemed that neither of them could ever drink in enough recognition to satisfy their unquenchable thirst for attention. When they looked for praise from their father, as children or as adults, they were more likely to receive another lecture about working harder. "I never got anything," he'd remind them, "and you guys are not going to get anything. You're going to work for every penny that you have!"

"Even when we were playing hockey, my dad was the guy out there screaming, 'Get going! Hustle! Hustle!'" Doug told me. "If we scored a goal, he'd buy us a milkshake on the way home. But I didn't score for the milkshake. I scored because I wanted to win."

—

Doug Jr. figured his own work ethic was largely formed by the time he was eight. "I'd wake up at five in the morning, by myself, and bring my dog with me, hop on my bicycle, and deliver newspapers all around the neighbourhood. And I had that paper route for about four years. Who would ever think of letting your kid in grade two wake up at five in the morning and go deliver papers by himself?"

At sixteen, he'd moved up to slinging carcasses at Canada Packers. "It was the best job I ever had, the most physical job. We were all young football players. We'd load eight hundred sides of beef and each side of beef would be three hundred pounds roughly, loading them into trailers and the freezer. I remember we'd have to change our coveralls in the first two hours. There was blood all over the place, the grease would seep into your shoulders. It sounds gross, but the next day you'd have whiteheads because all the grease was in your shoulders. It was terrible. It was a tough job. But man, were we in shape back then!"

The back-breaking work didn't earn the son any praise from his father, but it did please Doug Sr. "He loved that I worked at Canada Packers, not to mention that I was making $12.49 an hour. He was a hard-noser. The harder we worked, the better he enjoyed it. All of us had to work. We'd work sixteen hours a day and Pops would say, 'Why are you home early?'

"And then, if we were working, we were paying him $25 a week for rent. To show discipline. He never gave us anything for nothing."

"You're as tight as skin on a grape," the Ford sons would say to their father. "And that," Doug Jr. told me, "would put the biggest smile on his face."

I asked Doug whether his father, after becoming rich, still preferred to think of himself as poor. "A hundred percent," he answered. "He lived below his means." And Rob was like his father in that way. "Rob's tight as skin on a grape," Doug confirmed. Generous with others but won't spend money on himself, I suggested.

Doug was feeling left out of the competition to be the most like Dad.

"That's like me too," he interjected. "I shop at Walmart. That's my favourite store. In fact, the shirt I'm wearing is Walmart. The underwear is Walmart. The socks I wear are Walmart. Everything is Walmart! I'm serious."

Not your suits, I ventured. Doug always looked well tailored.

"My suits are a little bit more special," he said. "They're the next step up from Walmart."

—

After high school, Doug Jr. was primed to take on the world. He began a business administration program at Humber College but, within months, decided he'd prefer his dad's school of hard knocks. "I'll tell you the story," he offered in one of our interviews.

"The teachers went on strike—thirty days. So I showed up at my dad's office with a suit on. I think I was nineteen or twenty. He said, 'What are you doing?' I said, 'I can't sit at home. Can you bring me out on a few sales calls?' After the thirty days went by, I sat down with my dad and he said, 'You're going to finish your schooling.' I said, 'But Dad, I can learn more here in the business than I can in three years at college.' So he thought a little bit and then, typical Dad, he said, 'I've got to go talk to your mother.' So he came back and he said, 'Yeah. If you're willing to join the company, I agree you can learn more here.' He took me under his wing and the rest was history."

Doug combined his mother's social skills with his father's passion for customer service. "I loved sales. Once I got my feet wet, I just never stopped. I just absolutely loved going out and meeting people. I always say, 'The world's finest products travel with Deco Labels.' If you have a fancy label and a half-decent product, it's amazing what the packaging does to a product. That's key: packaging."

Over lunch one day, I'd witnessed Doug packaging himself perfectly. In December 2013, only a month after I'd orches-trated the removal of Rob's powers as mayor, Doug came out for a bite with the three "lefties" who sat behind him in council: Joe Mihevc, Mary Fragedakis and me. (Rob was not happy about it, later calling Doug out for it during a council meeting.) It was my turn to buy, but before I had a chance, Doug had given his credit card to the waiter, a young man with *Dennis* written on his nameplate. "Now *you* have a good day, *Dennis*," Doug said, signing the bill. "And if you ever need *anything*, Dennis," he added, handing him a business card, "you just con-tact Rob or me."

"It's such a pleasure to serve you, Mr. Ford," Dennis gushed.

Does this skill come naturally? I asked Doug during a later interview.

"That's through Dale Carnegie," he answered. "*How to Win Friends and Influence People*. It's the number one book in the world sold outside of the Bible. I've read that from front to back. I went on a Dale Carnegie course twice. I'm a *strong* believer that *everyone* should go to a Dale Carnegie course."

Intrigued, I got the old bestseller from the library. It's full of quaint ways to get people to like you and do what you want at the same time. Doug seems to have embraced some of the first set of rules, especially number three.

SIX WAYS TO MAKE PEOPLE LIKE YOU

Rule 1: Become genuinely interested in other people.

Rule 2: Smile.

Rule 3: Remember that a man's name is, to him, the sweetest and most important sound in any language.

Rule 4: Be a good listener. Encourage others to talk about themselves.

Rule 5: Talk in terms of the other man's interest.

Rule 6: Make the other person feel important—and do it sincerely.

Something may have distracted Doug as he studied the first ten items on the next list. But he was focused again by the last two.

TWELVE WAYS TO WIN PEOPLE TO YOUR WAY OF THINKING

Rule 1: The only way to get the best of an argument is to avoid it.

Rule 2: Show respect for the other man's opinions. Never tell a man he is wrong.

Rule 3: If you are wrong, admit it quickly and emphatically.

Rule 4: Begin in a friendly way.

Rule 5: Get the other person saying "yes, yes" immediately.

Rule 6: Let the other man do a great deal of the talking.

Rule 7: Let the other man feel that the idea is his.

Rule 8: Try honestly to see things from the other person's point of view.

Rule 9: Be sympathetic with the other person's ideas and desires.

Rule 10: Appeal to the nobler motives.

Rule 11: Dramatize your ideas.

Rule 12: Throw down a challenge.

—

At Deco, Doug Jr. was a star. A hard-working schmoozer, gifted in sales and business. At the end of 1998, he decided to expand the label business into the United States. "I didn't tell my dad," he said. "I wanted to surprise him." Doug spent a few lonely weeks by himself in Chicago, then returned to give his father the good news that he'd taken their business to a large new market.

"What the hell are you doing?" his father responded. "You need to stay in Toronto and take care of the business here." Doug went ahead with the Chicago branch of Deco anyway—with neither his father's blessing nor his money.

"He never showed up [in Chicago] for two years," Doug told me. "Then he came in, looked around, said, 'You guys are doing a good job,' and went out shopping. He'd tell everyone else how proud he was of us and he'd tell everyone else what a great job we're doing. But he'd never tell us." Doug laughed, but not the enthusiastic laugh he used to punctuate most stories. This was the shake-your-head kind. "'Cause he'd think that we're gonna slack off. I don't agree with that. I used to tell him that: 'I don't agree with your philosophy. I'll work my ass off no matter what.'

"He'd go brag to Jimmy—Jim Flaherty—and the rest of the guys, 'Dougie's doing a great job.' He'd never tell *us*. I said, 'Why don't you ever tell us we're doing a good job?' and he said, 'Because, you might slack off if you have it too good.'"

Did his father live to see how successful the US venture became?

"Not to the full extent," Doug responded. "But he came by. And, yeah, I'm sure he was proud. He was definitely proud of it."

But he never told you that before he died?

"No. No," Doug answered. "I'll never forget, he came through once and a big customer came in and said, 'You should be proud of your son.' And he said, 'Oh, I am. Don't worry.' And the guy goes, 'Have you ever told him?' And he said, 'No.'

"It is what it is," Doug concluded. "He'd tell my mother. He'd tell everyone else. He thinks it goes to your head. I don't know why he would think that, but . . ." Seldom at a loss for words, Doug let the sentence trail off.

Was his father the same with Rob?

"Oh yeah," Doug said. "Yeah."

—

The success of Deco labels, and the wealth that came with it, was critical to Doug Sr.'s plans for his family. Deco financed everything from political campaigns to the lawyers who dealt with Randy's and Kathy's brushes with the law. The boys each had a Deco job with a title and a good salary; Kathy eventually had a trust fund.

Doug Sr. enjoyed the trappings of success but still preferred to think of himself as the dirt-poor kid who'd fought his way up the ladder. He wasn't comfortable around the well-educated, well-spoken, moneyed class who thought they knew it all. Rob shared this discomfort, even as a child.

By the time he was in grade school, his mother was happily hosting splendid backyard parties, rubbing shoulders with the rich and powerful. But her youngest son wanted to be somewhere he could feel more at home. He asked his mom and dad if the family could move to Scarlettwood Court, the nearest assisted housing project.

"I'll never forget Rob telling my parents he wanted to move down to the Toronto Community Housing, 'cause that's where all his friends were," Doug said, then laughed. "Things haven't changed. All this time and things haven't changed.

"Rob was in grade one or two. All his friends went to Westmount Public School, and Scarlettwood Court was just down the street. So we'd go down there, hang out there, and spend a lot of time there."

Others who attended Etobicoke schools during those years say it was unusual for kids from wealthy families to hang out with kids from the housing projects. But Doug Ford described it as a "close-knit" area with no divisions caused by social class, family income, or neighbourhood.

"That's just the way my dad raised us," Doug said. "What makes us any better than the guy sweeping the streets? Everyone's equal. It didn't matter where you came from, everyone hung out together. Our best friends came from Toronto Community Housing at Scarlettwood Court, and up to today some of my best friends were raised in Scarlettwood Court."

I asked Doug whether his parents discouraged them from hanging out in the project, which, by the 1980s, had a reputation that went beyond poverty.

"Never," he said. "My dad was a tough son of a gun. He was a brawler. Not physically a brawler, but you wouldn't mess with him, put it that way. No, my dad loved it. My dad would have all the kids in and take care of them and treat 'em like gold."

—

Neighbourhoods in Etobicoke, much like the people who lived in them, tended to distinguish themselves by levels of wealth and status. Scarlettwood Court was designed with a single road that wound through the complex but led nowhere else. No streets, sidewalks or pathways connected the project to any other Etobicoke neighbourhood. A wide street, Scarlett Road, separated it from nearby pockets of affluence. But that wasn't enough for some of the working rich, who wanted an even greater divide between their children and the offspring of the working poor. Before anyone had even moved into the project, school attendance boundaries were shifted so that the kids from Scarlettwood Court went to Westmount instead of a closer public school in the more upscale Humber Heights.

Sheila Skinner was in grade one when her family of eight (soon to be ten) moved into the project. She didn't notice the class distinction until the nice couple from their Baptist church came by asking to adopt her youngest sister, thinking they could offer her a better home in central Etobicoke. Bookish and bright, Sheila was selected to start grade two in a gifted program. She was the only kid in her class who wasn't from a wealthy family. "When they'd talk at Christmastime, I'd think, 'Could they really have gotten all that stuff, or are they lying?'"

In the early years, neighbourliness abounded in the project. When a neighbour's child didn't have mittens, Sheila's mother offered up an extra pair belonging to one of her children. But by the time the Skinners left, in 1969, Scarlettwood had changed. As homes turned over, there were fewer working dads and more single parents. The poverty seemed greater, the project rougher. Drugs and drug dealers moved in.

Decades later, Sheila Skinner's mention of a Scarlettwood childhood sparked something in her new boss. Skinner was now Sheila Paxton, policy adviser to Mayor Rob Ford.

"Everybody's at me. You don't know what it's like," the mayor said to her after a difficult day at work.

"I know how people judge you," Sheila said in response. "I grew up in Scarlettwood Court."

She remembered how his face *lit* up. "You grew up in Scarlettwood Court!?" he asked, astounded.

"He was just so pleased. He hadn't been giving me the time of day. All of a sudden he listened to me, he talked to me, and I was his favourite person. A little while later, somebody came in to see him and he said, 'She grew up in Scarlettwood Court! She gets us!'"

3. FEW ARE CHOSEN

"Many are called, few are chosen. The Ford family was chosen."
Rob Ford

The children of Doug and Diane Ford were formed in their father's likeness, a united force even before Dad decreed that it be so, a brand even before Mom sent them forth so others could praise their name.

They were Fords above all else, as if their personal identities had been poured from a collective punch. They looked and thought the same, with extraordinary similarities in how they viewed the world and operated within it. Even when members of the family seemed different, they remained like branches of a tree, growing from, and dependent upon, the same roots.

I came to realize that I would not understand anyone in this family by examining them individually.

—

The Ford men were easily set off. For Doug Ford Sr., the face of Bob Rae on his television screen was all it took. "Socialist!" he would scream at Ontario's NDP premier of the early 1990s. "Communist! That lying SOB! They're taking over!"

"He'd be shoutin' and screamin' at the television every time Rae got on," Doug Jr. told me.

The family was already active in Progressive Conservative circles. So Doug Jr. decided it was time for his father to enter politics as a candidate for the provincial party in the election of June 1995. He told his dad, "You gotta run, rather than complain and sit at home yelling at the television. If you want to make a change, this is the time to do it."

"I'm not running," was his father's first reaction. "I can't stand those lying politicians."

"So I put his name forward without him knowing it. Came home and told him, 'You're running.'

"'Like hell. I'm not running.'

"'You're running, don't worry.'

"He said, 'Like hell' again and I won't repeat all his words. And so he ran. . . . He's so anti-politician," Doug said, explaining his father's reluctance. "Oh yeah. He's like me. I can't stand politicians."

I suggested to Doug that it was unusual that the Fords wanted to run the city, the province—the country even—when they are fundamentally against government and mistrustful of politicians.

"It's crazy," he agreed. "We're anti-politician. But that's just the way it is. It's weird. I can't figure it out. It just is."

———

"There certainly wasn't anything fancy about Doug Ford Sr.," observed Doug Holyday, Etobicoke's mayor when Doug the elder ran for office. (Later he became Rob Ford's deputy mayor.) "When I first heard that Doug Ford was running, I assumed it was Doug Jr." Doug the son had a folksy, outspoken manner, and he was a conservative who could talk like a populist while walking with the elite. A perfect Etobicoke politician. But his father?

"He was an unlikely politician, let's put it that way," Holyday told me, remembering an event he hosted at his home to introduce Ford Sr. to the constituency. The candidate addressed the crowd from the top of Holyday's spiral staircase. "He just went off on little tangents about why he should be the candidate and, in the end, you were left still wondering." Less puzzling was Doug Jr.'s wish that his father enter politics. "Doug was starting to run the business, wanting to take over from his dad at that time," Holyday told me. "He thought maybe he'd have a freer rein if his dad was into something else."

Doug the son said that his mother wanted her husband to have something to get him out of the house now that he was winding down his involvement in Deco. "You've got to understand how very traditional my parents were," he explained. "Dad would go out to work, come home at five, six o'clock, you'd sit down for dinner. Boom! All of a sudden my dad's retired, he's got nowhere to go but sit around and tell my mother what to do around the house. He'd be yelling at the television. Drove my mom crazy. She was talking to Mike Harris one day and she said, 'You've got to find him a job. No pay. No nothing. Just get him out of my hair.'"

Doug Ford Sr. was the type of character who left a lasting instant impression. "Right from the word go he came across as a different breed of cat," says John Parker, his fellow Member of Provincial Parliament (MPP). "I saw this weird old guy with a moustache and a green fedora with a feather, looking lost and confused, with his wife who looked quite composed and in control of herself. And I thought, 'Who are these people?'"

Parker is a thoughtful, moderate Conservative who became part of far-right regimes at both the provincial and municipal levels, first as a rookie member with Doug Ford Sr. in the government of "common sense" Conservative revolutionary Mike

Harris and, later, when Rob Ford was mayor, as the wry and witty deputy speaker of Toronto city council.

"Doug Sr. was the guy who sat right at the front of every caucus meeting, and he sat bolt upright and respectful. Whatever Harris said, he was all for it. If Harris said, 'We're going to take everybody's first-born and we're going to sacrifice them on the altar of a balanced budget,' Doug would say, 'That's exactly the right thing to do.' Because he was a true believer. He would follow the party line into a hail of machine-gun fire."

Despite such devotion, the government kept Ford on a tight leash. "He was never asked to speak on a matter, never asked to carry an issue," Parker recalled. "And the less the world saw of him, the better the premier's office liked it."

Parker said the one and only time Doug Ford was let loose in the Legislature was in 1997, during the debate over the Harris-imposed amalgamation of Toronto. "He was no more than three lines into his speech and he puts down his script, which had been handed to him, drafted by the premier's office. He puts that down, looks up at the gallery, and he says, 'You people up there.'" Parker mimics an irritable eccentric. "'You're always here! What's the matter with you? Don't you have jobs?'"

According to Hansard, the official parliamentary record, Doug Ford's speech began well enough, with a scripted homily about his childhood and his mother: "I watched this city grow from the dirt roads, the milk wagons and the service wagons. . . . I listened to some of the chatter as I was a little boy, and the greatest economist I ever met in my whole life was my mother. My mother had nine children and she didn't take any welfare and she had the kind of pride I haven't seen for many, many years.

"We're talking about living in two rooms with nine kids. The older ones took care of the younger ones. My mother worked every single day of her life. She used to brush my hair and I used to say to her, 'When I get older, you'll never have to work,' and she used to laugh. Every day I'd see her go out and I'd see her come back with a bag of groceries or something. Heating those two rooms—I used to go down to the coal cars down on Eastern Avenue, take the coal, put it in a bucket and bring it home on my wagon."

That was when Ford veered off script. "Some of you people don't even know what life's all about. You're always talking about more money, more money. It was disgraceful the way the NDP squandered the wealth of this province. You can smile, but you wasted that money and squandered it. As for *you* people"— he turned now to the Liberals—"you're the same and your government in Ottawa's the same."

Then he launched into the anti-government spectators in the public gallery. A verbal barrage came back at him. "Why don't you shut your mouth!" Ford shot back.

"He was a bumper-sticker kind of guy," Parker remembered. "He was part of the uneducated right, the part of the right wing that thinks it's all about kicking the lazy bums off welfare and getting government out of the pockets of the private sector. Let the private sector run wild and everything will be better." Ford had little grasp of government policy, Parker said, "but he could understand courage and he could understand a good slogan. So Rob and Doug Jr., they think it's all just a matter of having a good slogan and having the courage to stick with it."

On a personal level, Parker found Doug Sr. to be "a guy who was very simple and very unsophisticated, very much from a different time and place, but pure of heart and decent and wholesome."

Fifteen years later, serving alongside Rob and Doug Jr. on city council, Parker became part of the Ford team. He initially gave them the benefit of the doubt, as he had their father. But after two years of watching them up close, his views changed and his support wavered. Around that same time, Parker started to hear tales of a Doug Ford Sr. who sounded very different from the man he'd worked with. The stories—of drinking and angry outbursts, of loaded guns kept in the house, of special family treatment from the local police division—were at first whispered around city hall's second floor, where the councillors and the mayor have their offices. As Rob's problems became more public, so did the speculation about his father. Parker told me he didn't witness anything that would verify any of the stories during their time together in the legislature. "Although"—he paused— "he was eccentric. He was an odd duck. So it's not surprising that there are aspects to his life that are out of the ordinary."

—

Despite countless newspaper stories about the Fords' antics, the family remains shrouded in mystery and myth. Claims of all sorts—true, false and somewhere in between—obscure the family history even more. Ford Sr. did start up Deco, but not by himself in the basement of their Etobicoke home, as the family told reporters for his obituary. He was a marathon swimmer, but he did not try to *cross* Lake Ontario on the same day as Marilyn Bell in 1954, as was claimed at the time of his death.

Why make things up?

Well, if your aim is to start a dynasty, you need a founder whom others see as extraordinary, with rare qualities passed down only to the chosen few who share his last name. Self-aggrandizement seemed to flow naturally from the Fords, as did the manufactured evidence they used to support whatever case they were making.

"They're prone to exaggeration at the highest level. They can't help themselves," said Chris Stockwell, a former municipal and provincial politician from Etobicoke who has known all the political Fords. "They start flat out making stuff up. They make it up because they're *frustrated* they're losing the argument. When Rob said he saved [the city] a billion dollars, he thought it was true by the time it came out of his mouth. Even though it was never true. But he needs to say that in order to prove his black and white point."

Nick Kouvalis, who observed the Fords up close for several years, said, "If whatever is being said is offensive to the family—the mother, the father, the brothers—they'll just say it's not true. Once that comes out of their mouths, it's like the word of God, and it becomes true. Their brains, especially Doug's, are programmed that way. He could probably pass a lie detector test, he believes it so much, whatever the nonsense might be."

However deep or shallow their secrets are buried, the Fords go to great lengths to keep them hidden. While researching this book, I saw the fortress walls go up. Despite granting me four rollicking interviews of his own, Doug Ford cut me off from everyone he could. Sandra Pavan, a Ford family loyalist, at first agreed to talk to me, then wouldn't, then did, then wouldn't again. When I asked her what Doug had said to her to discourage her from talking to me, she replied, "Just that you were out to do dirt on Rob and the Fords. And don't trust you. That you had ulterior motives."

Why go to this much trouble to stop friends and family from talking to me? What caused the fear I encountered in people who had known the Fords in younger days? A prominent political figure was describing an incident involving Doug Sr. at a private Etobicoke country club when he stopped abruptly. He'd realized I was hearing this story for the first time and he refused to be the source, even off the record.

Several Etobicoke residents, with stories they were afraid to tell, noted that the Fords still have many ardent supporters, and tremendous influence, in the area.

—

Think of Rob Ford as a maze. The conventional approach would be to start from the outside and work in. But that route leads to the many dead ends the family has constructed. Maybe the best way to come at this mystery is from the place where Rob arrived, and then try to discern the road he took to get there.

In June 2014, while puzzling over how best to approach Rob Ford's childhood, I read a *Toronto Star* column on his situation written by the addiction expert and author Dr. Gabor Maté. "The most telling aspect of the Ford saga has been the absence of empathy toward a human being who is suffering and, clearly, has suffered all his life. Underneath Rob Ford's paper-thin hubris and achingly evident desperation to be liked is the pain of a child who was mistreated or, at the very least, deprived of acceptance and emotional nurture," Maté wrote.

In Maté's experience working with drug addicts, "this always proves to be the case, even with people who, owing to the power of self-protective denial, initially assert that they had a 'happy' upbringing. . . . For all the problems they inevitably create, all addictions begin as a person's forlorn attempt to solve the problems of shame, isolation, unbearable hurt and emptiness."

Or, as one city hall observer more succinctly put it, "You look at the children, and you've got to know there wasn't a lot of love in that family."

—

The Ford men came equipped with hair-trigger tempers and a birthright that declared them supremely justified in using their natural size and belligerence to establish dominance. When constrained by the need for civility, Doug Ford Jr. could assert himself with a look. By the time he began grade six at Hilltop Middle School, Doug already knew how to control a room. He was the absolute ruler of every school he passed through, the most popular kid in every class.

Dave, a classmate of his from grades six through ten, described Doug as "extremely self- confident and very controlling. He needed to be the leader, and he was very good at getting followers." Like almost everyone from Etobicoke who speaks about the Fords, Dave insisted that I not use his real name.

Dave remembered wanting to be just like Doug Ford. Doug was the cool athletic guy other cool boys wanted to hang out with, the strong, handsome guy the pretty girls wanted to date. Even as a kid, Doug seemed to get whatever he wanted. When he flashed that big smile, radiating an unstoppable self-confidence, the weaker, awkward guys like Dave didn't even try to compete.

"From grade six to grade seven, I had a wild crush on this girl. But I never even said a word to her because I was too shy," Dave told me. "In grade seven I found out that Doug Ford had started *dating* her. When I got home, I made myself a punching bag so I could pretend it was Doug Ford and punch him out. I hung it up in the basement and took a big swing at it." The homemade bag didn't stop his fist, which smashed into a cement wall. Dave broke his hand. "That's as close as I ever came to fighting Doug Ford, and I lost."

When Doug's smile didn't get him what he wanted, he shifted to the "don't mess with me" look that was his trademark even in middle school. Dave said that thinking about that look still made him shudder. Once, in grade seven history class, when the kids were divided up to work on a project, he found himself in the same group as Doug.

"Of course, Doug took over right away. He had ideas and he was going on and on about them. I had an idea *too* and I thought mine was better. So when I had a chance, I brought it up. I'll never forget the way he *looked at me*. Like, 'Are you a fucking idiot or something? Can you just shut up?' Then he turned his back to me and went on with his brilliant idea."

In Scarlett Heights, the high school they moved on to, it felt to Dave as though Doug Ford controlled everything. "I hated high school. Part of it was that I felt so *excluded*. I wanted to be an athlete. I wanted to be a cool guy like Doug Ford, hanging out with his cool friends." Dave had heard about the pool parties in the Fords' backyard. "I used to wish I could be invited, or some-one would take me there. But you had to be in his clique: the athletes and the kids from wealthy families. I don't remember seeing him hanging around with the less privileged people."

One afternoon at school, Doug Ford overheard someone make a derogatory play on Dave's last name. He used it when-ever he encountered Dave after that. Because Doug thought it was funny, other students started calling Dave the name too. "That was part of the reason why I decided to leave high school," he said. He was out for a year before he started over at a school where "I didn't feel like such an outsider because there was no Ford aura or Ford environment."

Decades later, when Dave saw Doug Ford on the news, "he brought the old chills back. Especially when he gave that look to his opponents—the same look he gave me in grade seven."

—

The youngest son, Rob, was a different kind of Ford, big and blond like the others but without the natural ability to dominate, as Fords must. In a family always trying to separate the winners from the losers, Rob couldn't compete. Thinking back to those school days, Dave had no memory of Rob except in relation to Doug. "Just after he entered Hilltop, I remember Rob running across a field with his big mane of blond hair and thinking he looked like a mini Doug Ford."

Up close, the similarities were less clear. Rob was chubby, and got teased for it. He wasn't particularly bright, charming, athletic or confident. The status seekers who flocked to Doug saw nothing of value in Rob. He wasn't comfortable around people like them anyway.

"He doesn't give a shit about status," said Fabio Basso, Rob's friend from the 1980s until Ford got caught on video smoking crack in the Bassos' basement in 2013.

In a 2015 phone conversation in which he extolled Rob's virtues, Basso told me that Rob held at least one big bash during each of his high school years. What made his parties stand out, in addition to the spacious backyard with the big pool, was Rob's "everybody's invited" approach. With other students' parties, "it was 'You, yes—you, no,'" Basso recalled. "With Rob, you didn't have to be invited. You could just show up. That was the whole thing about it. Not once did I ever see somebody say, 'You're not allowed in.' With him it was 'Come one, come all.' Fuckin' hundreds of people. As long as you don't cause trouble, everything is fine.

"Everybody came. Rockers, preppies—everybody was allowed," Basso recalled. "Rob was the only guy in high school who had parties like that. They were excellent parties. Just a good time. Laughing, joking, drinks, whatever. It was fun. Nothing crazy." Basso remembered that the Tragically Hip played at one of Rob's high school parties.

"I thought he was a healthy, well-rounded guy," said another schoolmate who, like Rob, came from a family of scrappers and was reluctant to say even good things about the Fords on the record. "He had all his buddies. Crabapple fights and street hockey—all the typical stuff you do." Kids teased him, but the ones he hung around with all had their weaknesses too. So Rob learned to dish it right back. In high school, "he had a solid group of loyal friends—the guys who hung around the shop doors. I don't know what you'd call them—the rock and roll guys."

Rob sometimes talked tough but was "more bark than bite," the friend recalled. "He'd say something like, 'You fuckin' greasy wops, I love you guys. Let me buy you a drink.' If you didn't know how he meant it, it might rub you the wrong way. It was all kindhearted and joking." Whether he offended you or not, "nobody messed with Rob," knowing how Doug and Randy might react to any perceived mistreatment of their younger brother.

Rob was a scrapper himself, especially after a few drinks. "There's no secret that I've had some donnybrooks," Rob told a reporter in 2014, adding that he was "brought up in a pretty rough-and-ready area." That's not how most people would describe central Etobicoke, but there were rougher areas not far away for those who sought them.

"Solid" is the word Fabio Basso used to describe the Rob Ford he met in grade ten. "He was a good guy. Straight up. He'd help anybody. Give you the shirt off his back. He'd be there if you were down and out. What's mine is yours."

I asked Basso what Rob thought of his father.

"He loved him! Oh shit, yeah!"

Even in high school, I pressed, sometimes a difficult period for fathers and sons?

"Oh fuck yeah," said Basso. "He was his hero."

Was his dad good to Rob?

"You'd have to ask him," Basso said.

And his mom?

"You'd have to ask her."

—

By the mid-1990s, Doug Ford Sr. was getting ready to turn his label business over to his sons, with Doug Jr. in charge. After he became an MPP, the chosen son decided to accelerate the succession process.

"I'll never forget what I did to him," Doug Jr. told me with a hearty chuckle. "He had 'Douglas B. Ford' on his door. We were running out of office space, and he'd come in for an hour or two, just sit there and then leave. So one day I chiselled his name off the door, and I grabbed his papers and got a twelve-by-twelve-inch box. I had his nameplate hanging out. He came in one day and I handed him the box.

"He said, 'What are you doing?' I said, 'You have no office

here. *You're retired.*' And he'd go back to all his buddies at Queen's Park and he'd say, 'Dougie just kicked me out of the company. Son of a gun. He handed me the box.' He'd be talking to Flaherty and he'd say, 'Jimmy, he handed me the box and it had my nameplate in it.' And everybody'd be laughing. But don't kid yourself, he still owned the company if any of us moved the wrong way. But he never interfered, he'd let us run the business, as long as it was profitable, and never said a word. And it was always profitable."

Doug Sr.'s new venture, politics, was another opportunity for the man to clear a path that his children could follow. A second term in office would make it likely that another Ford, Doug or Rob, would subsequently be able to hold the seat for the Fords, perhaps until one of them could lead the province. But his political hero, Premier Mike Harris, reduced the number of seats in the legislature and merged Ford's riding with that of another elected Conservative, Chris Stockwell. Ford decided to battle Stockwell for the right to be the Conservative candidate in the 1999 Ontario election.

The nomination battle had several unusual moments, according to Stockwell, including an extremely premature press release from Doug Ford declaring victory, and a CBC television interview in which Ford used the term "darkies" to refer to black people. Stockwell remembered Ford being full of bravado, continually taunting him: "Your clock is ticking. Your time's up."

Ford attempted a strategy that had worked for him four years earlier, bringing in busloads of supporters from some of the area's poorer high-rises for the nomination vote. Stockwell instructed his campaign workers to challenge every voter, demanding proper identification. Many of Ford's supporters were rejected. "That really pissed him off," Stockwell recalled. "He thought he could intimidate his way into getting these people accredited. I told my people, 'Stand your ground.'" When Stockwell won by three hundred votes, the Fords were surprised and angry.

"Doug Sr. never talked to me again. Diane gave me the worst sneer you've ever seen in your life."

—

With no provincial political succession plan in place, the Fords turned their attention to municipal politics. Rob had already run for council, unsuccessfully, in 1997. In 2000 he would try again and win. Ten years later, he would run for mayor.

Initially, John Parker thought the family steered Rob into politics to keep him away from the business. "I now see that they thought he was their foot in the door," he told me in 2014. "The message you get now is that they think they are a family of political destiny. If they aren't running the city of Toronto, they'll run the province of Ontario."

There are mixed opinions on whether Doug Sr. had specific political plans for his sons, but it's clear that he wanted them to move forward in his memory. When he died of colon cancer in 2006, he was eulogized as a humanitarian who had made a tremendous contribution to the success of the Harris government. The ceremony ended with the playing of "The Battle Hymn of the Republic."

"I think Doug Jr. and Rob were listening *a little too closely*," said John Parker. "They figured that a torch had been passed and that it was their mission on earth to carry forward the legacy of their father."

—

The face of a smiling Doug Ford shines out from the top corner of his tombstone in Riverside Memorial Cemetery, down the road from his Weston Wood Road home. It's the same portrait that overlooks the boardroom at Deco. The tombstone is inscribed with one of his numerous frequent sayings: "Of those who are called, few are chosen." It's a deviation, likely inadvertent, from the common translation of Mathew 22:14: "For many are called, but few are chosen."

In the Bible, the words are part of a parable about the "many" given the opportunity to reach heaven compared with the "few" who make the grade by doing God's will.

"Those who are called, very few are chosen," Doug Ford Jr. said to me, adding yet another variation. "My dad had that kind of religious side to him. He used to say it all the time."

When Doug Sr. died, the family sorted through his many sayings and picked the one they thought best suited a gravestone. What would their father have meant by it? I asked. "You know something, I'm not too sure," Doug answered. "I'm sure he had a few ideas in his head when he used to say that."

In a newspaper interview while running for mayor in 2010, Rob Ford had no difficulty explaining the inscription.

"Like my dad said," he told a reporter, "'Many are called, few are chosen.' It's on his tombstone. The Ford family was chosen."

4. BRAWLERS AND SCRAPPERS

"If somebody touches your little brother, you go beat the hell out of him. If they're too big, call me. I will."
Doug Ford Sr., as quoted by Doug Ford Jr.

The children of Doug Ford Sr. stood as one against the world outside. I asked Doug Jr. whether this was part of his early family upbringing.

"Oh, one hundred percent," he replied. "Our dad used to give us permission. 'Somebody goes after your brother, *you go beat the shit out of them*. I'll deal with the principal.'" Doug paused briefly for a chuckle. "You know, and that was just the way it worked in our family. My sister was the oldest, and he used to tell my sister, 'If somebody touches your little brother, you go beat the hell out of him. If they're too big, call me. I will.' So that's it. You've just got to stick together."

Did that permission only apply to protecting Rob, the baby of the family? I asked.

"All of us. Even my sister. When she was in grade five, someone was bothering my other brother in grade three. She'd go beat the hell out of the guy in grade three. Dad instilled in us, 'Don't let anybody ever touch your brothers or your sister. *Anyone* ever hits your brother, you go beat the shit out of him. I'll take care of the teacher. I'll take care of everything else.'"

Doug laughed at this tale of eccentric family solidarity. "Put it this way. You get in a fight with one Ford, you get the whole clan coming after you. That's just the way it is."

But who will protect you from your protectors? In a 2015 newspaper interview, David Price said that Rob was picked on by his older brothers "because he was the youngest sibling." Price added, "That's why he identifies with the little guy." Price, who would later work in Rob's office, describes himself as "kind of like the older brother that Rob got along with."

—

During the middle part of his term as mayor, Rob Ford hosted a Sunday afternoon radio call-in show with his brother. *The City* had bits of everything: Rob and Doug's analysis of the week at city hall, pro-Ford commentary by like-minded guests, phoned-in accolades from Ford Nation, even some public service announcements read out in a drone by the mayor himself. Interspersed with all this came moments of surprise, revelation and delightful irony.

One Sunday in March 2012, a discussion about schoolyard bullying got Doug reminiscing about his glory days at Scarlett Heights. "I couldn't stand bullies," he declared. "Actually, we never had bullies in our school."

"Not really," Rob chimed in. "We went to Scarlett Heights in Etobicoke."

"It was pretty good," Doug continued. "There were really no bullies there. We'd always take care of them if there was."

—

When the Ford brothers played hockey together in an industrial league back in the late 1980s, winning a scrap was as much fun as netting a goal. If there was a score to settle, you did it right there and then. "A guy takes a sucker shot at you. Boom! You've got to defend yourself," explained Doug.

Industrial league hockey was rough to start with. When the team from Deco Labels suited up, there'd be fights on the ice and, on a good night, fights in the stands. "We're scrappers," Doug said. "Bottom line is Rob and I are brawlers, scrappers. That's it. There's no secret."

You both seem to thrive on it, I suggested.

"We love it. Absolutely love it," he said with a happy laugh. "We love it."

It's not clear whether he was talking hockey or politics. Both, I think. "You gotta remember, John, no different than you—and that's what Rob said to me last week: '*Every one of those councillors* can drop the gloves. All of them don't. But if they have to, they can all hold their own.'" Both brothers admire a politician who isn't afraid to rough it up in the corners. During the chatter at council meetings, Doug often talked about "dropping the gloves" or "coming over the boards."

Both Ford brothers often brimmed with frustration at the constraints imposed by council's formal proceedings—as if the procedural rules should be amended to let them drag a smart-mouthed leftie into a corner and pound the crap out of him. At the start of each meeting, Mayor Ford would identify items he could turn into a political slugfest and "hold" them for a punch-up. "Holding" an agenda item means it must be debated, and the councillor who holds it gets the first punch.

Despite more than a dozen years of watching Rob Ford in action, many opponents remained surprised that even his wild punches landed solidly. Those foolish enough to go toe-to-toe learned that logic and facts are no match for the Fords' brute simplicity. In one exchange posted on YouTube, the ever-logical councillor Josh Matlow supposed a review of the pertinent facts might cause Ford to recant an obviously incorrect claim that a

Light Rail Transit (LRT) line through an existing grade-separated corridor would block traffic.

> *Matlow:* Mr. Mayor, how many streets, or how many traffic signals, will the LRT cross on the grade-separated line in Scarborough?
>
> *Ford:* I'm not an engineer.
>
> *Matlow:* Mr. Mayor, do you know about the line that we're debating? How many streets, how many traffic signals, will the current LRT . . .
>
> *Ford:* Councillor, I know one thing. I've listened loud and clear to the people in Scarborough. They're saying, "Rob, we want a subway."
>
> *Matlow:* Do you actually understand that it's grade separated— that it doesn't rip out traffic lanes?
>
> *Ford:* It *does* rip out traffic lanes. LRTs go down the middle of a road. They tear up your road.

Matlow became so apoplectic that the Speaker turned off his microphone and cautioned him to calm down. Then Matlow tried again.

> *Matlow:* Your Worship, my question is this, and I will say it in the most respectful and temperate tone. Do you understand, when you tell Torontonians that lanes are going to be ripped up . . .
>
> *Ford:* Absolutely they will be.

Matlow (voice rising an octave): Do you understand that this
specific one is grade separated, mostly along a hydro corridor?

Ford shrugged, exasperated by the councillor's inability to
grasp a simple concept.

Observers who knew nothing of the issue might conclude
that the mayor, speaking with such certainty, must have it right.
Some were in awe of what surely must be a brilliant political
performance. Others took it as evidence of the mayor's remarkable stupidity and lack of understanding of the most basic facts
about the most controversial issue of the year.

Few recognized the elements of Rob Ford's potent one-two
punch: a manufacturing of facts to match his argument *and* a
total certainty that his made-up facts were correct.

—

Adam Vaughan, who sat two seats to my right for eight years
before being elected to federal parliament in a 2014 by-election,
fared better in altercations with the Fords. A former television
journalist with exceptional speaking skills, he'd bob and weave,
mocking them with deft jabs, stepping aside while they swung
back, then landing a counterpunch. One afternoon, as Vaughan
lectured the Fords about squandering an opportunity to save
money, Rob Ford tried to disrupt him.

"Adam Vaughan talking about saving taxpayers' money,"
Ford said. "That's an oxymoron."

"At least I don't take Oxy," Vaughan shot back, bypassing
Ford's incorrect word usage to aim directly at his alleged substance abuse. "And I'm not a moron."

Later, as Doug talked about unflattering nicknames for
councillors, Vaughan interrupted him with a question, anticipat-
ing the answer that would set up his quip.

"What's your nickname for *me*?"

"Jackass," answered Doug.

"We just call you a Ford," replied Vaughan.

Still, while Vaughan was giving his farewell address in May 2014, Doug Ford became strangely emotional, declaring that he would miss the Fords' harshest critic.

"I like Adam," Doug told me later, his voice full of admiration. "You know why? He can take a political punch like I've never seen. You can go up to him and say . . . 'You little fuckin' prick, I'm going to tear you apart.' If I said that to *anyone* else, they'd be running to the Integrity Commissioner and they'd be filing a complaint. Adam, he looks at you, laughs, and then he'll give you one back. So that guy can take a political punch like I've never seen, *and* give it back to you.

"It's like in hockey," he added. "You drop the gloves and, afterwards, it's done with."

Almost weepy as Vaughan bade farewell to council, Doug called out to him: "I'm going to knock on doors for you, Adam."

The comment moved Vaughan to pause his speech and turn to Doug. "*Please don't*," he said.

—

"I'm a revengeful son of a bitch," Doug Ford declared, just as the doors closed on the elevator bringing a group of councillors down to their second-floor offices as council recessed for lunch. The Fords had just lost a close vote on a key transit issue. It was February 2012, just over a year into his four-year term, and the mayor was no longer able to control 23 seats on the 45-member council. Attempting to re-establish power, Doug couldn't allow anyone who'd crossed him to think the deed would go unpunished.

"I'm going to get Gloria," he continued to an uncomfortable elevator silence. "I'll never forget it. Mark my words." The Gloria in question was Gloria Lindsay Luby, a conservative councillor who represented the central Etobicoke ward in which Rob and Doug lived. She had begun the term voting mostly with the Fords, but now she was finding them too extreme and, well, just not very nice.

Still spouting venom after he got off the elevator, Doug charged to Lindsay Luby's office and delivered a message to her executive assistant, who later told me what he'd threatened: "I'm going to put up $20,000 of my own money to make sure you go down. I'm going to robocall the shit out of your ward. I'm going to paste it with posters. Every mailbox in the ward is going to get a piece."

In the 2010 election, the Fords had introduced Toronto municipal politics to the mass use of robocalls. Before then, automated recordings had been limited to candidate-friendly messages designed to get out the vote. Rob Ford used them as an electoral sneak attack with a new weapon. As Torontonians prepared to vote in 2010, the robocalls rained down in the wards of several incumbents who'd tangled with the Fords; one lost her seat and the others barely squeaked through. Lindsay Luby was one of the latter, a veteran conservative who won by a mere 309 votes after the automated onslaught. If it was intended to either take her out or bring her in line, it didn't work.

"I really don't care what he does, I really don't," she said of Doug early in 2014. "As long as they think they're going to get ya, they get ya. That's just the way they work. They're horrible, horrible, horrible people."

Doug Ford claimed Lindsay Luby started the fight. "She comes after us. Constantly. I've been polite to her. I've even invited her over for Christmas dinner. She's come. And all of a sudden she's writing these nasty things and putting out letters against Rob, and getting real nasty with Rob."

I asked Lindsay Luby how she enjoyed Christmas dinner with the Fords. She looked puzzled, telling me she'd never been invited for dinner and wouldn't have gone if she had been.

Lindsay Luby traces her Ford problems back to 1997, the "mega-city" election immediately following Toronto's amalgamation. That year, a 28-year-old Rob Ford unsuccessfully ran against her. Ask her about that election and she'll tell you the story of the missing stone dog. It was Easter morning when her family awoke to find the canine statue missing from the front of their Etobicoke home.

"So my family all went out and searched for it. Can't find it," she told me. "And then a couple of days later I received cut-out magazine letters, just like a kidnap note, saying, 'We have your dog. We want a thousand dog biscuits in a plain box. Leave it on your driveway.'"

At first she blamed it on pranksters.

"Well, then the phone calls started at 3 a.m. and I got the police involved. Then pictures kept arriving of my stone dog with a bandana on his eyes and a current newspaper under him. Oh yeah, it's pretty sick. And he had sunglasses on as well. *Sick*.

"And then another picture arrived, which was horrifying. They cut the head off and they must have stuck some newspaper inside the neck, because the picture was of the head on fire."

The picture she remembered most keenly was one of the dog "with what looked to be Rob Ford or Chris Farley—take your pick—wearing army fatigues and a bandana with a gun pointed at the dog's head. *Really sick!*

"Meanwhile, I had two dogs of my own. I'll show you a picture." She reached for photos beside her office desk. "You can see how beautiful they are. That's Duke and that's Peaches. And I was *terrified*, because I live backing onto a park and I thought they would try to poison the dogs.

"And I'm still not associating it much with the election until I saw the picture with the gun and I thought, 'Gee, that looks a lot like Rob Ford.' So then I started to twig."

When the election was over, the harassment stopped. But Lindsay Luby decided to bring the photos to a detective at the local police station. "He couldn't make heads or tails out of it," she said.

Later, she tried to retrieve the evidence from the police. "So I get it back and that picture—the one with the gun and the guy—is missing. It was the only thing missing!"

Being viewed as a Ford enemy is dangerous business for any politician in Etobicoke. Still, even after her narrow victory in 2010, Lindsay Luby said she rejected a 2013 ceasefire offer from Doug on the condition that she support the Fords "110 percent of the time."

"Oh, I'd *never* go under their wing," she said scornfully. "*Never*. That's how bullies get away with it. I've encountered it, and I've shoved it right back!"

Lindsay Luby contends that intimidation of all types has been part of the Ford brothers' playbook for many years. "When I was canvassing in 1997, knocking on doors north of Eglinton, people would say, 'Who else is running?' And I would say, 'Rob Ford.'" And they would talk about Ford family members, telling her stories about drugs and violence. "This is all well known in central Etobicoke," she told me.

Lindsay Luby acknowledged the extreme reluctance of witnesses—or victims—to say anything against the Fords on the record. "Maybe they're afraid they'll get a knock on the door late at night."

—

Tom Allison has run political campaigns since 1979, including Kathleen Wynne's successful run for the Ontario Liberal leadership in 2013 and John Tory's victory as mayor of Toronto in 2014. In 1995, he was the campaign manager for Dr. Jim Henderson, the Liberal incumbent who was defeated by Doug Ford Sr. that year.

Researching the opposition, he'd gone to Ford's nomination meeting at Scarlett Heights Collegiate and brought back a piece of his campaign literature, containing a family photo, to show Henderson. "I think we're in trouble," he remembered telling the candidate. "Look at the picture. Look at those men." It was Randy, Doug, Rob and a fourth man who he thought must have been Kathy's boyfriend or husband. They all looked like they played football. "Jim, that's a sign crew," Allison told his candidate. "That's a killer sign crew."

Allison told me: "They ran the most effective sign campaign ever run in the history of politics in Etobicoke. They kept bringing out bigger and bigger signs. This was at a time when the city had no bylaws about how big signs could be. They had signs that we called the garage door signs because they looked like they were as big as a garage door."

But another aspect of the campaign stood out even more starkly in Allison's memory. "Every two or three days, somebody would walk in off the street with a story to tell us about the Fords. And about every other day, Jim Henderson would come back from canvassing, close the door and tell me another story. A lot of people volunteered stories about the kids or the dad or about both. And the closer you canvassed to Scarlett Heights, the more stories you heard."

—

"How much is a political campaign like war?" I asked Doug Ford one day in his office.

"Oh, it's exactly like war," he replied. "Anyone who says it's not like war is so naive. It's political war. They try to kill you politically—not physically, so that's where you need to differentiate. But they'll pull every possible dirty trick to take you down. You know that, John. Anything they can do to *kill* you politically, they will *kill* you politically."

I asked if he felt sorry for opponents he defeats.

"No," Doug answered. "I don't feel sorry for anyone. Let me tell you something, John—and tell me if I'm wrong. . . . I've never started a fight down here [at city hall]. *They* come after *me*, and I hit back twice as hard."

Is it difficult to fight many people at the same time?

"No," Doug answered immediately.

What if they're all coming at you at once, like in a scene from an adventure movie?

"That's all right," he said. "We're used to it. Rob has skin on him like an alligator. You can call him anything and it just rolls off his back. Me—they call me a name and I'm dropping the gloves. I'm goin' at 'em. *Instantly*. But I *never* purposely went after anyone. Any argument I've been in, or a fight with anyone, I'll give you the whole history, and tell you where it started."

He challenged me on this issue again another day. "Try to find one fight that I started down there [at city hall]," Doug dared me. "I have no problem dropping the gloves. I actually enjoy it once in a while. But I won't go and look for a fight. Never. Even when I played sports, I never did that. But somebody goes out and cross-checks me . . . ? And there's always some cocky SOB down there who wants to be the big hero and challenge us. I feel like Rob's the Wayne Gretzky and I'm the enforcer, McSorley, covering his ass," Doug said, referring to the 1980s-era Edmonton Oilers tough guy and Gretzky teammate Marty McSorley.

"You know, John, there's an unwritten rule: someone goes after Rob, I'm going after him. It's very simple. It's just very simple. Like Kevin Spacey. He took a shot at Rob and everyone in that room thought, 'That guy's toast now.'"

Spacey had been a guest on *Jimmy Kimmel Live!* the night before Rob Ford's legendary appearance in March 2014. Spacey and Ford shared a dressing room briefly when Ford agreed to do a self-deprecating promo, pretending he'd shown up on the wrong night. On the show with Kimmel, Spacey joked that Rob

Ford had thrown up in the dressing room—a reference to his drinking problems.

"So he went on and right away he went after Rob and said he threw up in the dressing room. Right away, someone takes a shot at my brother, I'm going after him. I don't care if it's the prime minister. I just zoned in and thought, 'I'm going to get that SOB back.'" Doug hadn't seen *House of Cards*, the series in which Spacey plays Frank Underwood, a brilliantly manipulative and evil politician who'll stop at nothing to hold power.

Doug chose an episode of *Ford Nation*, the Ford brothers' YouTube broadcast, to settle the score with the actor. He accused Spacey of refusing to pose for pictures with fans.

"Kevin," Doug said on the show, "why don't you get off your high horse and be real and take pictures with the people?"

Rob appeared surprised by the attack. "You've got to be careful," he cautioned his brother, "because maybe he does take pictures and we're not aware of it."

Spacey responded by tweeting a Photoshopped image of himself posing with the Fords. "All you had to do was ask, guys. Here's your pic." The actor also tweeted a link to a site containing dozens of photos of him with fans.

"So then he spun it as if we wanted a picture with him," Doug complained to me afterwards. "I didn't want a picture with this character. He's an arrogant SOB. You can quote me on that one too." Although Doug knew the entire conversation was on the record, that was his way of punctuating a statement he wanted me to use. "I didn't want an autograph and neither did Rob. Rob didn't even know who the guy was.

"The real story about Kevin Spacey is Rob and I were outside, we came back in, and there were a group of people—I guess they were fans or something—and they said, 'Can we take a picture? At least you're nicer than Kevin Spacey. We were told we weren't allowed to take a picture with him, or we weren't allowed to speak to him. *You're* so real. *You're* open. *You'll* take a picture.'"

—

"Doug's first approach is to turn on the charm," I observed to Nick Kouvalis, "but if that's not working quickly, he—"

"Bullies," Rob's former campaign manager finished my sentence. "And if the bullying doesn't work, he threatens. That's the pattern with him. He threatened me two weeks ago at home." This was in the spring of 2014, after it became public that Kouvalis was going to work on the campaign of Ford's rival for mayor, John Tory. "Called me out of the blue. Eleven o'clock. I'm sitting on the couch with my wife. She could hear him talking through the phone. He threatened me, because I'm going to work for Tory. He said he was going to make sure that I'm fixed, taken care of."

Nick was offended as much by Doug Ford's lack of couth as anything else. "When people are civilized, it's implied: you cross me, I'm going to get you back. You don't *say* it!"

Kouvalis decided his best strategy was to respond in kind. "I told him, 'I'm not afraid of you. Come get me. Come.' And he kind of giggled, and I said, 'I'm serious. Don't be a pussy and send someone else.' When I say to him, 'Don't send some lackey,' I have stood up to him," Kouvalis explained. "'Cause if you say anything else, you're backing down to their bullshit. I said to him, 'Doug, you've got to cut this bullshit. Rob can't win. I've done the research. It's going to be humiliating for him, for you, for your family. He should run as a councillor. Maybe he can keep that together.'"

Then Doug said to Kouvalis, "What am I supposed to do, Nick? He's my brother." And Kouvalis said to him, "You're supposed to do what a big brother does: say no to the little brother when he's doing stupid things."

"He's my brother," Doug responded. "I can't go against him."

5. BREAKING FORD

"Now I knew what the Fords felt! I was put up on this pedestal and everybody kind of looked up to me."
Dieter Kiklas

T he thud of his skull against the cement floor numbed Glen's fear only for a moment. There wasn't time to consider himself lucky that the enraged young man with the heavy metal pipe had only grazed his forehead. Large and muscular, the attacker dropped the pipe and hovered over him. Glen looked up, into the eyes of Randy Ford. Glen continued the story only after I agreed not to use his last name.

"He sat on top of me and had his legs over my arms. I was helpless. His face was right above my face." The eyes came into focus, reigniting Glen's terror.

"His eyes," Glen remembered. "Unbelievable. Beady and just—lost.

"It was in slow motion. His mouth was coming down and I was moving my head from side to side, begging him not to do it. And he came down with his teeth and he got my nose in his mouth. I closed my eyes and begged him not to bite it off. And he bit right through until his teeth actually touched, and just the tip was hanging there."

Glen remembered it being a slow bite, as if Randy might be savouring the moment.

Did he say anything? I asked.

"No. Not a word. That's the thing about Randy—he doesn't say nothin'. Just holding everything inside him. He got up and he was happy. He was just smiling and growling at the same time."

—

It was February 1981. The evening had begun pleasantly enough, with what Glen described as a "drink and drug" party at Kathy Ford's apartment at Weston and Lawrence, in Toronto's west end. At the time, Kathy was the girlfriend of Michael Kiklas, who had been Glen's buddy since grade seven. "Michael and I were the best of friends. We went hunting together with my dad. We stayed over at each other's places. I always thought I could trust him, and that he would help me before he would ever help Randy."

As eighteen-year-olds still living at home, Randy, Glen and Michael were always on the lookout for a party house with no parents around. Kathy Ford, slightly older at twenty, already had a place of her own.

Randy was taller, wider and stronger than Glen. Michael Kiklas had introduced them, but the relationship had gone sideways after Randy traded Glen some bad acid for Glen's hash oil. Glen's buddies, who'd arrived with him from Brampton that night, expected Randy to make it right. "So Randy grabs a bag of this bright yellow powder, PCP, and he started making lines," Glen recalled. "And he said, 'Okay, everybody, help yourself.' Once we started snorting the stuff, we were fucked."

Still, if only the music had been better, Glen's nose might still be intact. "There was no good stereo system there, just a boom box." The Brampton visitors decided to head off in search of better sound and more scintillating conversation. As Randy was walking his guests out, one of them observed to Glen, "What a shitty party."

Overhearing the remark, the host took offence. "He just hauled off and started hitting the guy so hard," Glen said. "The guy's back was up against the wall and Randy just kept hitting him and hitting him and hitting him. His teeth went through his lip."

Glen ran for backup. Catching his friends before they left the building, he brought them back to the apartment, where a new fight broke out, travelling first into the hallway, then down the corridor and finally into the stairwell. Even outnumbered, Randy wasn't easily subdued. Kiklas, siding with Randy, had his teeth so tightly locked onto one guy's chest that someone had to smash a bottle of Tia Maria over his head to get him off. When Glen's friends finally got Randy on the ground, they took off.

Glen and a friend staggered to the parking garage to find his car, minds and vision blurred. Glen was still searching when the garage door opened and he saw Michael Kiklas and Randy Ford coming towards them, swinging metal pipes. Glen stared at Michael, his best friend. "It was like he didn't know me anymore," he said. His allegiance had shifted to Randy.

When Randy had finished with Glen that night, his nose was attached by a thread. Dazed and confused, Glen stumbled out to the street and into a nearby Chinese restaurant, looking for directions to the closest hospital. The nose felt plugged, so Glen blew into a restaurant napkin, spurting blood in all directions. Later, after his nose had been attended to, Glen returned to Kathy's apartment and buzzed up from the lobby, demanding to know where his car was parked. Michael, who had borrowed it earlier, calmly directed him to the lot across the street, as if nothing out of the ordinary had just happened.

—

The next morning, Glen's brother awoke in their shared bedroom to the sight of Glen's mangled face. "What the fuck!" he said, and ran to get their dad.

"My dad was fuckin' pissed," Glen said. "He wasn't going to let his son be treated like that without some retaliation. Got me up, gave me a shot to drink, and said, 'Phone every friend you have and get them over here.' So six or seven guys came over and we all had a couple of shots. My dad was a baseball coach. He got all the bats out of the bags and gave them to everyone. I had a five-pound hammer with me. Everybody had a bat or a hammer. And we had knives. We were going to kill the fuckers."

Eleven of them arrived in three carloads at Kathy Ford's building. When a woman opened the front door to go out, they walked in past her, weapons in hand, and took the stairs up. On the fourth floor, they lined up on either side of the apartment door. They knocked. When nobody answered, they kicked the door in. The apartment was empty.

"We destroyed the place. We broke *everything* in that apartment. I'm so glad today they weren't there, because I'd be doing jail time. Somebody would have been killed."

Glen explained to me why he never reported the attack that left him disfigured, and why he thinks the Fords didn't call the police either, after they discovered Kathy's destroyed apartment. "We didn't want a war."

—

Michael Kiklas had been dead sixteen years, blown away by a shotgun blast, when his brother Dieter met me in a Brampton pub, pitching a documentary he carried in his head. Dieter wanted his story out, stark and simple, before the October 2014 election in which Rob Ford was running to be mayor for another four years.

"I want to show the apartment building I grew up in, and I

want to show the Ford estate. And I want to say, 'This is where my family grew up and this is where the Fords grew up.'

"I'm going to do it very short, so I don't lose people's attention.

"And then I want to go over to my brother's cottage in Caledon and say, 'This is where my brother and Kathy Ford shared their little joyful life together, and this is where my brother was murdered.'

"Then I want to click over to show my brother's grave.

"But I want to do it as a melodrama-type thing, where it's pulling you in. You want to see the guy who shot Kathy in the head, in her house, and then got beaten in jail. Then I want me sitting in front of a church, or even me in front of my brother's grave. I'll say, 'Come October, make your vote count, because this is what happened to my family from growing up in Ford Nation.'

"Because we really did grow up in Ford Nation in a way."

—

Dieter's story begins in the late 1970s, when he was fourteen and living in an assisted housing project in Brampton, just northwest of Toronto. Everyone called him Dede. His brother Michael, sixteen, spent weekends in the city and came home Sunday, usually in time to watch *National Geographic*. Sitting on the couch, half watching the screen, Michael would tell his little brother about a world as different from theirs as anything on television. "He'd tell me stories of going away on this boat with these rich people, and of these big cars and this big mansion that they had, with this big pool. And about his girlfriend who was really rich and had these really cool brothers. My brother talked about these people. Constantly. Constantly. Constantly."

Dieter Kiklas described Michael as strong and athletic, with a mean streak nourished by violence. Michael practised it on little kids with lunch money, big kids with drug debts and, without compensation, on members of his own family. Kathy Ford seemed drawn to such men. A pretty face atop a large torso, she was herself controlling and aggressive. Two years younger than Kathy, Michael was captivated by her money and access to drugs. She'd let him have both, but first he might have to beg a little.

Back then, Kathy felt her Ford power. Dieter remembered her first visit to their home. "My mom went on a trip for a week and we had the place to ourselves. So next thing I know, my brother calls and says, 'Make sure there's nobody in the apartment. I'm coming home and I've got some pot.' And the next day this bumptious woman comes walking through the door with this boisterous voice. She took over the room. She literally took over the room and made the area hers. She exuded this power, like, *'I've got it!'* Maybe people with money exude this stuff. She was throwing around money like there was no tomorrow, and bags of home-grown marijuana." Dieter said it had been ripped off from a farm.

Dieter was impressed that Kathy travelled from Etobicoke to their place in Brampton by taxi. On one visit, he said, she dropped a bag of cocaine on the kitchen table and said, "Have a good time. Go for it." But when she left, the bag went with her.

Dieter blames his introduction to the Fords for the start of his thirty years as a middleman, buying and selling drugs. Early on, Dieter got his drugs from Michael, who he says got them from Kathy's family—the ones he was always talking about. After a year or two of only imagining the world these people lived in through his brother's stories, Dieter was finally allowed to visit it.

"Mr. and Mrs. Ford were gone away somewhere and they had the whole mansion to themselves." Before they arrived at 15 Weston Wood, Michael told him, "Just keep your mouth shut and hang around. Do what we do." Filled with excitement and drugs, Dieter obliged. "They'd scored all this hash. Lordy,

Lordy, Lordy! And that was my first introduction to the family. I left with my parcel and came back a few weeks later with their money. And that's how it went. But it was my brother handing me the packages, it wasn't Doug or Randy. My brother middles, and I middle after him."

What did Dieter see on that first visit? I asked.

"I'm seeing what I want to be," he answered. "I'm seeing where I want to go. I want to have a big house. I want a big swimming pool. I want what's raining on them to pour on me."

For a time, it seemed to be happening. "It was crazy. We had money galore. I was this rich kid. Everybody paid attention to me. I was highlighted in my community. I was elevated to a spot where I thought, 'I don't want to come off this pedestal.' *Now I knew what the Fords felt!* Everybody kind of looked up to me. *There's Dede! Hey Dede! Make sure you wave to Dede!* I was the one who got invited to the parties all the time now.

"And of course it brought addictions and divorces and stuff like that. My world changed forever."

—

In May 2013, the *Globe and Mail* published a lengthy investigative piece, quoting multiple unnamed sources who said that Doug Ford, roughly between the ages of fifteen and twenty-two, supplied hash to street-level dealers, sometimes from the basement of the family home. Ford threatened to sue the paper but didn't.

Dave, a druggie who attended Scarlett Heights at the same time as Doug, remembered buying his first gram of hash from Doug's friend David Price, who, years later, ended up working for Mayor Ford. Dave the buyer was in grade eight; Price wouldn't have been much older. "He was selling blond hash for $10 a gram. I bought it off of him a few times until I went to high school."

Later, at sixteen, Dave said he bought a gram of hash—once only—from Doug Ford, who sold it out of a car at James Gardens, a popular 1980s spot to score drugs in Etobicoke. Dave, like almost everyone who knew the Fords in high school, wouldn't agree to talk about them unless his identity was protected. Dave told me he bought more frequently from Randy Ford, who, he said, ran a retail operation with regular business hours in what is now called Douglas B. Ford Park, next to the Ford family home. "He was there every day between 6:30 and 7:00 p.m., and people would go and line up. Randy was always very *stoned*." Dave remembered Randy wearing a vest, a coat and a jacket, each with multiple pockets in which he stored hash, cash and scales to weigh the drugs. Dave noticed that Randy struggled to remember what pocket he'd put things into. "When I was next in line, I always watched to see where he put his scales and his money, so I could remind him."

Dave also got to know Kathy a bit, meeting her in the nineties as he lined up to score hash on Lemonwood Drive. Dave described Randy and Kathy as having a "down-to-earth" quality—like Rob. But *not* like Doug. "Doug is the anomaly of the family from that point of view: the arrogance and belittling of people."

All of Dave's drug transactions with the Fords were for small quantities, amounts high school students commonly purchased from other kids. There is no record of Doug Ford being charged with anything, nor are there any allegations that he dealt in, or consumed, hard drugs. By some accounts, he also tried to keep a safe distance from his brother Randy. "Doug, being as savvy as he was and as business-minded as he was, knew his brother was just too volatile," one former associate told the *Globe*.

Dieter Kiklas described Randy and Doug as a two-man fighting machine, although Doug was the brother with the self- control, relatively speaking. "They used to travel in a pair, because together they were a sword and dagger mixed together," Kiklas said. "And they were big boys." Michael Kiklas, who wasn't nearly as large as the Fords, studied martial arts and, according to his brother, took pleasure in gracefully beating people up. "My brother enjoyed fighting. If you fucked the Fords around for money, my brother was the unknown face" they might send to collect it, Dieter said.

At twenty-four, Randy was charged with assault causing bodily harm and kidnapping related to an unpaid drug debt. In his younger years, he was arrested more than a dozen times, with a long list of convictions for such crimes as assault, robbery and possession of narcotics.

Glen, whose nose is still scarred from where Randy bit into it, described the eldest Ford brother as "the most vicious guy" he'd ever met, "and I've hung out with some bad guys, bikers and everything, in my younger days."

—

With age, Randy Ford appears to have mellowed considerably, though not entirely. He is now the least conspicuous of the Ford siblings. From the 1990s onward, Kathy took over as the family problem child, plagued by drugs, alcohol and a brutal choice of men. In 1982, she married Jeff Pressley, about whom little has been written. They separated in the late eighties, soon after Kathy became pregnant by Michael Kiklas and gave birth to a daughter named Jennifer. Before long, Kathy was with an even more violent man, a drug addict named Ennio Stirpe. In March 1994, Stirpe fathered Kathy's second child, whom she named Michael.

The two addicts lived in the apartment above the garage at the Weston Wood Ford family home. But, as recounted by Robyn Doolittle in her book *Crazy Town*, in 1998 Doug Sr. noticed a large wad of cash missing from a tin can he'd hidden inside the house. All the Ford children denied taking it. Not believing them, Doug Sr. forced all his adult children, and Stirpe, to take lie detector tests. Kathy Ford and Stirpe failed the test.

When the couple split up, Kathy packed up her children and moved in with Michael Kiklas. Soon afterwards, Stirpe arrived at their home in Caledon, north of Toronto, with a sawed-off shotgun. Kiklas went to the door. With Kathy and the two children present, the father of her son murdered the father of her daughter. Claiming that he'd brought the gun along to defend himself against Kiklas, Stirpe was convicted of manslaughter and sentenced to thirteen years. For a time, Kathy spent most weekends at the penitentiary in Kingston, visiting him. She'd bring the children with her.

Stirpe was paroled after serving just two-thirds of his sentence, in 2009. But soon he was back in the pen, convicted of attempted murder, after bludgeoning a new girlfriend, almost disembowelling her and blinding her in one eye. His defence was that the woman, also a drug addict, had attacked herself with a knife.

Meanwhile, Kathy had taken up with Scott MacIntyre, another addict and seven years her junior. In March 2005, MacIntyre unintentionally shot Kathy in the forehead with a twelve-gauge shotgun, in the kitchen of her parents' home. According to several sources, the loaded gun was part of Doug Sr.'s collection, which was kept in the house. MacIntyre called 911, then fled in Diane Ford's Jaguar. The shooting was ruled accidental and he was sentenced to a year in jail. After his release, the couple got back together in a home provided by Kathy's parents, across from Scarlett Heights Collegiate.

On January 11, 2012, at 7:30 a.m., according to an agreed-upon statement of facts presented in court, MacIntyre entered Rob Ford's Edenbridge Drive home through an unlocked front door. "You owe me money, your sister owes me money. If I don't get it, they will kill me," he yelled at Ford. Rob yelled back, ordering MacIntyre out of the house. "You and your family are going to get it," MacIntyre shouted as he left. "You are going to pay for it."

When police contacted MacIntyre on his cellphone, he told them that he was going to shoot Rob Ford and cut his head off with a machete. Within a few hours, Kathy had another ex in jail. MacIntyre was arrested in a Mississauga motel, where police found heroin and cocaine. He was later convicted of uttering death threats, possession of narcotics, and violating a court order to not contact Kathy Ford. Prison officials had intercepted a letter to Kathy, dated January 22, 2012, well before the mayor's substance abuse problems became public. The letter, threatening to expose Ford family secrets, later became public as part of court documents.

> Hey Kay,
> Well Well here I sit in the Can because your Brother (The Rat) picked up the Phone & LIED! I never threatened him AT ALL! All of what is happening is YOUR FAULT! . . . Listen and listen GOOD! You and Your FAMILY have ONE chance to leave me the Fuck alone and stop this shit! Or I am going to start such a shit storm (By TELLING THE TRUTH! 100% ONLY THE TRUTH) that Politics is the LAST Thing they will be in! The MEDIA is Pounding down the Door here, THROWING SIX figure numbers at me for MY SIDE of not only this story, but they know I was BEHIND CLOSED DOORS! You and Your Family think I should play NICE! FUCK YOU! REMEMBER when I used to say "DON'T PUSH ME, AHAH!" Bring it the FUCK ON! MAD, you have no idea how mad I am! . . .
> People make settlements between each other all the time! If Im ignored Now there is NO LATER! NO PLEASE BE REASONABLE, SCOTT! SCOTT IS FUCKING ON FIRE MAD! ITS UP TO YOU TO PUT OUT THE FLAMES! NOW!

The next day, January 23, 2012, MacIntyre sent a letter to the circulation department of the *Toronto Star*, demanding that his newspaper delivery be redirected to the West Detention Centre.

To whom this May Concern

My Name is Scott MacIntyre and am currently at the Toronto
West Detention Centre awaiting charges of Threatening Death
on my EX-Brother-inlaw, The Mayor, ROB FORD! I Paid for a
Subscription of your Paper to be delivered to my Home, at the
time, 40 Trehorne Drive, ETOBICOKE, ONT M9P 1N9. The
subscription Started on Jan 1/12. I would like to have MY
Paper Re-Routed to M.T.W.D.C 111Disco Rd Rexdale Ont
M9W 5L6. . . .
    ALSO if the Toronto Star is interested in Uncovering some
of the Garbage our, So Called, Mayor is feeding the People of
Toronto have one of Your Investigative Reporters send me a
letter letting me know if the Star wants to talk! . . . You People
have NO idea about this man! . . . You just need a little More
AMMO for "THE FORD BROTHERS" AND WHAM ALL
OF YOUR REPORTING IS BONA FIDE!

ONE ANGRY EX-BROTHER IN-LAW (signed Scott MacIntyre)

Two months later, on March 22, MacIntyre was attacked in
the jail's shower. His teeth were smashed and one of his legs was
so badly broken it required two months in a cast and surgery to
repair ligaments and tendons. At MacIntyre's sentencing, the
judge described the beating as "jailhouse justice," which he
inferred "was visited upon Mr. MacIntyre because of his being a
bother to Mr. Ford."
    Three months after he wrote those letters, MacIntyre was
sentenced to five more months in jail, in addition to the five
months already served. At the sentencing hearing, both Rob and
Kathy Ford submitted requests asking the judge for leniency.
Kathy also asked that she be able to maintain contact with
MacIntyre "for purposes of assisting in his rehabilitation, if
needed." Justice Paul French described the Fords as "generous

and forgiving in not wanting Scott MacIntyre to go to jail" but denied Kathy's request as "simply a prescription for disaster."

Late in 2013, MacIntyre filed a lawsuit claiming Rob Ford had ordered one of his former football players, also an inmate, to carry out the prison beating. (That case had not yet been heard at the time of this writing.)

—

Dieter Kiklas blames the Fords, collectively, for two turning points in his life: the early introduction to the world of drug dealing and the murder of his brother. He was fifty when we met, clean for some time, he said, but still suffering the effects of decades of drug abuse and an emotionally painful childhood. Over a bowl of potato soup, he told me about a life that had been brutally unkind. It was hard to handle, even for the listener, but the retelling seemed to give him some temporary relief.

He described an early memory involving a neighbourhood bully who chased him, hoping to administer another beating. Small and passive, Dieter was trying to make it to that one safe place everybody needs.

"I was running home. We were in Unit 1 of the townhouses. I ran in screaming to my mom. Meanwhile the bully stood outside, taunting me. My mother threw me out the door, and I remember her fucking *smacking* me across the back with a stick, telling me to get my ass out there and fight that kid and get it over with. Life was hard, dude. Me and my brother had a hard relationship growing up. And when he became this martial arts guy, he did some terrible things to me and my sister, like injury-wise. He wasn't very kind to us growing up. Sort of like my father. When we moved away from my father because of the beatings, my brother took over.

"I always wanted my brother to be my best friend. You know how you strive for that and strive for that and strive for that?

You take the insults your brother would give you in front of Randy and Kathy—belittling me—and those were hard. I never got the respect from Randy or Doug that I deserved, because my brother belittled his own blood. It put bricks between me and my brother, big bricks."

Dieter turned to hard drugs in his early teens. "The needle goes into your arm and you feel that rush—either from the cocaine or from the heroin—and it's the most phenomenal thing. The heroin, it goes into your body and you start to feel it from your head down to your toes, and it's so warm and comforting. It's like you found home."

Did Dieter see similarities between himself and Rob Ford? I asked.

He pointed out the obvious differences: money, power, influence. Then he thought about it. "If you put us together as two human beings," he began, "drugs poured on both of us."

He thought some more, until his eyes brightened in a moment of revelation.

"Wanting to be loved."

6. THE AUTHENTIC ROB FORD

"This is a guy for whom all lies are equal to truth."
lawyer Clayton Ruby on Rob Ford

The Rob Ford who smokes crack is in the biggest jam of his life. It's November 1, 2013, the day after Toronto police have confirmed the existence of a Ford crack video. Talk radio host Bill Carroll invites listeners to call in their advice for the beleaguered mayor. Ford has avoided comment.

Ian from Etobicoke is on the line. "I don't think he has to answer to any of that. I think he has personal problems. And by the way, by the way, if you think you can fire somebody because they have personal problems with something like substance abuse, in a union, you can't. You can't."

Carroll points out that the mayor doesn't belong to a union.

"You mean at city hall they don't have a union in there?" says the caller, becoming angry. "Okay, so what's your name?" he asks the host of the Bill Carroll show.

"This is Bill," the broadcaster answers. "Is this Rob Ford?"

"Bill, okay Bill, answer me this: how many times have you been videotaped in the last week?"

"I've looked into the camera once," says Carroll.

"You looked into the camera once," the caller scoffs. "How do you know what you do exactly? There are cameras everywhere. Okay, okay, so you're telling me he goes around and videotapes himself smoking crack? Get a life! Smarten up!"

"Mayor Ford, I know your voice," Carroll says.

Ian from Etobicoke hangs up.

Carroll replays the conversation for his listeners. "I want you to listen for a couple of things: his expressions, some of the words he uses that are uniquely his, the little squeak he gets when there's an upper inflection. This guy, if he's not the mayor, could play one on the radio."

—

If you don't like who you think you are, you like to think you're somebody else. Perhaps Ian from Etobicoke. The need for a mask may originate in a childhood deprived of emotional nutrients, the ones that help you grow into an adult who can reconcile who he is with who he wants to be. After you've worn a mask for a while, it may fit so comfortably that you'll forget you have it on.

Rob Ford accepted the advantages of growing up wealthy but thought of himself as anything but a spoiled rich kid. He was far more comfortable among society's underdogs, to whom not much was given and from whom little was expected. His people were the common folk who couldn't quite make it to the next paycheque.

Former councillor Mike Del Grande told me a story about approaching the millionaire mayor, attempting to appeal to a sense of fairness, when Ford wanted to freeze councillors' salaries.

"I caught him in the back foyer, where the washrooms are, and I said, 'The standards you want to impose on other people are unfair. Because you're very rich and you don't have to worry about your next paycheque. But the rest of us still have a livelihood to make.'

"He turned to me, and he looked very serious and said, 'I'm offended by that. I'm poorer than a church mouse.'

"That's what he told me. He looked serious. He said he was offended. 'I'm poorer than a church mouse.'"

—

Boys playing street sports pretend to be their favourite player, providing their own play-by-play commentary as they zigzag through a crowd of defenders to win the game for the home team. Rob loved his father's game, football, and as a football coach he could try to be exactly like him: a relentless competitor, a hard-driving boss, a rugged disciplinarian, an unstoppable underdog who could climb his way from nowhere, up and over all those rich snobs, showing them he was more than their equal.

During one of our friendly sports chats, I asked Rob to describe what football meant to him. "That's too big a question. It's like the universe," he said, stretching his arms wide. He said nothing more, perhaps daunted by the immensity of the subject or not wanting to reveal too much, instinctively suspecting I saw football as key to understanding *his* universe.

To Rob Ford, football is so much more than a game. It's a source of identity and self-worth. It provides a comfortable entry point into an alien world, a 150-by-65-yard refuge within which he can display expertise and leadership, a place where he can feel respected and admired.

Inevitably, coaching football led him to interact with the world beyond the field, producing a heap of misadventures. After contacting lobbyists to support his football charity, the mayor found himself in a conflict of interest that got him temporarily removed from office. Because he left council meetings to coach his high school team, Ford was widely accused of shirking his duties. When he diverted a city bus in rush hour, emptying it of passengers so his football players could get an early ride home, Ford's detractors had a field day. Football prompted the firing of his chief of staff, Mark Towhey, because he refused to let staff organize a farewell party for Ford's team after a school board fired him as coach. That dismissal as coach, accompanied by claims that he'd mistreated his players, sent Ford into a drunken tailspin.

Ford had made his coaching debut at Scarlett Heights in the early nineties, when his former high school needed a volunteer to revive its football program. Rob started out with an inexperienced ragtag collection of players, lacking size and skill. The new coach believed such adversity could be overcome by determination and grit, especially against teams full of spoiled rich kids.

"He hated Richview," remembered Alan, a player on that first team who asked that his real name not be used. Richview Collegiate was the upper crust of Etobicoke high schools. Canadian prime minister Stephen Harper was once a student there. The school's winning football tradition was based on discipline and smart coaching.

"Rob would say, 'These rich kids, they can't play. They're a bunch of rich pussies.' At the time, I didn't know *he* was rich. For some reason he saw himself as the underdog fighting the rich kids at Richview. It's almost like he doesn't see himself as rich. He sees himself as a tough blue-collar guy, even though he's not."

Alan transferred from Richview to Scarlett Heights just in time to play for the new coach. "At Richview it was all professional, like a machine. Every play is ironed out. I remember one time they wouldn't let me play because I was wearing black socks instead of white socks. You go to Rob and it's chaos.

"He had this one drill: he just stands people fifty feet apart, two players, they could be any size, like a big guy against a small guy, it's got nothing to do with football, and they just *sprint* at each other. A lot of people would *fear* it. People would get injured. You'd just sprint at each other and *nail* each other from like fifty feet away. That's kind of Rob's style."

In their first game against Richview, Ford's team lost 52–0, Alan recollected. Ford was undaunted, "very Chris Farley–like, hands on his knees and shouting." When the playoffs came, first-place Richview was matched against last-seeded Scarlett Heights.

"The week leading up to the game, he had us run all the way to Richview and go onto their field. So we're jogging around Richview's track while they're practising, getting ready for the game against us. He's *staring the kids down*, and I'm thinking, 'We suck so bad and we're supposed to be intimidating?' Just a bunch of losers running around the track, and they're laughing at us."

On game day, the coach was even more on fire. "He had us line up in their end on purpose. So their players are lined up beside us. Rob said, 'Don't move!' Then he starts going back and forth along their line. He was not afraid to get into scraps with kids on other teams. He was right up into kids' faces. 'None of these guys get scholarships,' he belittled them. 'They're just well organized. They're just a bunch of rich pussies.' So one of their players goes up to Rob—'You fat fuck.' Rob just goes ballistic. Then the big guy on our team tries to fight that guy. It was just chaos. Rob just loved it, eh?

"He wasn't a good playmaker, but he was good at screaming and slobbering and getting everyone psyched to do damage. *Rah rah RAH!*"

Ford got his team so pumped up that, midway through the playoff game, they were leading Richview.

"We were in the dressing room at halftime," Alan continued, "and then Doug Sr. comes in and Rob—you know he's *so* proud of his dad—Rob goes, *'HERE'S MY DAD!!!'* He's so totally pumped up that his dad's there to watch. And his dad's giving us a pep speech—'I'm proud of you, bah bah bah.'

"But then we came out for the second half and ended up getting whooped. After the game Rob's so drained, 'cause he's been shouting so much. It's almost like he's hungover."

Alan and a few of his friends thought Coach Ford was totally odd, especially for an adult. "It was like he wished he was on the field as a player." But most others saw him differently. His players mostly loved him, and those from other teams wished they could have a coach like Rob Ford.

—

I've seen most of Rob Ford's qualities, few of them constant, and many of which seem to contradict others, as if they shouldn't belong to the same person. He's shy but friendly, insecure but good-natured—unless you push the wrong button. Helping others makes him feel better about himself. He uses sports and politics to dip into a world that seems otherwise strange and unfriendly. He has a sense of humour and he likes music. Despite the self-absorption, he can be generous and appreciative. He wants to be a loyal friend. He can be a caring father.

Rob rarely allowed the sum of those qualities to appear, especially after becoming mayor. Both Doug Ford and Nick Kouvalis told me that Rob has very low self-esteem. He apparently tries to hide it with a lot of pretending. But who can keep that up? The pressure becomes too great, the failures too unbearable, the humiliation debilitating. The personas became deranged and ugly, their meanness encouraged by alcohol, their delusions promoted by drugs.

—

Even with four of them attending to nothing else that evening, the mayor's staff couldn't make the mayor calm down. He was already the drunkest any of them had ever seen anyone. Just past midnight, they managed to shuffle him out of a bar and into a cab, back to the presumed safety of city hall.

It was St. Patrick's Day, 2012, around the time Ford's

increasingly erratic behaviour sometimes brought a carnival-like feel to his office—all crooked walls and spinning floors and mirrors that distorted everything. Back at the funhouse this night, the mayor went straight for the fridge and pulled out a bottle of St-Rémy French brandy. He chugged it like you would an ice-cold pop on a hot summer day.

"Liberal hacks," he berated the three male staffers who were with him. Policy adviser Olivia Gondek was there too, but Ford talked about her as if she wasn't in the room. When his crude sexual comments about her were later made public, Ford would famously respond in the same vernacular—this time on live television.

Alcohol opened Rob Ford's chasm of needs. To someone offering him attention, he might be gregarious and generous—a big, huggable, stupidly drunk teddy bear who would spend hours happily posing for pictures. But his mood could change in an instant, based on how he interpreted a look, a phrase, a situation. When that happened, you'd best get out of the way.

If a foe was present, Ford the aggressive drunk would take him on. If only subservient staff members were available, out came the bully: mean, angry, abusive. The staff members who bore the brunt of his alcohol-induced personality swings could either shrug it off or leave. Most eventually quit. But tonight there was no time to consider anything other than how to pacify the beast. (I've pieced together what happened this night from police documents, a security report and the recollections of people who observed parts of it.)

"Why don't we sit down and have a bottle of water," a staffer suggested.

Ford responded with rage, interrupted by meltdowns in which he would wail in self-pity, mostly about his father, followed by more rage. Restless, Ford grabbed a list of constituents to call back and started to dial from the desk phone. That sent special assistant Brooks Barnett scrambling to unplug the line from the wall, which really made the mayor mad.

The well-dressed, well-spoken Barnett had such difficulty relating to Ford at the best of times that a senior Ford staffer suggested he learn something about football. Barnett had been the first to be pulled in that night, halfway through the weekend. City hall was closed, the mayor had no events scheduled, and he hadn't answered or returned any of Barnett's calls asking if he was needed. But Barnett waited at home, even as day became evening. Just in case.

About 7 p.m., Barnett got the call from chief of staff Amir Remtulla. "Why aren't you at city hall?" Remtulla told him to get over there fast.

When Barnett arrived, Ford was in his office intermittently swigging vodka from a large bottle and doing football sprints from a three-point stance. With Ford was Peter Kordas, one of his buddies from the neighbourhood, and Alana, a much younger, attractive new friend. Unable to control the bedlam, Barnett called Remtulla. The chief of staff then called communications assistant Isaac Ransom, who rushed over from a nearby office where he was writing a script for the mayor's Sunday afternoon radio show.

By this time, Ford was halfway through the forty-ouncer and wanted Ransom and Barnett to help him finish it off. With the situation still deteriorating, it was Ransom's turn to phone Remtulla, who sent Earl Provost to the scene. Provost, Ford's director of stakeholder and council relations, arrived in time to observe the mayor adding a pill to the mix. Then Ford decided to take the party on the road. A fourth staffer, Olivia Gondek, was pulled in to meet up with them. It was now a party of seven, more than half of whom were minding the mayor.

By the time they arrived at a bar called the Bier Markt, Ford was beyond drunk. He charged the dance floor, bumping into patrons, barely able to stay upright. The staff got him back to a table. When he sprang from his seat a second time, Ransom and Barnett grabbed an armpit each and shuffled him out the door, not caring how many bystanders they knocked into as they got him to the cab that a bouncer had already summoned.

Back at the office, Ford became more messed up by the minute. He demanded they contact yet another staff member. Barnett told the mayor the staffer was out of town and unavailable—nothing he could do about that. Something about the comment enraged his boss. Barnett was standing with his back to the mayor, unaware of what he had triggered.

Like an enraged football linebacker, Ford charged the slightly built Barnett, sending him sprawling. He landed on a couch. Ford then raised his fist, as if about to pulverize him. Ransom and Provost intervened before a punch was thrown.

Barnett got himself up. "Fuck this," he said. "I've had enough of this shit." He left the office and walked home.

Provost's night from hell wasn't over yet. It took until 3 a.m. to get Ford out through the ground floor lobby—barely able to walk, sweating profusely, swearing at Provost and making lewd comments to a female security guard. Provost got into the taxi with him. On the drive to the mayor's house, Ford told him to get out so he could make a private call. Provost refused. When they reached Ford's home, the mayor bolted from the cab and into his own car. By the time Provost got out of the cab, Ford was already pulling out of the driveway, so quickly that he almost ran Provost over.

—

Dr. Gabor Maté is the author and physician whose column on Ford I quoted earlier, and whose book *In the Realm of Hungry Ghosts* explores the relationship between addiction and childhood trauma. In an interview, I described to him the Rob Ford I know—the ten-year-old looking to make friends—and asked him to reconcile that with the person whose awful behaviour had, by that point, been extensively chronicled in the media. "Which is the real Rob Ford?"

"No, no," Maté corrected me. "You say 'real.' They both exist. But which is authentic? That's the question. I mean, if I manufacture a mask that I put on my face, the mask is real but it's not authentically me. Even if I wear it so much that I think it's me, it's still not me. So the mask is real, but it's not authentic. It does not express the real self. Underneath the mask is a normal human being. He has feelings, he cares about people. He probably has some feelings for the little guy because he was the little guy who suffered a lot. When he's not threatened, I'm sure he can be quite generous.

"Which is authentic?" he rephrased my question. "It's the ten-year-old insecure, hurt little kid."

The authentic Rob Ford.

—

There were *so many* jarring twists and turns in Rob Ford's mayoralty that it's easy to forget a few of them, even some that were big news for weeks or months. In November 2012, Rob Ford was ordered removed from office over that conflict of interest involving his coaching activities. Ford had voted on a recommendation from Toronto's Integrity Commissioner that he pay back $3,000 he had raised from lobbyists for his football charity. Instead of removing himself from the debate and decision, Ford gave an impassioned speech on the good he had done with the money. When a private citizen filed a conflict charge against the mayor, the high-profile criminal lawyer Clayton Ruby agreed to take the case pro bono, seeing this as *his* opportunity to do some good.

Ruby loves the courtroom, a place where you can publicly poke and probe the brain of a witness to get at the truth. With Rob Ford, Ruby told me, he saw an opportunity to "show the world—I think successfully in this case—that the man was making it up as he went along, that much of what he was saying was not true and could not possibly be true. . . .

"No one can press you the way a cross-examiner can. That was an exercise Ford had never engaged in before, and you could see how terribly uncomfortable he was with it. You could see in his face and his body how *miserable* he was."

Clayton Ruby won the case by convincing a judge that Rob Ford hadn't been truthful. Ford was removed from office, but the decision was stayed and then overturned on appeal. Ruby came away from it with a new understanding of the mayor.

"What I saw—the insight I had at the end—was that this is a guy who has a very narrow *interest span*. I'm not talking attention span, but interest span. His psychological peculiarity is what I call that narrowness of interest. He cannot cope with the complexity of the world he's not interested in. It's all very dangerous from his point of view. Can't cope with it. Can't understand it. It's out there. It's weird to him."

—

When dealing with the small number of topics he finds interesting—football, property maintenance problems, political contests—Rob Ford can navigate the intricacies of an issue. Otherwise, most of life seems incomprehensible to him. As mayor of Toronto, he constantly had to cover up an inability to understand much of what was happening around him.

That's why he preferred looking at a tenant's broken window to meeting with a business leader. It wasn't only the grey areas he couldn't fathom; entire subjects did not exist for him. When he asked a simple question, he wanted a simple answer. Complexity, related to anything except football, confounded and frustrated him.

"I was trying to understand, 'Why is he getting so angry at me?'" recalled a bureaucrat who was often called upon to explain something to the mayor. "He'd flip his papers down and say, 'I don't need to listen to all this shit. Tell me straight.' That's when

I started realizing, 'Okay, I have to really dumb this thing down. No big words. Very, very simple.' He might say, 'Why should we do this?' Both him and Doug: 'Why should we do this?' One of the ten reasons might be 'because we're engaging the private sector, they can do it cheaper.' I know that's what they want to hear and that's how I can get them to agree that this is the right thing to do.

"You've got to be really into their mantra—the private sector, respect for the taxpayer. As long as you fall within those bounds, you're okay. Otherwise, it's no. Even with that, you only had a few minutes to get to yes. I had to be able to summarize the problem and the solution within one sentence. If I don't do that, he can't pay attention long enough. He gets frustrated, and that frustration builds so he doesn't want to do what you are asking him to do."

—

"That narrowing is an interesting observation, and a very astute one," Dr. Gabor Maté remarked when I told him what Clayton Ruby had said. "That narrowing happens to addicts in general. They're just uncomfortable with anything beyond their immediate area of expertise. The addict is a very insecure person, threatened by anything they can't control.

"But really, what it speaks to is the person who is alienated from themselves so that large areas of their own psyche are unavailable to them. Emotions, real human interest—the many exciting aspects of life—is not available to them. To defend against a whole lot of emotional hurt, they really have to narrow themselves. Too many areas are vulnerable for them. So what Ruby is describing is not Rob's real nature, but how Rob has come to function in the world, and how he's come to define himself."

At some point relatively early in his life, if one accepts Maté's approach to understanding addicts, Rob Ford redefined himself and the world around him. After a while, he could no longer recognize the difference between what was real and what he had created.

The narrow interest concept, and the redefining of oneself to match it, would explain a lot about what baffles observers of Ford. Why does he stare blankly when you try to speak to him about something unfamiliar or uncomfortable? Why does he answer a question you didn't ask? How can he not understand the difference between an LRT train on a rail corridor and a streetcar on a main road? When he says something that is obviously not true, how can he speak with such conviction?

"One of the things I learned in the two examinations was that he absolutely has *no concern* if he's caught in a lie," said Ruby. "There's a momentary embarrassment. It's *slight*. You can see it in his face. He gets a bit flustered and red, but after a few seconds *it doesn't matter to him*. It's over. It's *gone!* Literally *gone!*

"It's much like you see him with the apologies in the public. In *his* mind, once he's apologized, *it's gone!* Not just over, finished! It's off the universe! It's a very tiny proportion of people who may be able to lie well enough that you can't tell that they're lying. Almost everybody has *some* kind of reaction to telling a lie. As a cross-examiner, you learn how to spot that.

"But this is a guy," Ruby said of Ford, "for whom all lies are equal to truth."

What did you see in his face when he was lying?

"You saw a momentary, very slight, embarrassment *at being caught*. But you didn't see anything in his face when he tells the lie. *These are very rare skills*—or psychological peculiarities. It's very, very rare."

Which is it, a skill or a psychological peculiarity?

"I think it's both," he said. "I think he has worked out his life to make this skill work, and it's easy for him because of his psychological peculiarity."

"He's become impermeable," Gabor Maté said of Rob Ford. "The lying has become second nature because that's likely how he survived his childhood. So it sounds like it's become his modus operandi. He's not even perceiving himself as lying. It's totally automatic."

I asked Dr. Maté to explain how that works.

"Well, if the lie becomes your way of surviving, then there's no longer a value judgment, a negative value to the lying. It serves the larger truth. That completely unfeeling and automatic way of being is just a way to survive."

I asked Maté if Rob Ford's sense of survival would be threatened by a person who accused him of lying, or tried to unmask him.

"Well, exactly, yeah. He becomes indignant because his very existence is being threatened. He's so identified with his lies and everything else. And when you are attacking a lie, you are actually attacking *me*."

—

The theories of Ruby and Maté may explain a lot about Rob Ford's behaviour. But what explains why a large percentage of Toronto's population believes everything the Fords say, and thinks that the Fords are, in fact, the *only* politicians who speak the truth?

"Reality bends around Rob Ford," the *Toronto Star*'s David Rider observed to me in 2014. He gave an example. "Rob and Doug have said, 'Nobody has done more for Toronto's black community than Rob Ford,' even though he's voted against a bunch of measures that would help communities where there are a lot of black people. By buying crack cocaine, he participated in Toronto's drug and gang problem that regularly leaves young black men dead. Why does a lower-income black person in Toronto Community Housing identify with a rich white guy who has never been in their circumstance, and has never gone out of his way to improve their circumstances? It shouldn't make any sense, but to a lot of those people it makes perfect sense."

Rider marvelled at the Fords' strange skills, in much the same way I do.

"The ability to stay on message and stay focused is a huge political benefit. I've been in lots of scrums with politicians where you point out the flaws in their logic and they're sort of taken aback, it puts them off. The Fords, you can point out to them every which way why it doesn't make sense, and they won't be shaken off of it. . . .

"People have said to me, 'Oh, they're just dumb, or like hill-billies.' I say, 'No, you couldn't be a simple person and have the ride that they've had.' Some people think they understand the Fords—they're this or they're that. I'm always telling them, 'You know more than I do, because I've been watching them for a long time and it's very complicated.'"

———

Both Maté and Ruby told me that psychopathic tendencies are not uncommon among the population subset known as politicians. "*You* see that a lot," Ruby told me about my own profession. "You've got to have something that drives you to do that job. . . .

"One of the characteristics of psychopaths, from a layman's point of view," he continued, "is that they *genuinely* can't see beyond themselves. It's me me me me. My interests, my interests, my interests. They can't tread very well through the complexity of ordinary human reasoning and motivation. They stop at their own skin, essentially. That's where their interests begin and end."

Ruby told me a story.

"I once talked to a psychopath—a murderer—and I said, 'If we opened the cell door right now and I stood between you and freedom, would you kill me?' We were having a friendly talk, lawyer and client. He looked at me and said, 'Clay, the truth is you're not quite real to me. And yes, I would kill you.'

"So I think there's that element of, 'Nothing is real but *me*.'"

Rob Ford, he said, "goes beyond his own skin. He cares about those kids [playing football]. Although there's an element of self-love in it: 'I'm the saviour of these kids.' But he *does* care about things that are outside himself."

I asked Ruby how one figures out who somebody is if he doesn't know himself.

"You can't ask him to explain it. He's not capable of it. To him, this is all normal. From his perspective, this is the way the world is. It's only to us looking at him where we say, 'This is not like ordinary people.'"

I commented to Ruby on how intriguing it is that someone like Rob Ford became mayor of Toronto.

"That's an aberration," Ruby said. "Who the hell knows how that happened?"

7. ROBBIE'S TURN

*"We'll support you this time, and you'll serve for a while.
And then it will be Robbie's turn."*
Diane Ford to John Tory, 2003

"Twenty dollars says you're too chicken to run for mayor,"
I said, leaning closer to the large man two seats over.
Within seconds he was all over me.

"I'm not chicken to run for mayor," Rob Ford thundered.
"I'm going to run. Not twenty dollars—make it a hundred dollars! No—" He stopped himself. "Make it a thousand dollars!"

Could a bet lure Rob Ford into a political contest he couldn't
win? Was this how we could get rid of him? Rob and I often
made $20 bets, usually on football or politics. It was a friendly
way to pass the time during tedious stretches of long meetings.
But a thousand dollars? "That's not a friendly bet," I said.

"A thousand dollars! A thousand dollars!" Ford became
more insistent. "You're the one who's chicken!"

After ten years of Ford's tirades on such subjects as the
wasteful watering of plants in city buildings, almost all of his
fellow councillors wanted him gone. Would they join me in a bet
we would hope to lose?

"Is it worth a hundred dollars to you to get rid of Rob Ford?" I began asking my colleagues. The first nine councillors I approached gleefully signed on. I knew Ford hated losing even a small bet. Once he'd bet that he was going to run, he wouldn't likely back down. And if he ran, what chance could he possibly have?

The man couldn't articulate even the far-right positions he championed. He was prone to outrageous gaffes, like blaming cycling deaths on cyclists. And lies, like when he at first denied even being at a Maple Leafs hockey game at which he eventually admitted he had been drunk and disorderly. And his demeanour! Dangerously overweight, the tips of his shirt collar pointing in all directions, bombastic to an extreme, without *any* of the statesmanlike qualities I assumed most Torontonians were looking for.

The thousand-dollar bet broke down in December 2009 when Rob wanted it cancelled if potential candidate John Tory entered the race. But by the time I next spoke with Ford, the following month, he was well into mayoralty campaign mode. Did he understand something the rest of us didn't?

Apparently so.

Perhaps his home base of Etobicoke, the epicentre of anti-downtown, anti–left wing, anti–city hall sentiment, gave him an exaggerated sense of his chances against a downtown candidate. Or maybe he simply stuck his finger in the wind and felt which way it was blowing—something most politicians had forgotten how to do.

—

Legend has it that Rob Ford's father was the driving force that compelled him to run for councillor and then mayor. It's evident that Rob did whatever he thought would please his father, or might earn his praise. It's also clear from several media interviews given by Doug Ford that their father wanted his children to do as he had done, surpassing his milestones, as both a tribute and a legacy.

Less clear is whether Doug Sr. actually encouraged his son, or if he was willing to show approval for anything Rob did. The story of what really happened between father and son is presumably known by Rob, his mother, and probably his brother Doug as well. That none of them will talk about it perhaps says as much as you need to know.

"When he ran for council in 1997, it was with the intention of becoming mayor of Toronto one day," Nick Kouvalis told me, citing a family source. "His dad said it, it was set in stone, and then it had to happen. You have to admire them for that."

But according to one of Rob Ford's friends from those days, Rob's father stung his son in 1997 by telling him he had voted for one of his rivals, Dennis Flynn. Voters could choose two councillors for each ward in that election, so it was possible for Doug Sr. to have voted for Flynn *and* Rob Ford—even though all candidates asked their strongest supporters to "plump" the vote by choosing only one. The storyteller wasn't clear on that point, only that Dad had told Rob he preferred the more experienced politician.

According to brother Doug, their father's influence was mostly by osmosis. The father "caught the bug," explained Doug, "and then Rob just followed suit." Over the course of three interviews, I asked Doug Ford several times how much his dad wanted Rob to become mayor. Each time, I got a one- or two-sentence answer, followed by a change of subject. "Conversations took place a few times before he passed," was the most he would say.

I asked whether the mayoralty would have been something their dad wanted for Rob. "I think he would, yeah," Doug said, and offered nothing more.

However muted, non-existent or negative his father's enthusiasm may have been, the idea that he could make his father proud would have been enough to set Rob on any path.

"He idolized him," said Chris Stockwell, one of many, including Rob, who have used that word to describe what the son saw when he looked at his father. "Definitely idolized him, and worked to replicate him. He just thought he was one of the brightest and most successful people he had ever met in his entire life."

Knowing that others didn't see Doug Sr. that way, I asked Stockwell, "On what basis?"

"He was his dad."

—

After Doug Sr.'s death, the Fords became a matriarchal society.

"Mom was in charge. Whenever there was a fight between the brothers, they would go to Mom's house and she would resolve it," Nick Kouvalis told me. "So I knew that she was in charge. Very quietly. Very stealth-like. She was in charge. Always."

Her husband's will gave Diane Ford what amounted to a veto over most family financial matters. No one of them made a move without a nod from her. But even while Doug Sr. was alive, Diane had taken charge of the family's political destiny.

"The father was the icon," said Val Wilson, who started volunteering for Rob in 1997. "But he wasn't the driver. Diane was. Mom worked like crazy on the campaign. She would do anything—whatever needed to be done."

"There was no limit to what she thought they could achieve," said Stockwell, who in 1995 helped Doug Sr. get elected and, four years later, sent him into retirement. "She thought there could be a dynasty. The father started it. The son was moving in, and it would carry on."

"She was very politically motivated," said Leonard Rudner, who worked with the Fords at Deco during the 2010 campaign and met Diane on several occasions. "Since she couldn't do it herself, she did it through her sons—to continue the progress that her husband had made in government."

Rudner described Diane as "a fine lady, really upper-middle class or higher. Very positive, very confident. Well dressed. In control. I remember Randy getting drunk at some affair and she admonished him and he got up and actually apologized."

Neither Doug Sr. nor Diane Ford ever spoke with Stockwell again after he defeated Doug Sr. in the 1999 nomination battle. He had interrupted their path to family political power. *Premier Ford*. Diane liked the sound of that, and so did Doug Jr. Rob thought, too, about *Prime Minister Ford*.

"My ultimate goal is not mayor," Rob Ford told the *Toronto Sun* in 2010 while seeking the mayoralty. "It's prime minister." Ford acknowledged he wasn't quite ready for the job just yet. "I've got to learn French first." In a 2015 interview with Global News, Ford set his sights a bit lower. "I'd love to be a finance minister," he said.

Who put *those* ideas in his head? His father seems to have issued the command that his sons not merely follow in his footsteps but climb past the spot where he'd fallen. "I started from nothing and came this far. And you guys have to take it to the next level," he instructed his children, according to an interview Doug Jr. gave the *Toronto Star* in August 2014.

Doug elaborated during a 2015 interview with me. "He always said, 'We've got a gold mine'"—the gold being the undefined but unlimited Ford potential. "'You've got to mine the gold.'"

Wherever he stopped, you have to keep going? I asked.

"We *have* to," Doug said. "We bought here in Etobicoke when it was farmland, and we grew up in the community. Sponsored every school team, every Rotary Club—you name it. You're *entrenched* in the community. People *rely* on it. It's [like] a big family. You rely on each other. They support us overwhelmingly, and in return for that, we respect them. When they call, we show up to their front door. That's just the way it is."

—

Doug Jr. was the obvious political heir. But he was too valuable to the family's label business, which financed their ambitions. Besides, Doug always got *everything*. It was his little brother's turn to shine.

Rob first set his sights on a council seat in 1997, the year the provincial government forced the union of six separate cities into the new "megacity" of Toronto. On that first attempt, the 28-year-old Ford finished fourth. But three years later, he unseated a lacklustre incumbent and began ten years as city council's in-house outsider.

When it came to getting one of her brood elected, Diane Ford was both skilful and tireless. She organized Rob's campaign office, schmoozed volunteers, checked the wording of speeches, got the coffee and went door knocking to round up votes. And she loved it.

"We were talking about campaigns one day," remembered Val Wilson, "and Diane said, 'I'm a political junkie. I could go from one campaign to the next. We political junkies live for elections.'" Sandra Pavan, another early volunteer, agreed. "Diane had the final say on everything. There isn't anything that goes on in a campaign that she doesn't know about."

Other family members helped out with varying amounts of enthusiasm. Doug Jr. got involved when he wasn't in Chicago. Randy pitched in, mostly with signs. By the start of the 2000 campaign, Rob was married to Renata, who was eager to help her husband. "She would come straight down from work, pick up literature and say, 'Where do I go?'" recalled Pavan. "And she'd go and go, even in the dark. That dedicated, oh yes."

But where was the presumed inspiration and leader of the Ford political dynasty? Where was Doug Sr.?

Pavan recalled him putting up a few signs in 2000 and wanting to climb on the roof of the campaign office to erect a banner in 2003. But Rob's father never went canvassing, she said, and the campaign was instructed not to disturb him, especially in the evening. "Don't bother them at night," Pavan said Diane Ford told her, "because they like to sit and have a drink together—referring to Kathy and Doug Sr."

I asked Pavan how Rob's father reacted on the night of Rob's first victory in 2000, the greatest accomplishment of his son's life to that point. "He wasn't at the campaign that night," she told me. "He was at home. And he wasn't there in 2003." Val Wilson confirmed Doug Sr.'s absence. Nobody offered any reasons for it.

Diane Ford would have to be pleased enough for both of them. What she wanted for her son—for the family—was coming true. "He was her golden boy, as far as politics was concerned," Pavan said.

In the summer of 2006, near the beginning of Rob's last campaign as councillor, Doug Sr. was diagnosed with terminal colon cancer. The annual backyard barbecue—an enormous political and social event for the Fords—was scheduled for September.

"The long weekend in August, Diane phoned me and she was upset, so I said, 'Do you want me to come down?'" remembered Sandra Pavan. "That's when she asked me if I'd be around and help with the campaign because she wasn't going to be. But they wanted the FordFest. I says, 'Why don't you just cancel it?' She said, 'No, Mr. Ford wants it to go on.'"

The night of the event, family members took turns keeping Doug Sr. company. Former premier Mike Harris and federal finance minister Jim Flaherty came by and went upstairs to show respect. In the backyard, FordFest carried on as usual, complete with the hoarding of free cheeseburgers and complaining when the free T-shirts ran out.

—

During John Tory's first run for mayor of Toronto in 2003, he made the pilgrimage to Etobicoke to seek the Fords' blessing. "I was told they were the kingpins of Etobicoke politics and that they had this amazing capacity to do things, especially with signs," Tory told me years later, during his second run for mayor—this time *against* the Fords.

Tory thought his meeting would be with "Mr. and Mrs. Ford," as he politely referred to them. He was surprised to see the whole clan waiting when he arrived at a private room at the west-end Board of Trade. After the usual niceties, Diane Ford invited everyone to take their seats. The Fords were already familiar with Tory, but he went over his background for them and said why he wanted to be mayor. They asked a few questions and discussed his campaign. Then it came time for the family to render a decision.

"It was Mrs. Ford—Diane—who spoke up," Tory recalled. "'Well, we think you're okay,' she said. 'We'll support you this time, and you'll serve for a while. And then it will be Robbie's turn.'

"'That's fine by me,'" said Tory, concealing his surprise that the family thought Rob was mayoral material. "They then did support me in the way that the Fords did. They had an event in the backyard. I was very much treated like a special guest, and they brought me up to the front and made a fuss over me. The Fords were very helpful."

—

Around the time he became the *Toronto Star*'s city hall bureau chief in February 2010, David Rider decided to spend a day with Rob Ford. He knew the renegade councillor was already talking about running for mayor, but hardly anybody was taking that very seriously. Rider wanted to check out Ford's legendary constituency work.

They started early in the morning, with Rider following Ford on a whirlwind tour of six homes where residents had sought his assistance. One guy had a problem with an addition; on another stop Ford investigated whether a strip mall owner was stealing power from a church. "There was just this hectic pace," recalled Rider. "He'd take off like a bat out of hell and he obviously knew every shortcut in Etobicoke. I lost him a couple of times. I was struggling to keep up. After three hours of that, I was exhausted. I said to him, 'I think I've got enough for the story. That's great.'

"Then he said, 'No, we've only got one more place to go and you have to come.' So then we rolled up to a factory and I thought, 'What are we doing now?' All of a sudden we're on this plant tour, and Rob says, 'We're going to show you the machines.' I'm still wondering what's going on, and then Doug pops out a door. I do a double take. It's another big blond guy. I didn't know Rob had a brother. I'm still trying to figure out what this is all about and then a second door opens and Randy pops out. These three giant blond guys are taking me on a tour of a label factory. I'm thinking, 'This is weird, this is bizarre.' Then they take me into a boardroom and they say, 'Rob is going to run for mayor.' I'm surrounded by nine hundred pounds of blond Ford laying out their battle plan to take over the city."

Rider wrote it up and the *Star* ran it with a memorable photo of the three brothers standing in front of the boardroom portrait of their father. They had the look of brothers accustomed to getting what they wanted, full of smiling domination, as if waiting for either a championship belt or the keys to the city. "I'm sure a lot of people read that and thought, 'They're all deluded, this is crazy,'" Rider said. "But, actually, it came to pass almost exactly as they said."

—

Doug Ford remembers precisely where he was when the call came in January 2010. "I was at 83 and Busse going into our plant [in Chicago] and I almost hit a telephone pole," he told me. "Rob called and said, 'I need your help. I'm going to run.'"

"Are you sure?" Doug asked.

"Yeah, I'm sure," Rob told him.

Ford had delayed the decision until John Tory announced he wouldn't run in 2010. Tory was a well-known moderate Conservative, and Ford wanted an open field on the right. Tory's announcement was the second of three gifts. The first was Mayor David Miller's announcement he wasn't seeking re-election. The third came when Miller's designated left-of-centre successor, Adam Giambrone, abandoned the race ten days after entering it. Giambrone was caught cheating on his girlfriend with a university student who, upon learning he was engaged, headed straight for the nearest newsroom. Toronto's media, which as yet had *no idea* what really bad behaviour by a political leader might look like, branded Giambrone a cad of the worst sort and kept the spotlight on him until he dropped out.

But that still left the early prohibitive favourite, former Ontario Liberal deputy premier George Smitherman. Doug asked his brother a pointed question. "Can you beat him?"

If Rob had any doubts, he kept them to himself. "I can sense it," he told his brother. "I can *feel* it. I talk to the people on the street and I think I can beat him."

Doug had learned to respect his brother's gut. "I call him the walking pollster," he told me. "He talks to every demographic, every political stripe, every religion and race you can think of— in a day. He's been doing it for years and years and years and years. It's just automatic. Rob Ford is no dummy, I'll tell ya. He may come across sometimes as that, but believe me, he *shocks* me sometimes. His instincts are better than mine. He gets the pulse from every person."

Every person, Rob's gut told him, had been waiting for an everyman.

8. THE WIND IN OUR SAILS

*"Every time they attacked Rob for being the average Joe—
everyman—that would put the wind in our sails."*
Nick Kouvalis, Ford campaign manager.

Anger came easily to Rob Ford. So did the resentment, the mistrust, the gnawing in the gut that you weren't getting something you deserved. Those same feelings festered across the city, especially around its outer edges, where the poor and the marginalized struggled to make ends meet, where crime was higher, health rates lower, transit services poorer, jobs harder to find. In 2010, these people looked at Rob Ford, a new candidate for mayor, and thought they saw somebody just like them.

Though born into privilege and a veteran of city council, Ford was an outsider to the bone. He'd never fit in anywhere, but especially not with the know-it-alls on Toronto city council who, from 2000 to 2010, mercilessly mocked and heckled every time he rose to rail against them. During those years as a councillor, his motions to cut spending routinely lost 44–1, or 43–2 when fellow Etobicoke tax fighter Doug Holyday took his side.

Located not far from the luxury condos on the waterfront and the gleaming bank towers of Bay Street, city hall was seen by downtowners as a beacon of local democracy. Ford saw it as a target, and strung it up so high that anyone who felt mistreated, for any reason, could get a clear shot at it.

Political observers trying to make sense of Ford's 2010 victory often point to three factors: lingering discontent over the forced 1998 amalgamation of Toronto and its former suburbs; the stench hanging over from the summer garbage strike of 2009; a pendulum swing to the ultra-right Ford from the left-leaning previous mayor David Miller. Add to this the inept campaigns of each of his rivals and an anti-gay bias that Ford passively exploited, particularly among some of Toronto's older ethnic residents. Ford's main rival, George Smitherman, was not only openly gay, he and his partner had adopted a child near the start of the campaign.

Still, all these factors combined can't fully explain how a man like Rob Ford became mayor of a city like Toronto, or why the Ford brand still attracted one out of three voters in the 2014 election—after his catastrophic mayoralty.

—

Toronto's population is the fourth largest in North America, its budget larger than those of several Canadian provinces combined. The mayor of Toronto is directly elected by more people than any other politician in Canada. A leader hoping to hold so powerful a position would normally possess some minimal combination of eloquence, charisma, charm, intelligence, strategic ability, analytical thinking, higher education or leadership skills. For reasons that defy conventional political understanding, Rob Ford turned his lack of such traits into a campaign asset. He possessed that perfect absence of aspirational qualities—perfect for the anti-politician campaigning to throw the bums out, a leader hell-bent on dismantling the government he would lead.

Ford didn't need to play the victim. He'd lived the part.

Ever been picked on? So had Rob!

Ridiculed? Humiliated? Him too!!

Made to feel stupid? Unloved? Vote for the poster boy!!!

His vindication would be yours, his triumph your triumph. What better way to tweak the noses of the intellectuals and big money earners, the uncaring bureaucrats and self-serving politicians, than to put Rob Ford in charge? Imagine how aghast they'd all be if this oversized outcast became Mayor Rob Ford!

—

At council, Rob Ford didn't simply speak to the city's simmering discontent. He raged and roared at it, his thick neck turning a bright red that spread quickly to his sweat-soaked forehead, as he bellowed and squeaked, so puffed up you feared he might explode right there in front of you.

This man's affinity for anger and alienation was all too real.

Among the disenchanted, attacks on Ford by other politicians only made him more of a hero. "I think everyone who opposed him in the end were the ones who made him: the left and the *Toronto Star*," said Doug Holyday, Ford's deputy mayor for most of his term. "They created an image for him that they couldn't unravel."

Holyday's many years of relentless penny-pinching had gone largely unnoticed outside Etobicoke. Rob Ford turned *his* thrift into a contact sport the media couldn't ignore. Ford's status as the defender of the taxpayer was cemented in 2007 when colleagues attacked him for *not* spending his office budget. Ford outdid Holyday's parsimony by spending *nothing*, paying for office expenses from his own pocket or through the family company.

An auditor's report supported most councillors' view that politicians with personal wealth couldn't be allowed to privately purchase whatever level of office support they could afford. That principle, however, was lost on a legion of taxpayers who cared only that, at long last, there was a politician who *didn't* want to spend their money. Ford battled on, making municipal news at once interesting and stupid. Readers, listeners and viewers were drawn to a great big angry protagonist and a simple storyline. The cheers and jeers gave Ford a city-wide prominence.

Under any normal circumstances, creating the profile to run for mayor requires years of promoting righteous causes, presenting new ideas and forming relationships. Ford merely stood his ground and let his attackers do the rest. "The media made him," continued Holyday. "I don't think they thought it would go as far as it did, but they kept making him every step of the way. They just created this guy, who never could have done it by putting forth ideas or championing things."

Next, all Rob Ford needed was someone who could distill the essence of his unusual appeal, package it up and market it to a broader range of disgruntled Torontonians.

That person wouldn't be found among Toronto's political backroom elite.

—

Nick Kouvalis was three when his parents divorced and his mother moved into west Windsor's social housing. They lived in ramshackle homes in the shadow of the Ambassador Bridge, below the grinding sound of transport trucks, next to the freight trains that rumbled along the tracks behind them. Kouvalis wasn't just poor, he was the child of poor immigrants. Barely educated, his mother and stepfather spoke no English in the home. His kindergarten teacher wrinkled up her nose at the sight of his first name—Nectarios. She changed it to Nick.

"I couldn't speak a word of English, they weren't using my real name, I was fat. I just didn't fit in. I'd walk home from school and almost every day there was trouble. Somebody would pick on me or somebody would pick on my sister, they'd want our lunch money. It was just that kind of a neighbourhood. If you had a bike, it would get stolen."

High school—"J.L. Forster, the toughest high school in the city"—didn't make his life any better. "I wasn't a good-looking rich kid. I wasn't the teachers' favourite, because I was always challenging them." To relieve his boredom and isolation, Nick became the class troublemaker, spending so much time in the vice-principal's office that he eventually spotted an opportunity there.

"He had these notepads with his signature on them, a pass so kids could get out of class. I grabbed a stack and I would sell them. So if you wanted to get out of school early, I would write you a note for thirty bucks and then you would give that to your teacher." Eventually, Kouvalis was caught and expelled. He finished high school at night while working towards the goal his parents had set for him: a permanent job on the Chrysler assembly line.

Had Kouvalis grown up in Toronto, his profile as a poor, overweight immigrant kid with working-class parents, living in social housing, feeling that he'd never been given a fair chance in life, would have made him a prime candidate for Ford Nation, the legion of Rob Ford supporters with mostly similar backgrounds. But Nick had a will to succeed and a confidence to break through any obstacles, which had been nurtured by his summers as a sea cadet.

In 1988, an oppressively hot summer in Windsor, a 13-year-old Kouvalis went looking for a place to shine and found it in nearby Lake St. Clair, and eventually on the waters of Lake Ontario, through the sea cadets programs run out of Kingston's Royal Military College. "All paid for by the government," he pointed out years later. "So I'm *not* against government programs. People *say* that, but it's just not true." It's a recurring theme for Kouvalis: not being recognized for who he really is and what he is capable of.

Sea cadets set Nick on a new course by teaching him the joy of fair competition—and the excitement of winning. "There was discipline and order and everyone was equal, so you got rewarded on the merits, not who you were or what your last name was. I didn't just go out for a sail. I wanted to be next to another boat and to go *faster* than it—having the same boat and the same sail and the same everything—but going faster than the other guy. That's the part that I like. Going *so fast* in a boat that it's beyond the boat's capability and the mast snaps in half, or the mainsail breaks and the mast falls. One time the boom hit me in the head and knocked me out of the boat. I was in a coma for two weeks. I love that stuff, right?"

After those experiences, welding bumpers onto minivans in a Windsor assembly line wasn't a long-term career option. "I'm with guys who got hired twenty-five years earlier. They're lazy. They've put in their time. And then, when you'd get a break and go for a smoke, it's mostly men, they're all divorced twice over, they're all poppin' pills or doing drugs to get through the pain in their elbow, and they're all negative. And I thought: 'I can't do this. I can't do thirty years like my dad did.'"

Trying to break free from the line's crushing routine, Kouvalis started up several businesses, one of which developed an insurance problem. His lawyer told him to seek the advice of an insurance executive who could be found Monday nights chairing a Conservative Party meeting at a local restaurant, Tunnel Barbecue.

"I told him my problem and he said he'd help, but first I would have to become a member of the party. So I paid my ten bucks and became a Conservative."

What if the insurance man had been Liberal?

"I would have joined the Liberal Party."

And if he was NDP?

"I'd probably still be working at Chrysler and running the union."

—

Nick Kouvalis became a Conservative—but one with his own definition of what that meant. "I make enough money to live in a nice house, right?" he explained. "But I don't need it. I'm a Conservative, and I believe in being conservative about things like that."

He dislikes pretenders of any stripe, and has no time for "elites" of any political persuasion. He thinks he can spot them by the champagne they drink. But his litmus test is attitude. "An elite is someone who just doesn't know what it's like for this guy in North York who has to work to pay his bills, and how the month is just a little bit longer than the bank account. They just don't know. They don't care to know. And they think they know all the answers.

"Oh yes," he continued. "Conservative elites. Liberal elites. Lefty elites. They all need to stop making so much money. But the lefty elites drive me particularly crazy because they're always talking about people who are poor, and shelter beds, and all that stuff. They have the money to make the investments themselves. Why don't they do it? They don't care who they walk over to make their next million bucks, but they want me and everyone else making a lot less than them to pay for it."

In late 2003, Kouvalis was recruited for his first campaign, playing a minor role in Belinda Stronach's unsuccessful bid to become leader of the newly formed federal Conservative Party. But a few months later, running an uphill campaign for Conservative Jeff Watson in the Windsor riding of Essex, where the federal Conservatives hadn't won in forty-six years, Kouvalis tasted political victory. "I really like this," he told himself. "I wonder if I could do it full-time?"

The success reminded him of sea cadets. He could feel the wind in his sails.

—

The first time Nick Kouvalis met Rob Ford, in March 2010, he thought, "Wow, this guy is really rough around the edges." Being from Windsor, he knew almost nothing about Toronto's maverick councillor. By now, Kouvalis was co-owner of Campaign Research, a polling, research and political strategy firm. His partner, Richard Ciano, a prominent Conservative, had joined the Ford team but would leave by May, unable to work with Doug Ford.

Nick was initially apprehensive about taking over from his partner. "Okay, how much money do they owe us for what we've already done, and are we going to get paid?" he whispered to Ciano, eyeing the Ford brothers at that first meeting. "Should we be getting our money upfront?"

Doug Ford thought Nick seemed a bit rough himself. But he liked that. "We started with his partner, Richard. He lasted about two weeks before we chewed him up and spit him out. 'Cause he was the prim and proper guy. And then Nick came in and he was more our style, kinda rough and ready. And he enjoyed it. He slept on the floor for months—in the campaign office or wherever."

For most of the campaign, Kouvalis lived in a makeshift bedroom at Deco Labels. The Fords liked that he didn't want to spend money on a fancy hotel, or any hotel for that matter. Here was a guy who rolled up his sleeves. Before long, Nick discovered he had a lot in common with the candidate.

"I related to Rob right away. I wasn't the smartest kid in school. I'm very protective of my family. I grew up poor, really poor. I grew up in social housing. So his affinity to going into these places and helping them with the holes in the walls or the bedbugs or whatever, I could *relate* to this, because that's where I grew up, in these shithouses."

Kouvalis began gathering information, starting with scoping

out Rob Ford himself. He followed the candidate on several long days of door-knocking. "He saw things differently from everybody else, and I wanted to see what he was seeing. We started at seven in the morning and went until midnight. House to house to house to house. The fence, the grass, the sod, the city cut a hole in the road, the this, the that. He had a list of all the city staff and the department heads and he just made calls from the car *and he got things done.*

"After three days, I'd figured out how he approaches things and how his mind works. It was a good chance for us to bond a bit and try to build respect." Building trust with the Fords would prove difficult. "They'd say it right to your face: 'I only trust the person I see in the mirror in the morning. I only trust the person I see when I'm shaving.' All the time. Both of them. Rob and Doug used that line over and over. All their lines go back to their dad."

But soon the brothers had Nick wondering whom they mistrusted more, him or each other. "I had no idea of the animosity between the two brothers. I had no idea. Doug wouldn't miss a chance to take a shot at his brother, and his brother wouldn't miss a chance to take a shot at him. *Constantly* undermining each other and trying to win over staffers to their points of the argument. *Every day* on every issue, *every* little thing. *So much* drama, and so much *stress.*"

No matter how he tried to resist the Fords' gravitational pull, it was hard not to get drawn in. "I don't know how many times I told everybody in that family, 'I work for Rob Ford, he's the candidate, and this is what he wants. So I'm doing what he wants.' And Doug would often say to me, 'No, you work for the Ford family. That's who you work for. This is the Ford brand, and that's who you work for.'

"And I would say no, and he would say yes."

Partly to reduce Doug's influence, Kouvalis looked for ways to spend more time with Rob, to keep building a relationship. "He wanted to lose some weight and was going every day to the track. And Doug smokes a lot and is out of shape, and this was an opportunity for me to get another two hours with Rob every day, without Doug. And so I started running with him. We would walk and then we would jog and then we would walk."

For two hours each day, they talked. "About everything: 'When did you start as a councillor? You lost your first race? Tell me about your dad. So what did he think? How'd you guys come to the conclusion that you should run for mayor?'

"I don't think Rob Ford has a lot of real friends, so I became his friend, and then I was able to convince him that the campaign needed structure. And these are complicated things, for Rob. He resisted structure and putting people in charge. He'd say, 'All they want is a title and then to just sit around.' And I'd say, 'Not the people who work for me. I won't let that happen. Do you see me sitting around?'

"And he would say, 'I've never met anyone like you, Nick. I've been doing campaigns all my life with my father and brothers, and you're the first campaign manager who actually did any work.' So then I'd say, 'The people will work harder for me if they see that there's no light between us. But if they think they can go to Doug and get their way, and you then support Doug, I can't make them work.'"

—

Both Rob and Doug Ford had little understanding of the sophisticated data-based campaign Kouvalis wanted to run. They knew there was political value in the phone calls Rob returned, and his many visits to people's homes. "These are gold," Rob Ford said to me one day, brandishing a fistful of papers containing the names and numbers of constituents with problems. But they didn't understand that the gold was of limited value stashed away in old boxes of lists and business cards and scraps of paper. Kouvalis used the information to start a database.

But contrary to popular myth, those boxes were only the very small beginning of their data collection, said Mitch Wexler, who joined Ford's campaign team in early April 2010, as the person in charge of creating and managing a database. Wexler had been active in Conservative campaigns since his university days. As soon as Rob Ford unofficially entered the race, he called to offer his professional services. True to form, Ford called him back, close to midnight. But it was Kouvalis and Ciano, who'd bought his first Conservative Party membership from Wexler years earlier, who brought him on board.

Kouvalis and Wexler worked as a team. Nick mined most of the data, collecting phone numbers, e-mail addresses and other supporter info through telemarketing and telephone town halls. Wexler sorted and analyzed the data, which in turn gave Kouvalis information about where he should look to identify more supporters. By the time the official voters' list came out in early September, Ford had about 80,000 known supporters. By election day, the number was up to 350,000.

Who were they?

"When we did the demographics, it showed he brought out a group of people that I termed 'bread-and-butter Canadians,'" said Wexler. "They go to work every day, they work hard, they don't want to worry about politics. They worry about putting the food on the table and they want to spend time with their family and they don't want to have to worry about things like garbage pickup. Rob was able to speak to those people. He had a very, very strong appeal.

"We didn't analyze it during the campaign. I think we just understood that this was something different—that Ford appealed to people as a regular guy. The people who were fed up with the elites and the 'smart' people downtown saw a lot of themselves and their daily struggle in Rob Ford."

—

Meanwhile, candidates with grandiose policy pronouncements were befuddled that their campaigns faltered while Ford's star ascended. Even more baffling, his numbers took a bump every time an incident of misbehaviour hit the front pages.

"You've got to take the negative stuff they will throw at Rob and make it the energy of the campaign," one adviser told Kouvalis and Ciano. "The wind in our sails," Kouvalis thought, remembering a phrase from sea cadets. "This was our code name. Every time they attacked Rob for being the average Joe— everyman—that would put the wind in our sails."

Rather than trying to present Rob Ford as something he was not, Kouvalis worked with what he had. Ford's limited understanding of complex issues matched that of most voters. Let the opponents attack his ignorance, then let the average guy decide who sounded right.

"I never try to make a candidate say something he wouldn't do normally or naturally. This is the difference, I think, from other campaign managers. You work with the attributes you have. His weaknesses were that he wasn't articulate, he was boorish, he was fat. He didn't like to spend money. So why put him in a nice suit? I enjoyed watching the wrinkled collar all the time. I think that played well. It was *natural* for him. And every time someone mentioned looks, his appearance, his deportment, the way he carried himself, we said, 'That's the wind in our sails.'"

Kouvalis figures the Wind in Our Sails effect was already happening before Ford ran for mayor. In a 2008 speech at council, in a city where more than half the population was born outside Canada, Ford had this to say about Asians: "Those Oriental people work like dogs. They work their hearts out. They are workers non-stop. They sleep beside their machines. That's why they're successful in life. . . . I'm telling you, the Oriental people, they're slowly taking over."

Thinking he was paying tribute to the "Oriental" work ethic, Ford couldn't comprehend the demands for an apology afterwards or the protests outside his office. "At no time did I ever offend the Asian community by giving them a compliment," he offered in his own defence, introducing, as exhibit A, a supermarket flyer advertising "Oriental-flavoured" sauce.

As Kouvalis told it, "He started it by saying, 'The media makes fun of me for saying Orientals work hard—but they do work hard.' And the media would say, 'He just said it again.' Wind in our sails.

"They made fun of him for saying 'roads are for cars and for trucks.' Wind in our sails."

—

Toronto mayoralty campaigns are gruelling ten-month marathons in which the winner is often the one who makes the fewest mistakes. Most contenders couldn't survive even one major slip-up. Take the example of Adam Giambrone, forced from the campaign for cheating on his girlfriend. It was hard to imagine that someone as volatile, controversially opinionated, and indiscreet as Rob Ford could possibly survive so lengthy an examination. Towards the midpoint of the campaign, there were several moments when Ford appeared to teeter on the edge of self-destruction.

The first major incident involved a tape of Rob Ford, made in June 2010, in which he agrees to try to buy OxyContin for Dieter Doneit-Henderson, a gay man living with HIV. The Fords had befriended him a month earlier in a short-lived attempt to demonstrate that Rob wasn't homophobic. (During a 2006 council speech against funding for AIDS prevention programs, Ford had declared, "If you are not doing needles and you are not gay, you wouldn't get AIDS probably.")

During the campaign, the *Toronto Star*'s David Rider was doing a feature on Ford's most outrageous statements. He invited Rob to explain himself. When they got to his AIDS comment, Rider mentioned that a gay man had contacted the newspaper to say how offended he was that Ford's campaign hadn't called him back.

"Rob got really agitated," Rider remembered. "'Nobody got back to him? Let's go over there!' The next thing I know, there's me, a photographer and the Fords in this weird motorcade."

When they arrived at Doneit-Henderson's apartment, Rob Ford told him and his husband, "I feel terrible. I feel hurt if I offended you in any way." Not to be outdone by his brother's uncharacteristic display of gay-friendliness, Doug Ford added: "I've had my gay friends come and visit me in Chicago. Gay men have slept in my bed."

"With you in it?" asked Doneit-Henderson.

"Now you're trying to get me in trouble," Doug answered with a chuckle.

As a result of the meeting, Doneit-Henderson signed on to the Ford campaign. A month later he was on the phone asking Rob to score him some OxyContin, a prescription painkiller and street drug. Doneit-Henderson taped the conversation, then turned it over to Rider.

Kouvalis and Ford were on the running track when the candidate told him to expect a call from the reporter.

"About what?"

"Wants to know if there's some conversation I had where I offered to buy someone OxyContin."

"What are you talking about?"

"Oh, nothing. Forget it."

They ran a bit more, then Kouvalis resumed the conversation.

"You didn't tell me that for no reason."

"Talk to Rider."

"Well, give me some information."

"Nothing. Rider says he has a tape of me."

Figuring Rob was too embarrassed to tell him the truth, Kouvalis called the campaign's deputy communications director, Fraser Macdonald, and told him to do whatever was necessary to get a copy of the tape. Macdonald, then twenty-four and social media savvy, set up a Twitter account for a made-up George Smitherman supporter calling herself Queen's Quay Karen.

"So, Fraser's a really smart guy," Kouvalis recalled. "He dressed 'Karen' up as a downtown female lesbian who was into George Smitherman and couldn't stand Rob Ford. He then befriended Doneit-Henderson, who, like Rob, had no friends, and let Doneit-Henderson go on and on about how he had the goods on Rob. Eventually, Doneit-Henderson, like Rob, needed to be appreciated and respected so much that he gave our guy, Queen's Quay Karen, the tape.

"So he brought it to me. I couldn't believe what I was hearing.

"I went to Rob and said, 'Okay, I've listened to the tape. It's bad. Like, you actually offered to buy him drugs, illegal drugs. Why would you do such a thing, Rob?'"

"It didn't happen. It's not true," Ford told him.

"But I have it on tape. I've just listened to the damn thing twice."

With Rob still denying what Kouvalis had on tape, Nick asked for a family sit-down. The meeting was held in a board-room at Deco Labels overseen by the large portrait of Doug Sr. Kouvalis played the entire 52-minute tape for the family.

"Doug was angry as hell. Randy wasn't saying anything. Diane—furious. And Rob's got his head buried in his knees, you know, ashamed. Diane is saying, pointing to the picture of his father, 'If your father were here right now, God help you, Robbie. Unbelievable. You're letting the whole family down.'"

Fearing the *Star* would wait until just before the election to release the tape, Kouvalis proposed leaking it immediately. On the tape, Doneit-Henderson had said he could see Rob's house. It was late at night and Rob was home with his children. His story would be that he agreed to try to help the man because he felt threatened. The family opposed Kouvalis's plan to leak the recording. He did it anyway.

"We couldn't let the *Star* have this in their back pocket in October. The Fords, I was convinced, couldn't think that far ahead. So I just did it. I mean, what was the worst thing they were going to do to me? Fire me? Well, the campaign was over anyway, if we didn't leak it. I wanted to win."

Kouvalis didn't know that a *Star* editor had already decided to kill the story—at least for the time being—fearing it would look as if the newspaper was targeting Rob Ford. Following his instincts, Kouvalis gave the tape to a Ford-friendly columnist at the *Toronto Sun*, who accepted Rob's story that he'd felt threatened and was just trying to get off the phone. Whoever leaked the tape, Ford said, was trying to set him up.

"I don't know any drug dealers," Ford told the columnist. "I don't even know what this shit—that's what I call drugs—what this shit is."

Within a few days, the story had blown over. After his strategy had obviously worked, Kouvalis told the family what he'd done. They all had a good laugh.

"The OxyContin thing wasn't planned, but it fit right in," said Kouvalis. "Wind in our sails."

But even before this incident, Kouvalis was wondering what might be buried in Rob Ford's basement. "Anything you haven't told us?" he had asked Ford.

"No. Nothing."

"Are you sure?"

"No. Nothing."

"I asked Doug, 'Is there anything we need to know?' I asked Diane, 'Is there anything we need to know?'

"'No, no, everything is fine.' Like, you'd think Diane, who was in her seventies, is not lying to you."

Kouvalis had already seen enough of the Fords to not trust what they were saying. He hired a private investigator, who turned up a police report on one Robert Bruce Ford, arrested for drunken driving in Florida in 1999.

"It's not me," Ford told Kouvalis. "It's a different person."

A few days later, Kouvalis was in the campaign motorhome with Ford when a reporter called asking about a Florida DUI conviction, and also a dropped charge for marijuana possession. The political pundits swung into action, predicting that this was one Ford scandal too many.

FORD'S DRUNK DRIVING CHARGE COULD STEER HIS CAMPAIGN INTO THE DITCH, read an August 19, 2010, headline in the *Globe and Mail*. "Until now, Mr. Ford has been an unstoppable everyman," the story read. "Despite his history of gaffes and buffoonery, he has marched up the polls with a rallying cry against taxes and waste, flummoxing his more polished opponents. Although his hard-core supporters won't budge, the incident could turn off undecided voters and send his campaign into freefall . . .

"'This really is a train wreck,' said Myer Siemiatycki, a municipal politics expert at Ryerson University. 'I think for many Torontonians, this will be a game changer.'"

But many Ford supporters saw it as another set-up by his enemies and their media friends, desperate to gang up on the populist front-runner.

"Wind in our sails," said Kouvalis, who called a press conference at which Ford declared, "This campaign is not about mistakes made eleven and a half years ago, by me or by any other candidate. I am not perfect. I have never claimed to be perfect."

Eventually, most Torontonians would grow tired of Ford's "I never claimed to be perfect" line. But in 2010, it struck many as new and refreshing: here was a politician who puts his flaws on display, even as he courts your vote. Days after the DUI revelation, a new poll showed that Ford's lead had increased.

"The bump was because of the scandal," said Mitch Wexler. "Because people saw him as real. He was exactly as he was presenting himself to be, which was imperfect. He was authentic, and he was straight-up. He said he made a mistake, and that was it."

—

For Kouvalis, the final, defining Wind in Our Sails came during a televised all-candidates debate on August 17. Rob had been prepped for the usual issues, and had his default answers at the ready. But debate moderator Stephen LeDrew was cueing up shots of refugees from Sri Lanka on board a boat heading to Canadian shores.

"So they go back to the candidates and start getting commentary," remembered Kouvalis. "And Smitherman says, 'Well, of course we're going to let them in the country. They're political refugees.' And they turn to Rob and Rob says, 'NOPE! NOPE!'"

When they cut to a commercial break, Kouvalis raced onto the studio floor. "I ripped the mic off his jacket and pulled him into the corner and I said, 'We don't have the road capacity to handle more people, we don't have the school capacity, we don't have the hospital capacity. We've got to provide good services for the people who waited in line properly and filled out their papers and came into the country legally. And once we do that, then we're open to new people. Go.'"

Ford followed the script. "Right now, we can't even deal with the 2.5 million people we have in the city," he said. "I think it is more important to take care of people who are here now before we start bringing in more people. We've got enough problems already. We're gonna deal with what we have here."

His opponents were delighted. George Smitherman declared it "a turning point in the election" that would "awaken Torontonians to what he's all about." Opponent Rocco Rossi held a press conference to declare, "I am offended. I am appalled. And I believe this man is unfit to be mayor."

Five days later, Ford's support rose to 44 percent.

"The immigrants, he was already good with them because he'd helped so many of them, but this was when it solidified," explained Kouvalis. "Because they had waited in line. They had filled out papers. They worked hard and they paid taxes. They don't want people coming over here as freeloaders. That's Rob's gut political instincts. When the man is sober, he has got amazing gut instincts. He understands how people feel. He can't articulate it, but he knows how they feel."

—

Controversy kept Rob Ford at the centre of election coverage from June through August, by which time his core vote had solidified. "There was no oxygen available for any of the other campaigns," observed Mitch Wexler. "None of the other candidates—in particular, George Smitherman—could get a word in edgewise. They couldn't present their campaigns. There was simply no room. He had basically won the election by August, and subsequent to that it was just a matter of steering the ship into shore."

But as Ford was less in the news and the battle against him seemed to have subsided, Ford Nation took a nap. It started to look as though Smitherman was making a comeback and an "anybody but Ford" movement might gain traction. Although Ford's internal polling and growing database were positive, as election day neared, Wexler was concerned that Ford's followers hadn't yet shown up for the final month's critical day-to-day work.

"We weren't able to build the door-knocking side of the field operation to the extent that we wanted to. We knew we had tons of voters identified and we had to pull out our vote." On election day, the campaign needed to reach 350,000 identified supporters. To do that, it had to assemble, by hand, a volunteer kit for each of the city's more than 1,800 polling stations.

"To do the operation on the ground, we needed over three thousand volunteers. That's a really, really difficult number to raise up in a single municipal campaign—especially when many of these people hadn't really done anything. We were skeptical we'd be able to achieve it. But we went ahead with the plan. We rallied people, we told them, 'It's now or never.'"

The election was held on the last Monday in October. By the middle of the week before, Wexler was watching as volunteers poured into the Etobicoke office. The same thing was happening at a second office in Scarborough. "It was just an amazing thing to see. All of these people who said they would help out—they showed up at the end of the campaign and made it happen. It was against all probability, and so I will always remember how fantastic it was. On election day, 3,500 volunteers materialized out of nowhere and we were able to completely execute our plan."

—

As the thought sunk in that Rob Ford would likely become Toronto's next mayor, some members of the Ford team felt twinges of apprehension. Wexler remembered standing in the campaign parking lot with a veteran organizer.

"We looked at each other and I said, 'Can you imagine if we actually elect this guy?' We knew that there was something—*wrong* is not the right word, don't use the word *wrong*—but there would be something unusual, risky. We couldn't, we just couldn't imagine having him as the mayor.

"I don't think we were having second thoughts as much as we were bracing ourselves for what could possibly happen. And I guess, in hindsight, we were right to think that. We were expecting controversy, we were expecting hyperbole, we were expecting bull-in-a-china-shop-type governance. We weren't expecting the addictions and the full scale of the sideshow."

9. STOP THE GRAVY TRAIN

"Everybody had their beef against city hall. 'Stop the gravy train' encapsulated all of them."
Nick Kouvalis, Rob Ford 2010 campaign manager

It was a nugget of political gold, a four-word sentence that would become the rallying cry for every voter who felt shunned by previous politicians. Nick Kouvalis uncovered it while reviewing clips of Rob Ford's blustery speeches at council. In one of them, Ford scolds his colleagues: "It's nothing but a gravy train."

Kouvalis and Richard Ciano used focus groups to test that clip, along with several others. "I didn't know that the 'gravy train' one was better than the others until we showed all of them," Kouvalis told me. "When that one was played, we watched the body language. We just *saw* a reaction. So we took a break and I said to Richard, 'Play that one again and then have them talk about it for five minutes. Let's see what they say.'"

"Gravy train" struck a dissonant chord, the perfect accompaniment to Rob Ford's anti-establishment screed. "Everybody in the room is going '*councillors*,'" said Kouvalis, mimicking their scorn. "'We should just cut all of them. They're all on the gravy train.' I couldn't believe it. Call in another group, just women, same thing. Call another group of downtowners. Same thing.

"I thought, 'Wow! This is powerful!'"

The slogan could be used to attack almost anybody or anything. But it also had tremendous defensive potential. When Rob Ford was criticized for bad policy and even worse behaviour, he could dismiss the attacks as entirely predictable. Of course they were coming after him! Rob Ford wanted to derail the gravy train, so it wasn't surprising that everyone riding it would stop at nothing to protect their power and privilege.

Kouvalis spun the narrative. "They're going to say, 'Rob's just terrible because Rob's going to stop the gravy train' and they don't want anyone to touch that little gravy train they have. The environmentalists and the activists, and all the trough feeders and all the poverty pimps. And that was the kind of language we used, and it worked. I was shocked at how everyone just took the bait. It was really simple. It didn't take a lot."

Stop the Gravy Train would help propel Rob Ford to Toronto's highest office. It was his own thought, in his own words: the perfect slogan to capture anything and everything anyone was angry about.

"*Stop the Gravy Train* meant different things to different people," Kouvalis said to me three years later. "Everybody had a different beef against city hall: service was poor, slush fund for councillors, sole sourcing of a contract, the vehicle registration tax, the land transfer tax, the wildcat strike with the TTC, the garbage strike. Everybody had their issue. And *Stop the Gravy Train* encapsulated all of them."

—

Ford needed no prompting to bellow this message. But Kouvalis trained him in *how* to use it, a task made easier by the candidate's simplified view of every issue: good or bad, right or left.

"Rob's not like a John Tory, who is really smart and well versed and educated and who wants to *explain* to everyone how he knows every little bit of the file—which is *really bad when you're campaigning*, 'cause you get in the *weeds*," Kouvalis explained. "So one of the first things I said to Rob when I took over the campaign was, 'If a reporter asks you a question, why do you answer the question?'

"'Well, they're asking a question,' he replied. 'I've got to answer the question, buddy.' And I said to him, 'No, these are your six answers. You pick the one you think is best for the question. You never say anything but these six things. And when you're in trouble, you use number six. Even if it doesn't make any sense.'" (Number six was promising not to spend taxpayers' money tearing down the Gardiner Expressway, a crumbling eyesore that carried many thousands of motorists each day along the city's lakeshore.)

"What do you think about the Peter Street shelter?" a reporter might ask. And Ford would offer up one of his six answers. "And then they'd say, 'But you're not really answering the question!'" recounted Kouvalis. "And he'd get a bit flustered and then he'd say, 'Well, I'll tell you what I'm *not* going to do: I'm not going to spend $300 million to tear down the Gardiner!' That was number six, and he'd say it all the time. It was never coherent, but it *worked*!"

Kouvalis also utilized Rob's street fighting experience. Look for the opponent's weakness and exploit it. George Smitherman had an open wound: the money wasted by the province, while he was minister of health, on a program known as eHealth. Kouvalis, from the corner of the ring, coached Ford on how to exploit that.

"'EHealth, it's the cut. It's open. Focus on the cut. Forget the ribs, forget the body blows, focus on the fucking eye!' It was a game and he played it. So the question would be, 'Are you tearing down the Gardiner?' And the answer would be, 'No, I'm not spending $300 million to tear down the Gardiner. But George Smitherman, he'll spend a billion dollars to do it 'cause he just blew a billion dollars on eHealth.'

"He just kept doing it, and it was great."

—

Ford officially launched his risk-filled campaign on March 26, 2010, in Etobicoke's massive Toronto Congress Centre. His opponents had cautiously staged their kickoffs in small, easy-to-fill rooms. Ford picked a space so large that anything less than the adoring throng that turned out would have looked like a flop. Along with the vast amounts of free food and booze, Ford served up promises of lower taxes and better service, invoking the simple ideology of his father. "My idol. I know you're with me, Dad," he said, choking up onstage. "I know you're with me."

Only two councillors showed up, and only two Conservatives of any prominence: federal finance minister Jim Flaherty and his wife, MPP Christine Elliott, both family friends. But the size of the crowd—1,600 people by *Toronto Star* reporter David Rider's count—heralded something new for Toronto politics.

Rider was the only mainstream journalist who considered the event significant enough to cover. "It wasn't because I thought he could be mayor," Rider told me four years later, "but because I thought he was a fascinating guy. I wanted to see what kind of turnout he'd get and what sort of people were interested in him."

Everyday people, it turned out. Lots of them. Before long, news outlets that skipped the launch would be examining his every word, certain to find an easy news story in his rancorous and unfiltered thoughts.

—

If the simple messaging of Rob Ford's even simpler message was essential to his campaign, a second key element was keeping track of the people who liked what they heard. "The data was our lifeblood," said Mitch Wexler. "It was how we reached people and how we drove them out on election day."

The least sophisticated, least technologically savvy of all the major candidates for mayor since the new city had been formed thirteen years earlier, Ford lucked into a team that knew how to use data and technology to identify supporters drawn to his intuitive political approach. The database allowed the campaign to assemble important pieces of information in one place, and then to combine it for multiple purposes.

For provincial or federal elections, a political apparatus gathers data between elections. In Toronto campaigns for mayor, with no formal political parties, any candidate who isn't an incumbent starts with little or no data on some 1.5 million potential voters.

Wexler constructed Ford's database from basic blocks of publicly available information, starting with the voters list, which he then merged with a phone directory list. He divided the combined data into postal codes and then merged that with Statistics Canada profiles on who lived within each code: average household income, education levels, ethnic background, family size.

Using automated polling and telephone town halls—techniques never before used on such a scale in a Canadian municipal campaign—Kouvalis continuously populated the database with the names of likely supporters. When residents responded to a polling question by pushing a number on their phone keypad, the Ford campaign knew where they lived and what they thought. Data was collected on anyone who contacted the campaign office, went to its website or attended an event. Ford supporters were remarkably willing to give his campaign their name, address, e-mail and postal code.

The profiles showed, for example, that Ford's support was highest among those with lower incomes and less education. As a result, Wexler searched for other postal codes where similar people were concentrated. This told the campaign where it should focus its limited resources to collect the greatest number of votes.

The database also logged those willing to volunteer for various tasks, take a lawn sign or make a financial donation. It stored individual voters' opinions on particular issues. Once gathered and entered, the data would be pulled off, one field at a time or in combinations of fields. Wexler could, for example, instruct the database to provide a list of identified Etobicoke voters who shared Ford's opposition to the land transfer tax but hadn't yet made a campaign donation.

Kouvalis used polling to verify patterns of support. This, in turn, allowed him to identify more probable supporters. To use a simple example, once a statistically valid sample showed that Ford had 80 percent support in Etobicoke's Ward 2, where he had been councillor, the campaign decided to remind the entire area to get out and vote. "It didn't matter if we pulled up one of Smitherman's votes in the course of pulling up four extra Ford votes," explained Wexler.

The same technique worked with any identifiable group. Kouvalis obtained a list of 14,000 real estate agents, likely allies because of Ford's promise to cut the land transfer tax, which increased the cost of buying a home. "I would do a quick poll of those 14,000 numbers. It might cost $500 and I might only get a 5 percent response rate. But if 80 percent of them answer they're voting for Rob Ford, I'd take all 14,000 and call them on election day."

The database allowed Ford's team to assign a numerical value to each possible voter, indicating their level of support. If a voter e-mailed a positive comment or requested a lawn sign, that gave them a score. If they responded well to a telemarketing call, or attended a candidate's event, that raised the score. At election time, they targeted those with the highest scores. A volunteer was dispatched or a robocall programmed to encourage them to get out and vote.

When the 2010 voters list was released by the city in September, Wexler combined his data with the million and a half entries on the list. "I crawled into my data dungeon and stayed there for two or three weeks and then came back out with everything merged."

—

When the data was analyzed, it stood Toronto politics on its head. Ford, the extreme right-wing candidate, was strongest in areas that traditionally voted for centrist or left-wing politicians. This matched his high support among blue-collar workers and immigrants. Kouvalis directed the campaign to focus on specific geographic areas where these populations were concentrated: the former suburbs of Scarborough, Etobicoke and North York.

Ford voters also included another surprising category: people who don't vote. Unless it's for Rob Ford. "There are a lot of people in every election, when you go to the door, they say, 'All politicians are liars.' That's the common phrase," Wexler said to me. "The people who thought that way, by and large, were supporters of Rob Ford. And still are supporters of Rob Ford."

In 2010, the number of voters jumped more than 25 percent from four years earlier. "It was a lot of the same demographic we had detected," Wexler concluded. "A lot of new Canadians, a lot of blue-collar, lower-income people who don't normally feel represented by the system and therefore haven't typically voted."

—

Back at city hall, where council meetings continued during the lengthy campaign, councillors noticed a very different Rob Ford. Gone were the hostile explosions, the red face, the angry rise in the pitch of his voice. Even below-the-belt comments about his late father didn't provoke the usual furious response. Councillors speculated that he must have been medicated.

For the last few months of the campaign, Kouvalis shadowed Ford; he maintained to me that the candidate was focused, sober and likely not taking drugs. But knowing that Ford was capable of completely losing control, even during a televised debate, Kouvalis employed techniques to reduce the likelihood of that happening.

"We practised the Dad stuff a lot, goading him in debate prep. I went after his brothers. I went after his *mother*. He knew we were practising, he knew why I was doing it, and he'd still get mad. One time I said to him, 'Don't talk to me about your father, your father called these black kids darkies not ten years ago.' He got really mad at me.

"I said, 'Someone's going to say that to you, are you going to get mad at *them*? You're *not* going to get mad at them. You're going to take a deep breath and you're going to say, 'I love my father.'"

Kouvalis often resurrected Doug Sr. as a motivational tool. "When I was in a jam and needed something done, I'd figure out a way to bring his dad into the equation and get my way on it. But I had to use it carefully. If I didn't like something he was saying, or if I didn't like the way he was thinking about something, I'd say, 'What would your dad say? How do you think he would feel? How do you feel he would think?' I'd use those words *feel*, *felt*, *thought* and *father* and I'd use them together."

Four years after his death, Doug Sr. remained extremely influential with the candidate.

—

By August 2010, Ford seemed unstoppable, vulnerable only to a coordinated and concerted effort by his opponents to get behind one candidate. Co-operation of this sort seldom happens in Toronto politics, and George Smitherman had chased after Ford so far to the right that supporters of the left-wing candidate, Joe Pantalone, weren't inclined to move to him.

Toronto's "progressive" leaders were in a state of shocked disbelief at Ford's increasing lead in the polls. The Conservative hierarchy, which at first kept their distance from the uncouth, uneducated Ford, now wanted to reserve a seat on the new gravy train. "Near the end of the campaign, a lot of Conservatives were coming in to say, 'We support you, Rob,'" Kouvalis recalled. "I was like, 'No you don't! Get the fuck out of here!' Including Mike Harris," he said, smiling. "Do you want to know that story?"

I did.

In Ontario, Mike Harris is a Conservative icon, the former premier who twice led his party to majority governments under the banner of his "Common Sense Revolution." In office, Harris had cut spending and slashed government programs. Ford was looking forward to doing the same at city hall.

"All right, it's August," Kouvalis began, with enthusiasm. "We've spent a lot more money than we've raised. They were desperate to raise money. Here comes Mike Harris. Calls up Doug Ford and says, 'Doug, you and Rob should come down to my office, we should have a meeting.'"

It has taken Kouvalis weeks to wrestle control of the campaign from Doug Ford's grip. "There've been so many meetings that I didn't know of, that have all turned into a disaster, that I'd made a rule: no fucking meetings. None of you fucking guys are fucking talking to *anybody* unless I know about it. *I need to fucking know everything.*' I was swearing like that at them. And so Doug says, 'Oh, we're going down to Mike Harris's office for an afternoon coffee, just to chat with Mike.'" (The late Doug Ford Sr. had served that one four-year term in Harris's government. An enormous photograph of Ford Sr., posing with Harris, would later dominate the wall behind Rob Ford's desk in the mayor's office.)

"So I said, 'I'm coming,'" Kouvalis continued.

"Doug says, 'Oh, you can't come. You weren't invited.'

"I said, 'I'm coming! I know what he wants, and I'm coming. Because you guys don't have the balls to stand up to him. I'm coming.'

"'What does he want?' Doug asks.

"I said, 'He wants to offer you money, he's going to raise you money so he can get in on the campaign. Right?

"'These guys are all in business to make money. These are the fucking people we're running against. These downtown elites include Conservative elites. We're running *against* these people. We should not be spending one minute of our time with them. I'm coming.'"

Doug Ford didn't share Kouvalis's aversion to elites, especially if they were influential Conservatives with money.

"'Don't create a scene,' he warned.

"'I will if I have to. I'm coming.'

"'You're not coming. You're not coming.'

"So I just went anyway," Kouvalis told me. "I showed up.

"We get into the elevator going up and Doug is telling me in front of Rob, 'You don't say a word in there. You don't say *a goddamn word* in there. You shouldn't be here.' And Rob is, 'C'mon, Jones [the brothers' nickname for each other], leave Nick alone. He's part of the family.'"

Rob was tired of being outmuscled by his big brother. Grabbing the chance to make it two against one, he sided with Nick.

"So we go in and they have this long chat about their father in Harris's caucus, and what a great guy Doug Ford Sr. was, how much Mike Harris appreciated him. You know, the niceties, it's all nice, a nice chat, everybody feels good about it. Then they get down to brass tacks. Mike asks, 'Where are we at with numbers?' Very official. 'What's the spread? Do you think you've peaked too soon?' And then he gets into, 'Where is the spending at? How are you on the campaign funding?' And then he offers, 'I'll do a quarter-of-a-million-dollar fundraising for you.'"

Kouvalis had remained silent as it unfolded as he expected. He knew Doug would happily give Harris whatever he wanted in return for a much-needed cash infusion.

"Doug's like, 'Great!' I'm waiting to see what Rob says. If Rob says great, I'm not going to say anything, 'cause he's the candidate and I work for him. But if Rob shows *any* bit of discomfort, I'll just jump in and I'll be the bad guy, not Rob. So Rob says, 'Well, you know, I'm not sure we need a fundraiser right now.'

"'What are you talking about?' Doug jumps back in. 'We're bleeding all over the place!'"

And so Kouvalis interceded. "What I think the candidate for mayor is trying to say—even though Mike Harris in all of our eyes is a Canadian patriot—he would be a fucking disaster for us at this point in our campaign."

Kouvalis looked right at Harris and continued. "We will win, and you will raise three-quarters of a million dollars. After we win—but not before."

Harris can't believe he's being spoken to like this. "Who the fuck are you?" he asked Kouvalis.

"I said, 'My name is Nick and it's a pleasure to meet you. I'm a big fan of what you did as premier in the nineties. But you, and all the people that you associate with, will not be associated with this campaign until *after* we win, and then you will help us raise money.' Doug and Rob were just shocked, and that was the end of the meeting. Mike was furious, *furious. Still furious. Still.*"

Years later, Kouvalis remained disturbed by the opportunists-come-lately who tried to join the campaign at the end. "Yeah, well they all wanted to be on the winning team. All of them. All of them who said Rob Ford is a knuckle-dragging animal who couldn't tie his own shoes and should never be the mayor of Toronto, they were all lining up to literally put their fricking lips right on his ass. It was disgusting to watch all of it, and I'm happy if you quote me on that. Because it was disgusting."

When the campaign ended, Kouvalis and Doug Ford continued their tug-of-war for control of a mayor who listened to no one. Kouvalis became Ford's chief of staff; Doug asserted his lifetime role as Rob's smarter, more capable big brother. For Kouvalis, ending the gravy train required a mayor who showed up every day ready to lead the government in a new direction. When that kind of mayor didn't materialize, he left city hall, unable to accomplish what he wanted to with the Fords. Disillusioned, he would eventually turn against them.

10. FORDS AT THE GATES

"He's gonna be the greatest mayor this city has ever, ever seen. Now put that in your pipe, you left-wing kooks."
Right-wing kook and hockey commentator Don Cherry

The matronly voter narrowed her eyes. "Are you with the city?" she asked the man supervising an Etobicoke polling station on Election Day 2010. Her tone was more accusatory than questioning.

"Yes," he replied politely.

She thrust her ballot into the box. "Well," she said, "we're comin' to get ya."

And come they did, the fearsome Ford brothers, entering through city hall's tall wooden doors, holding a key to the mayor's office but still taking the place by storm.

"Remember *Braveheart*, where *all* the people were standing on the hill, and the army came *whipping* down the hill going crazy?" Doug Ford said to me one day, wanting to capture the fervour of the Ford followers. "That's Ford Nation."

—

On October 25, 2010, Toronto's electorate split in two, one part fearful that this barbarian of a mayor would ransack everything that they valued, the other part rejoicing that a man of the people had arrived, finally, to make everything right.

Voting ended at 8:00. By 8:08, Rob Ford was declared the winner. Buoyed by a record-high turnout, he received 383,501 votes, or 47.1 percent, as much as his two main competitors combined. George Smitherman, the former Ontario deputy premier, was a distant second with 35.6 percent. Joe Pantalone, the former deputy city mayor, had 11.7 percent. In the end, his opponents' impressive resumés meant nothing against a guy who had bypassed the usual selection committee.

Displayed on a map, the results showed a city deeply divided along pre-amalgamation boundaries. Ford took the former suburbs of Etobicoke, Scarborough and North York. Smitherman won a cluster of wards in the old City of Toronto.

"Do you know what it was?" asked Doug Ford, who won Rob's old council seat the day his brother became mayor. "It was the power of the people. We had over three thousand volunteers. Staggering. So we had everyone out there banging on doors."

"The right candidate at the right time focusing on the right issues—things that were top of mind with people, that were bugging them," summed up Nick Kouvalis, who, to Doug's chagrin, received much of the credit for Rob's victory.

"Rob Ford was a bad candidate running a great campaign in a field of bad candidates running bad campaigns," summarized journalist Jonathan Goldsbie.

"He returned your call," said Fabio Basso, Rob's friend from high school. "Something so little means a lot. You know what I mean? He believed in what he said, obviously. Half of the people didn't like it. They were, 'Oh, God forbid—him! He's not a doctor, he's not a lawyer. He's not educated. He doesn't fucking fit in. Whereas the blue-collar working person is, 'Yeah! Right on!! Finally!!!'"

At his victory party that night, Ford told an adoring crowd at the Toronto Congress Centre, "Four years from tonight, you'll look back and say, 'Rob Ford did exactly what he said he was going to do.' This victory is a clear call from the taxpayers, 'Enough is enough! And I want respect!'" Ford shouted above the cheering, "And that's exactly what we're going to give them."

He blew a kiss skyward, as he had at his launch, in the same room, seven months earlier. "Dad, this one was for you."

It was easier for Rob to imagine his father smiling down from heaven than to wonder if he would have been there in person to tell his son, the mayor-elect, that he'd finally met his expectations. This night, Diane Ford was the proud parent, the mother of both a mayor *and* a city councillor. She smiled approvingly as Rob talked about tax cuts, but she beamed as she raised the arms of both sons into a large V for victory. At Rob's other side, Renata Ford applauded and nodded at all the right times—a perfect political wife, it seemed.

"It was a beautiful moment for the Ford family," recalled Tom Beyer, a Ford friend and campaign worker who that night drove the family from Diane's house to the congress centre in the campaign's dilapidated motorhome.

Behind Rob on the crowded stage stood an exuberant giant of a man in a cowboy hat: Randy Ford. To Randy's left was their sister Kathy, looking bewildered and overwhelmed. Next to her, applauding eagerly, was her son, Michael Ford-Stirpe. With encouragement from Diane, who'd helped raise him, Michael would drop the Stirpe so he could run as a Ford in the 2014 election, extending the political brand at least one more generation.

—

As the date for the official takeover of power crept closer, many of the city's top civil servants got the jitters, knowing Rob Ford would be unlike any mayor before him.

Mel Lastman, the amalgamated city's first mayor, was a populist guided by political instinct, with no patience for detailed policy briefings or the minutiae of day-to-day operations. But Lastman assembled a talented and congenial office team and dispatched them to build relationships. He reached across political lines and geographic boundaries to create at least the appearance of a unified government.

The Harvard-educated David Miller, Lastman's successor in 2003, was bright, articulate and policy driven. Miller employed strategic thinking and careful vote counting to get his policies through council, then relied on senior officials to implement them. When a councillor complained that a city department was uncooperative, Miller would send the politician back to work it out within the bureaucratic framework. He was a bureaucrat's dream.

With Ford, the public service had seen enough over the years to predict the direction he would storm down, but they couldn't tell who or what he would knock over.

—

On his first official day in office, December 1, 2010, the new mayor held a press conference to announce the end of Transit City, the $8-billion cornerstone of the previous regime's rapid transit plan. He acted without council authority, and offered no replacement plan other than a pledge, without details or funding, to build subways in place of Transit City's Light Rail Transit. Ford had wasted no time making this his signature wedge issue, already intending to campaign non-stop right through to 2014. "The very next day we were already talking about the next election," remembers Tom Beyer, who worked in Ford's office for more than three years, beginning that first day. "So *everything* we did was in the lens of the next election. Immediately, they were thinking of 2014. Immediately."

Further evidence of Ford's "Rock 'em, sock 'em" approach to government came at his December 6 inaugural, kicked off by "special guest" Don Cherry, the outspoken hockey commentator. Previous mayors ushered in their terms with inspirational advice on wise and compassionate governance. Cherry, resplendent in a pink and white silk jacket, got right to the point. "I'm wearing pinko for all the pinkos out there who ride bicycles and everything. I've been bein' ripped to shreds by the left-wing pinko newspapers out there." Cherry said he'd been in Ford's corner "because Rob's honest, he's truthful . . . he's gonna be the greatest mayor this city has ever, ever seen. Now put that in your pipe, you left-wing kooks."

Seated at the front of the room, the chain of office around his neck for the first time, Rob Ford looked happy and proud—feelings that didn't come often to him and, when they did, didn't stay long. With most of the audience still recovering from Cherry's rant, policy adviser Mark Towhey handed the mayor his speech. "Oh, that was good," Ford told him, referring to Cherry.

—

Just dealing with the transition from Miller to Ford would have made bureaucratic heads spin. But Ford arrived with a brother who thought the Ford family now ran the city, and that their power knew no bounds. Kouvalis, now the mayor's chief of staff, was moderate by comparison, but was as ready to rumble as a Ford, scrapping with Doug one minute, taking on the civil service the next.

Kouvalis described to me his early interactions with the city manager. "I was very honest with Joe Pennachetti. I said, 'Joe, I didn't go to university, never worked in government, not a good reader—don't fuck me around, right? Shoot straight. Teach me what I need to know. And I'll protect you—if you're doing what we want.'

"He goes, 'Well, I work for council.' I said, 'Yeah, *I under-stand that*, right? The Fords might not like it, but *I* understand that. So you tell me what's possible, what's not possible, what's impossible, and I'll tell you what we're going to try and do anyway. I'll work with you and your people.'"

As leader of Ford's transition team, Kouvalis remembered, the bureaucrats at first "tried to bury me in paper. Literally, I would get two thousand sheets of paper a day. It came to a point that I would leave the paper in the box and just move it to the next office." Kouvalis chuckled. "I wouldn't even read it."

Without prompting from me, Kouvalis acknowledged that, in normal times, his skills wouldn't have matched the job description. "I say that without *any* shame, though lots of my opponents or enemies like to say, 'You see, even he doesn't think he should have been in there.' But the fact of the matter is that I was the best person for that job with the Fords."

—

I asked Pennachetti when it first struck him that Rob Ford would be mayor. "I'll be honest," he said. "I did not believe that he would be elected."

Pennachetti had been at city hall since 2002, first as the CFO and then, in 2008, as city manager. He was professional but flexible, well liked by everyone. He spoke often with most councillors, but there was only one subject Rob Ford was comfortable discussing with the well-educated bureaucrat in the well-fitting suit. "His parking spot in the garage was right next to mine," Pennachetti told me. "One night we happened to be going to the garage together, and he had all these Riddell football helmets jammed into the back seat. He opened the trunk and more were in there too. I said, 'Boy, you've got some great equipment there, Riddell helmets.' He said, 'How the hell do you know that?' I said, 'Well, I played football, I know the game.'

"That became our only contact point. So if he saw me in council, once in a blue moon he'd pull me aside and we'd start talking football. That was the only real common ground we had." Ford had played centre, Pennachetti was a quarterback. Ford tried, unsuccessfully, to recruit him to coach high school football.

For the most part, after he became mayor, Ford avoided the city manager. Meanwhile, the mayor's staff and brother were hatching plots to replace both Pennachetti and the city's chief financial officer, Cam Weldon.

"First day in there, Doug wanted to fire Cam Weldon," Nick Kouvalis told me three years later. "He was the CFO under Miller and they wanted to set the tone." Kouvalis fought Doug on it. "No, we're not going to fire a guy who knows how the place works. We're going to win him over and get him on our side."

But Kouvalis himself was toying with the idea of finding a new city manager to replace Pennachetti. He had his eye on a high-profile business executive with Conservative credentials. "I was in private conversations with John Tory," he told me. "I wanted John to come in and be the city manager. Not that I wanted to fire Pennachetti. But I could see that he was really struggling.

"The Fords would blast Ford propaganda, like, 'There *are no* homeless people.' And Joe would leave the meeting visibly shaken. So I didn't think Joe was going to make it. That was the biggest surprise for me—the man is tough as nails." The Fords supported bringing in Tory, Kouvalis said, but the politician-turned-radio-talk-show-host thought better of it.

Pennachetti, meanwhile, had a contract and wasn't planning to leave. "I had a couple of dozen staff come to me and say, 'At least stay on a year. Please help us do the transition.' It meant a lot that they supported me," Pennachetti told me, "and, quite frankly, I wanted a term of council anyway. I felt that I could make some change no matter who the mayor was."

At their first meeting, the mayor surprised his top officials by demanding a zero tax increase. It hadn't been part of his campaign platform and wasn't part of the budget preparations. "Mr. Mayor, you know we've got a $350-million problem," Pennachetti responded. "Are you *sure* you want zero?"

"I want zero," Ford repeated.

Pennachetti covered the sudden shortfall with the prior year's surplus, pushing an even bigger problem on to the following year. With the mayor in his honeymoon period, council approved the 2011 budget Ford wanted, setting the stage for a 2012 financial crisis the mayor's office would use to justify the elimination of programs and services.

—

During the first few months, Rob Ford must have felt like a kid bringing home his first-ever straight-A report card. In rapid succession, he axed the unpopular Vehicle Registration Tax and got Toronto's public transit deemed an essential service. He pressured councillors to reduce their office budgets and to forego their annual cost-of-living salary increase. He delivered a 2011 tax freeze and privatized garbage collection on the west side of the city. Not that these were necessarily good public policy, but they were political wins and they were popular. Ford's approval rating soared.

Perhaps the most tangible money-saving achievement was the contract his administration negotiated with the city's largest unions, early in 2012. Ford's hardline bargaining team, controlled by a handful of headstrong councillors and a few professional negotiators, obtained huge concessions by being prepared to run the city without its unionized workers if they didn't get the contract they wanted. The plan was to force the issue in the winter, when the garbage could be stored outside, the parks weren't used much and it wasn't tourist season.

Previous mayors had rejected such an old-school strategy, fearing severe labour turmoil. The Fords and their allies loved the "Bring it on!" approach. "It was gutsy, but it needed to be done," said Doug Holyday, who chaired the negotiating committee. "If the mayor hadn't been onside with any of this, it wouldn't have happened." The gambit worked but could just as easily have turned the city into a massive labour battleground.

Mike Del Grande, Ford's budget chief during these negotiations, told me in 2015 that there was support among a small group to lock out the employees for two years.

What might that have meant for the city? I asked Del Grande.

"Well, if we didn't have a contract, it could have meant—*could* have meant—that we would open up the CNE and start taking applications from people who didn't have jobs."

On whose instructions? I asked. Had a small number of councillors and negotiators gone rogue?

"It's an untold story, John," Del Grande said. "You count your votes. It's a bit of a crapshoot. . . . My first question to the negotiators was, 'What did you have for breakfast?' 'Eggs, toast, cereal,' they would answer. 'That's not what I want to hear. I want to hear that you had nails for breakfast! Because, in these negotiations, we're not taking any prisoners. We're going to win, and we're going to do what needs to be done.'"

With many residents still angry over the 2009 garbage strike, union leaders knew the crowd would have cheered as Ford beat them to a bloody pulp. With Toronto headed towards the type of labour unrest gripping Madison, Wisconsin, that same year, the union blinked. The city saved millions through a contract settlement that wouldn't have happened without the spectre of Rob Ford, club in hand.

—

At the end of Rob Ford's first year as mayor, Dave Nickle of Metro News interviewed him to ask where he wanted to take the city. "I said, 'I know you want to cut the gravy and build a subway. What's your vision for the city past that?' And he said, 'I just want to cut the gravy and build a subway.' He couldn't talk about what he wanted the city to look like. He didn't understand the question."

"I think he's afraid to deal with the big picture," observed one senior administrator. "I've never seen him show an ability to look at a business problem, analyze it and come out the end with a solution. A mayor should be leading the way, setting the course with big-picture issues like transportation and where's the city going in the future, how do we become sustainable. Meanwhile, he's spending most of his time dealing with minutia that can be taken care of by staff."

—

Rob Ford dealt with the city's problems like a salesman for a small company trying to build a client base. When he visited homes to see problems up close, residents welcomed him. They showed him respect, gratitude, admiration. They made him feel smart and he made them feel valued.

"He phones them and says, 'You called, what's up?'" Kouvalis told me. "But he also talks to them. 'What do you do for a living? How many kids do you have? Are they playing football?'"

Routinely, Ford dragged senior staff away from their desks to accompany him.

"I felt he used staff for a show of power," the same bureaucrat told me. "I remember one time we were called to a meeting in an industrial area in North York. There were at least fifteen of us in a room to deal with a garbage issue, and we sat there for almost two hours while conversations went on between him and the person who owned the building.

"By the time you travel out there, have a two-hour meeting and have to get back to the office—that would be half of a day gone. That happened numerous times a year. It takes you off what you're actually supposed to be doing. Staff ends up not handling issues that they should have handled. Or they're too late on an issue and it becomes a bigger problem."

Joe Pennachetti tried to establish regular weekly meetings with the mayor, in his office, as he had done with David Miller. Ford resisted. The mayor wanted the city manager to come to where *he* felt competent.

"From day one, when he got elected mayor, he wanted me to meet with him on the street," Pennachetti remembers. "I said, 'No. I'm not going.' I think I went to one meeting. It had to do with a fence, that's all I remember. It was an argument between two neighbours over a fence. And then I said, 'Mr. Mayor, I'm not doing this anymore. You can have the divisional supervisor, or the manager for transportation, if it's a sidewalk issue. At most it's going to be a general manager or director. But you're not dragging out the city manager and deputy city manager to these one-offs with residents, fixing a sidewalk out in front of the house.'"

Pennachetti said of Ford's approach to customer service, "You've got 2.8 million residents out there. You can't go out and meet with every one of them."

Rita Davies, former executive director of cultural services, remembers being summoned to the mayor's office for an important arts matter. "There was a woman who had contacted him. She was dotty as all get-out. Deep red lipstick, huge black hat. Dolled up like she was going to a cocktail party, *circa* 1956. She came with page after page of handwritten notes in plastic file folders and proceeded to go through them one by one. She was just going on at length about the horrible arts organizations, like Toronto International Film Festival, because she lived in the Manulife building and she never got to meet any of the stars."

The mayor was writing down everything she said.

"The board of TIFF should be fired!" the woman with the big bold hat told Ford.

Davies told me, "He looked up with great anticipation and then wrote down, 'Board should be fired!' And the reason was that she hadn't met any stars. About forty minutes into this, I stood up and said, 'I'm sorry, but I have another meeting to attend.' And I went."

—

"I would say to him, 'Rob, all you've got to do is try hard,'" recalled Nick Kouvalis. "'Nobody expects perfection. Everybody thinks you're going to fuck up—and you *are* going to fuck up, because you're not an articulate guy. But if you make an effort every day to be as good as you can, you can be mayor as long as you want.'

"But he didn't actually want to govern. He wanted to be in an election so he could win. But to prove what? To whom? He wanted to become mayor so he could prove to his father that he could become mayor."

After the election, Ford seemed motivated by only two things: customer service, Dad-style, and planning for the next election. "I never thought he actually understood what the mayoralty was," said one former staffer, adding that Ford saw most duties as a chore. "The mayor of Calgary, I've got to see that guy," he grumbled before a scheduled meeting with Calgary's smart populist, Naheed Nenshi.

"I think he hates being mayor. I really do," one senior bureaucrat told me during the final year of Ford's term. "I've always said the mayor should love the city—actually love it—love the people who are in it, love the complexity of it, love the challenges. The mood when he's around is nothing but negativity."

Many of those inside Ford's mayoralty observed that he loved the attention he got as mayor but disliked everything else about the job, especially the embarrassment of speaking with people who were book smart.

"Imagine you're running one of the most complicated organizations in the country, trying to figure out problems that don't have any solutions. You're going to these Board of Trade events where people are expecting that you've got pearls of wisdom and solutions to solve the city's problems. And you don't understand half of them," a member of Ford's executive committee said to me not for attribution. "How insecure Rob must have felt, going to those things. You'd feel like the dumbest person in the room. And I feel sad for Rob Ford the person, knowing he'd have to sit there *without any clue.*"

During her four years as chair of the Toronto Transit Commission, Karen Stintz didn't have a single one-on-one meeting with the mayor to discuss transit. Typically, she found herself pitted against the Ford brothers and the mayor's staff. Conversations were about subways, even when none were planned and no money was available to build any. "The very idea that I had to fight with the Fords about the concept of having to *fund* transit, basically for the entire four years—who would have thought that would be a point of argument? Any time I'd say, 'You need a funding source,' I'd be seen to be obstructing. They would basically suggest that you were either incompetent or you were not up to the task. 'Just get it done. If you can't get it done, we'll find someone else who will.'"

Stintz, who spoke with me just after abandoning her run for mayor against Ford, recalled a 2011 discussion between the mayor and a senior executive of Bombardier. The city had placed an order to buy streetcars from the Canadian manufacturer. Now Ford didn't want them. "He wanted to cancel the streetcar order and put the money towards subways. I said, 'What subways? We don't have an approved subway plan, and we've already approved this contract for streetcars.' And I sat in his office while the senior vice president of Bombardier patiently explained that he's already spent money on studies, contracts, labour. The mayor said, 'What if I just cancel the contract right now? What am I going to get?' 'You'll get a set of plans,' the vice president answered. 'For $350 million, you'll get a set of plans.' I doubt he has ever had a similar conversation with any mayor *in his life*— and I can't imagine any other $11-billion corporation having that representation at the top."

Mike Del Grande said the mayor wasn't interested in budget details. "He would only scream about taxes no higher than this, or no TTC increase. 'I'm the mayor and that's what I want.'" A few times, Del Grande tried to explain the numbers. "But you figured your clock was between two and five minutes, as far as attention span. He was gone."

"There's no depth there," former councillor Peter Milczyn said to me. "Cut off the coffee and tea and cut the office budgets: that's pretty simplistic. But how do you maintain service and cut costs at the TTC? That's a little bit more complex. I don't think he ever really delved into that, and certainly as mayor he wasn't prepared to."

———

While Ford was in control, there was no middle ground on council. The right was defined as those who supported him. Everyone else was seen as left, a group that, at first, struggled to get past denial so they could start plotting the mayor's downfall.

On the right, councillors who for years had treated him like a big dumb lug were now reconsidering that opinion. As difficult as it was to comprehend, he was now the guy who got to decide which of them held power and influence. Like his predecessors, Ford used that power to line up supporters. With only one vote of his own, Toronto's mayor needed a bare minimum of twenty-two steadfast followers. Observed retiring councillor Howard Moscoe, "Without the support of council, Rob Ford won't be able to pass wind." But any local politician with the nose and stomach for it could drift along with the winds of power, whichever way they were blowing. Some were adept at it.

Norm Kelly, one of council's veterans, had stayed to the right under right-of-centre Mel Lastman, then changed course under left-of-centre David Miller. Whenever Kelly rose to defend Miller's policies, I'd turn to Rob Ford, two seats away, and profess confusion. "I thought Kelly was one of your guys." This scene was repeated many times, always with the same dialogue. I'd pretend to be bewildered by Kelly's ideological conversion and Rob would mutter under his breath.

Knowing Ford possessed the deluded—or so I thought—belief that he might one day be mayor, I'd present the silver lining. "When you're mayor, you'll get Kelly back." Every time I said it, Rob would correct me. "I'm not going to do it that way. It'll be different."

As for Kelly, he offered a simple explanation: "I'd rather be on the inside than the outside." When Ford offered to make him chair of the parks committee, Kelly thought to himself, "Let's see where this will go." As part of the Ford cabinet, Kelly felt duty bound to defend his policies as ardently as he had supported David Miller. "How can you serve with this man?" a left-wing councillor scornfully confronted him one day.

"Leadership has many styles," Kelly replied.

—

Back in November 2010, Rob Ford controlled the game, the only kid with a ball, picking and choosing from among those who wanted to play. Lefties were excluded, as was anyone in the centre unwilling to embrace his entire agenda. But there was no shortage of councillors with their hands up, waving for his attention.

"We had a lot of people begging for jobs, and everybody was trying to show Doug Ford that they were the biggest conservative in the room," Nick Kouvalis told me. "Nobody wanted to look weak and liberal because everyone was concerned about what Doug thought of them, because they thought Doug was in charge."

In Ford's honeymoon period, even some councillors who saw him as reckless went along for the ride. Several were already contemplating an exit strategy for whenever Ford's predictably extreme behaviour caused public support to plummet. Opponents also anticipated a time when Ford would get himself into a big mess.

"We should figure out which path he'll be taking and dig a pit," I suggested to Adam Vaughan, always the most articulate of the anti-Ford voices on council. Vaughan sat two seats away from me, on the opposite side from where Rob Ford had sat.

"We just need to wait until he falls down," Vaughan replied. "Then we don't let him up."

11. BEING ROB FORD

"If you're offended, I'm not apologizing.
Because, put yourself in my shoes, if somebody
said that about your husband or your wife."
Rob Ford, after his own comments about marital life chez Ford

---

Imagine aching to be noticed, searching for yourself in the eyes of a father who turned away while you looked up, reaching for comfort in the arms of a family that remained distant, even as it came to your rescue. Your sister is an addict, your oldest brother as tough as your father. Another brother, the one who has everything, seems jealous of what little you have. When he comes to your side, everyone can see which of you stands taller.

Imagine being Rob Ford.

After Rob's election as mayor, his family was exalted as never before. Soon his behaviour became disgraceful, but the Fords refused to be disgraced. Rob was left out there, taking the beating, until he could stand no more.

—

The family that craved respect lacked the ability to step outside itself, even for an instant, to see how others saw them. Rob especially. Drugs and alcohol released the impulses that led him to trouble. But just as often, he simply didn't know any better. It was painful to watch.

"He's so unaware of what's around him, or other people's feelings, or other people's reaction to what he does," said his former policy adviser Sheila Paxton. "Like, I'm sitting in his office and he says, 'My balls are so itchy. I've gotta scratch my balls. I've gotta scratch my balls.' And Earl Provost says, 'Mayor, Sheila's sitting right here.' And he says, 'Okay, I'll turn my back.' He gets up and does it, turns his back. Oh my God! He's just so unaware."

Even those who expected unfiltered comments from him were unprepared for what came out of Rob Ford's mouth on the morning of Thursday, November 14, 2013. It was the day after the release of court documents containing police interviews with former staff members in the mayor's office. They claimed Ford was frequently out of control, binge drinking, taking drugs, behaving violently. They said the guy who promised to stop the gravy train skipped work and used his office staff to run personal errands. Ford didn't respond to any of that. What disturbed him most were allegations that he'd partied with a prostitute and made crude sexual remarks about a female staff member, Olivia Gondek, during his St. Patrick's Day bender of 2012. The portrayal of Ford as a bad family man clashed with how he needed to see himself and to be seen by others. It was all lies, Ford proclaimed.

When he got home that night, Renata was furious—at the media, for reporting these stories. Rob wanted to put the reporters in their place, using a clever quip, like other politicians sometimes did.

"It hurts my wife when they call a friend of mine a prostitute," Ford began the scrum outside his office the following morning, before that day's council meeting. "Alana is not a prostitute. She's a friend. And it makes me sick how people are saying this."

Wearing his Toronto Argonauts jersey, he switched the conversation to football. Then he must have remembered the line he and Renata had thought would make it clear that he would *never* make a lewd comment about a woman.

"Oh, and the last thing was Olivia Gondek. It says that I wanted to eat her pussy. Olivia Gondek. I've never said that in my life to her. I would *never* do that. I'm happily married. I've got more than enough to eat at home. Thank you very much." Ford turned and walked calmly into his office.

"I know we're live right now, but I don't know if we can . . . I . . . uh . . ." stammered CP24 reporter Katie Simpson. "Mayor Ford speaking as Mayor Ford does—very plainly—now using language that I don't think we can broadcast on TV, but we just broadcast that on TV."

"What? What?! What?!! What??!! Whaaaaat!!!!!!" late night comedy host Jon Stewart commented that night, advising Ford to make that his last line as mayor. "That is what we call, in my business, a closer!"

In thirteen years of listening to Rob Ford, I had never heard him even attempt a play on words—offensive or otherwise. That, plus the way he introduced it, told me this was no slip of the tongue.

For confirmation that Rob Ford's worst-ever comment was premeditated, I went to Sheila Paxton, who had driven Renata to city hall that day. "He was just trying to make a joke," Renata told Sheila during the drive. "We talked about this last night. It was funny. Why couldn't they see that? It's none of their business what our sex lives are like. It's none of their business to get in the middle of our marriage."

Paxton was a good listener, and full of practical advice. Renata spoke openly with her, as if she needed someone to confide in. Paxton listened but didn't want to know too much, in case the mayor asked about the content of her conversations with his wife. She didn't want to be in a position where she would need to choose between lying and betraying a confidence. Much of what Renata and Sheila spoke about remains private. But Paxton chose to let it be known that, in the latter part of 2013, she regularly drove the mayor's wife to her Thursday appointments: urine testing in the morning and counselling in the afternoon. "I never kept it a secret," she said to me, explaining that there should be nothing hidden about her roles in the mayor's office. The information was there for anyone who asked, but nobody did—until I spoke with her in December 2013. During a year when Paxton walked several times a day through the dozens of reporters camped in front of the mayor's office, how was this possible? I wondered.

"I don't mean this disparagingly about myself at all," she explained, "but when you're an overweight woman, people think you're stupid. So they ignore you. They don't think you're the person running the show or holding it together. They just ignore you. For the first while I was in the mayor's office, nobody knew my name. Nobody knew what I did. They'd come in and talk to other staff.

"Those people weren't there as reporters," she said about the crowd outside the mayor's office. "We were a reality show. They were there for sound bites. They weren't there for a story."

Had anyone asked, Paxton would have answered truthfully. "It's just better to answer than to lie or to cover it up. I felt if I'm doing this on work time, then it's not a secret."

I asked her about the origins of her predisposition to tell the truth. "Probably an incident with my dad," she said without hesitation. "I lied to him once and it was a nightmare, and I always felt guilty the rest of my life." Paxton began a story she had trouble finishing. It was about three cents and the self-inflicted pain of a lie. The change was left over from a purchase she made for her father.

"I was probably in grade two at the time. I'd spent three pennies change and I didn't tell him." More than fifty years later, she cried at the memory. "I lied to him once and I felt guilty. It's hard for me to talk about it. It's just so much easier to tell the truth."

As an adult, Sheila offered the truth to anyone who asked, even if it might get her in trouble. Of the more than seventy-five people I interviewed for this book, Paxton stands out as the one who answered *every* question as if *nobody*, including herself, should ever have anything to hide.

—

On the day of the cat comment, Paxton had picked up Renata for her regular Thursday appointments. Sheila had arranged the counselling program and registered the mayor's wife under a false name, her identity known only to the centre's director. When Ford's chief of staff first asked Paxton to drive Renata to the appointments, she had refused. But when the mayor asked her personally, as a favour, she relented.

"I hated it. Not because I didn't want to help her but because it took a whole day out of my week. I was trying to do policy, read the agendas, attend meetings, be at council, and then I'd have to stop whatever I was doing to go and drive Renata. I didn't feel it should be necessary that the mayor's staff do that. I was really resentful of that."

"There's a change of plan," Renata had told Sheila when she arrived at the house that day. "We're going down to city hall." Sheila thought that was a bad idea; Renata seemed too fragile to be going anywhere near the pandemonium of that place. But Sheila did as Renata insisted. As soon as Renata got to the mayor's office, she and Rob began to squabble. Rob criticized what she was wearing and how she had fixed her hair. She fought back with a critique of *his* fashion sense. Then Doug arrived, so that there were now enough of them for a family fight. Doug complained that Renata didn't do enough to keep Rob out of trouble.

"He does what he wants, you know that," Renata yelled back. "You're always telling me what to do. Don't tell me, tell him!"

"Don't talk to her that way," Rob joined in against Doug.

"You're going to rehab," Doug shouted back at him. "You shouldn't have said what you said. What are we going to do now?"

"Why should I take time off?" Rob asked. "I'll just be sitting at home doing nothing."

"Can you excuse us for a minute," Doug finally said to Paxton. She stepped outside but told me later that "the fighting continued, mostly Doug yelling at Rob. They never lowered their voices. Doug and Rob would just go at each other. You could hear the shouting. Not listening, just shouting. It was very uncomfortable. It was just seeing people dysfunctional. It was sad."

—

After the comment about his domestic life wasn't well received, Rob Ford reacted as if an unseen enemy had caused this latest fiasco. "If you're offended, I'm not apologizing," he announced at the start of that day's council meeting. "Because, put yourself in *my* shoes, if somebody said that about *your* husband or *your* wife. Okay? Enough is enough!" He seemed not to notice that almost the entire chamber of councillors had literally turned their backs to him.

Soon afterwards, he agreed to an early afternoon press conference. An adviser thought Renata's presence might add a nice touch. She stood off to the side, hands clasped in front of her, while the mayor solemnly apologized to the city—but not to her—for his "graphic remarks."

"The past few months I've been under tremendous, tremendous stress. I used unforgivable language," he read from a prepared statement. "These allegations are 100 percent lies. When you attack my integrity as a father, and as a husband, I see red. Today I acted on complete impulse in my remarks."

Ford neither mentioned his wife nor acknowledged her presence. Not once did he look at her, or she at him. He concluded with a request that the media "respect my family's privacy"—as if *their* words had disrespected it.

When it was over, Paxton was ready to take Renata down the back way to her car. But her husband marched her to the elevator through a crowd of reporters. In the parking garage, he handed Renata over to Paxton while he went to the gym. "Just left me standing there with her," she said. Reporters had already spotted them. Sheila hurried Renata to the car, stepping in front of anyone who got too close. "Nice block," Ford told her afterwards, having seen the replay on television. It was the only compliment she ever received from him.

Thinking back on her year in the mayor's office, Paxton is more incredulous than judgmental. Amid the daily shock of seeing Toronto's ruling family up close and personal, she saw characters with human frailties. "The mayor always reminded me of Bart Simpson: 'I didn't do it!'

"It's hard to judge the mayor as a bad person. I think he just doesn't know better. He hasn't seen any role models."

—

People have spoken to me of a warmth between the Ford men and their children, of the closeness in Doug's family, of Randy's protective caring for his mother. But among the Ford brothers and sister, there's often open hostility. Various pairings of siblings have not been on speaking terms for long stretches. That includes Rob and Doug, before Rob ran for mayor, several insiders told me. There has been so much animosity between Doug and Randy that, even at the family business where they are partners, they've settled differences with a fist fight. Leonard Rudner, a former executive with Deco, heard about the fighting from multiple employees he spoke with right after he was first hired in 2010.

And the relationship between Rob and his mother wasn't easy. "Rob is always angry at his mom. I wouldn't call it a good relationship," Paxton said. " There's just an overall lack of affection and respect when they talk to each other. Having met his mother, having met his wife, and having had quite a bit of interaction now with both of them, I don't think he has a healthy relationship with a woman. I definitely think, in watching him, that he was very uncomfortable talking to women, even to staff."

"Rob has a *serious discomfort* interacting with women, which became obvious," Councillor Jaye Robinson offered without me asking. "He never really made eye contact with me."

"He's got some mom issues," a former Ford friend and staffer, Tom Beyer, told me. "He did tell me once, 'My mom comes across as being nice and everything, but you know . . .'" Beyer decided he had said enough.

Sheila Paxton described the lack of contact between Diane and Rob and his family at the 2013 FordFest in Etobicoke. "Diane spent a lot of time in the beer tent entertaining people, you know, like a butterfly, the social butterfly type. No interaction between her and the mayor at all. No interaction between her and the grandchildren."

Does Diane Ford seem proud of her son, the mayor? I asked.

"I think she was proud that her son *was* the mayor, but I don't think she was proud of her son," Paxton replied. "It was her own personal pride: 'My son's the mayor.' Not, 'Rob, you're mayor, that's great.' So it was about her pride, not his."

And brother Doug?

"Again, it's 'My brother's the mayor.' It's not about Rob Ford, what a great person. It's a different way they have of seeing it."

"These guys are absolutely so jealous of one another," Nick Kouvalis told me about Rob and Doug. "It's a love-hate relationship. They will defend each other in the face of some of the worst behaviour while at the same time hoping the other falls down so they can get a leg up."

"They have a *huge* rivalry. *Huge*," Beyer said of the brothers. "They're a very complicated family. I'm from a big family. You're always seeking attention from your mom and dad. Sometimes parents can play you off, one against the other, to *encourage* a rivalry shall we say. I'm surmising that's what happened. They certainly did have lots of 'got ya' moments. Rob would undermine Doug. And Doug would undermine Rob. On a regular basis. All the time. It happened *all* the time. . . .

"I think in Doug's mind it should have been *him* as mayor," Beyer continued. "Look, they've got a big brother–little brother relationship. Doug is the only guy who can scream and yell at Rob. And he did. In the office sometimes I could hear them when I was at the front—yelling and screaming from the back office. That was how loud it got sometimes. But the Ford family— hey—he's going to support his brother, no matter what, if it's upholding the Ford family brand."

"When they get into the room, they remind me of my brothers when they were young, like, you know, fighting over a toy— as opposed to being two adults who had grown up and now had a collegial adult relationship," Sheila Paxton told me. "There's no adult relationship between them. There were many times when the mayor would say, 'I don't want Doug in this office, get him out of here.'"

What was the toy they fought over? I asked.

"The toy was the family name. It's all about the name. Yeah, it's all about the name."

———

Of all the tempestuous relationships within the family, the stormiest was between Rob and Renata. The 911 calls from their home started well before Rob Ford ran for mayor. In 2008, police charged him with assaulting and threatening to kill his wife, after a call from Renata brought them to the home. The charge was later dropped, due to "inconsistencies" in Renata's statements to police. Ford gave his version of events to the *Toronto Sun* in a 2010 interview. "I came home one night. She was drunk and she said, 'If you fucking touch the kids, I'll call the cops and say that you hit me.'" Ford said she made good on the threat after he left the house with his two children. "I have never laid a hand on a woman in my life," he told the reporter. "My father never touched my mother."

By 2012, Etobicoke police were frequently responding to emergency calls from Rob Ford's home. Renata's mother, who was often at the house to help care for the children, sometimes called the police to deal with a drunk and disorderly son-in-law. Rob's family was equally fond of Renata. "When she was at the FordFest, they just totally ignored her," remembered Paxton. "In my conversations with Renata, I got the impression that there was no love lost between them. The mother was too pushy. She didn't think the mother cared about Rob."

Around this same time, Rob and Renata's mutual problems made it difficult for their household to function. Staff members were pressed into service, taking the kids to soccer practice, bringing them lunch, babysitting when Rob left the house with them and checked into a hotel. In late August 2013, following another 911 call, Rob checked into the Grand Hotel, next to an area known to locals as "crack central." While he asked some staff to do his laundry, the mayor asked Sheila Paxton to look after back-to-school clothes shopping.

"I come from a large family. If one person can't cope, everybody else steps in, and that wasn't happening in this instance. Afterwards, the grandmother said to me, 'Oh, I saw the clothes you bought for the kids. It's nice to see them dressed properly. They looked quite cute.'"

—

However estranged the Fords frequently were from one another, many insiders I spoke with talked about the united force they immediately became when some collective action was required to honour and protect their heritage.

"There's a lot of animosity and fighting between the two brothers. But if you get in between them, you'll get squeezed, you'll get hurt," observed Nick Kouvalis.

"The one thing about the Fords, they stick together no matter what. You don't mess with them," said long-time Ford volunteer Sandra Pavan. "They fight among themselves. But as soon as somebody on the outside says something—boom!"

Their father fused his family into an indivisible unit, bonded by the Krazy Glue of collective ambition. After they'd outgrown schoolyards, politics provided the place where Rob and Doug could assert Ford dominance. When they cloaked themselves in the Ford banner, members of this family did not doubt themselves for a minute.

"There is no grey at all in the Ford world," observed Chris Stockwell. "You couldn't have a conversation, logically, with Rob and explain to him why his position was at least *intemperate*. And the father was the same. And the mother was the same. It struck me as passing strange that *all* these people are together and they have the same philosophy on politics and, frankly, *on life*. It goes back to the old saying, 'Show me four people who think *exactly* the same and I'll show you *one person* who's doing *all* the thinking.' The father instilled it, and the father gave them all the thinking."

—

In 2013, Diane Ford commissioned a portrait of Rob. "I stand back and look at it and I can see ten personalities," she marvelled at the unveiling. "I can see all of Rob's personalities in that picture."

Would she be commissioning portraits of her other children?

"Maybe," she answered, "when Doug becomes premier."

12. BULLS

"'If he's not with us, kill him.'
It was that kind of mentality."
Councillor Josh Colle on the Fords

Lacking Dad's single-minded ambition, Mom's cool charm and intelligence, and brother Doug's extraordinary confidence, Rob Ford was blessed with none of the Ford attributes that might have prepared him for his unlikely role as the political master of a large city. Unable to recognize complexity in any form, he treated this new job as if it had none. As a city councillor, he had eagerly reached out to the common folk in his ward, dropping by their homes to solve every little problem they called him about. Now he was excited by the larger challenge of doing that for 2.8 million residents.

For him, there could be no greater calling, and those who believed in him saw their problem miraculously move to the top of a bureaucrat's pile. When the busted fridge in their Community Housing project became like new, they would praise Rob Ford's name. As word of him spread among the poor and the powerless, he opened his doors to the dispossessed. The possessed were welcome there too.

Did a lot of *unusual* residents contact the office? I asked the mayor's receptionist, Tom Beyer.

"Yeah. Yeah," he responded. "We had all kinds of strange characters. I've got a whole book full of them." Beyer went to find the book. "Let me see here. I've even got the dates," he said, randomly flipping pages until he landed on September 13, 2011.

> 9:48 a.m. "Can you get Toronto Community Housing to give me patio stones for my backyard? My dog's head keeps getting caught in the fence when he digs in the yard. Patio stones would fix that. TCHC says they have no money."

> 9:49 a.m. "Nobody believes in the ten commandments. And I'm no prostitute!"

He flipped to December 13 of the same year.

> Guy comes in wanting help to lodge complaint. There's a foreign body in his bloodstream, put there by the CIA. It's an alien substance that the CIA was able to put there through the soles of his feet. Was at hospital last night and they didn't take it seriously. Sent him to CSIS headquarters.

Beyer closed the book. "That gives you a little bit of a flavour."

Those folks were easy compared with the ones promising to kill themselves if Rob Ford couldn't fix their broken lives. Beyer remembers the mayor successfully talking one guy down, but he wasn't there when someone else threatened to set himself on fire in the outer office. Beyer reported that incident. Later that day, a helpful bureaucrat delivered a fire extinguisher.

"I realized very early on that the people calling the mayor's office had long-term outstanding issues that councillors would not touch anymore," said former Ford policy adviser Brian Johnston. "These same people would call every week, always trying to get the mayor to meet with them. If they got hold of him, he probably would have."

Midway into the term, Doug Ford contacted me in my role as chair of the board of health to ask how we could help the mayor's office deal with the large number of unbalanced people who visited. When I mentioned the problem to Rob, he didn't know what unbalanced people Doug was talking about.

—

Unlike the guy with the broken fence, a city business leader hoping for an audience with the mayor was typically told that Ford couldn't fit him in. The mayor before Ford spent *his* time crafting policy, pouring through agendas, tackling issues like climate change. A lot of good *that* did him when people got pissed off that their garbage wasn't picked up for six stinking weeks! Rob Ford saw everything from street level, and many people loved that about him.

Councillor Frances Nunziata described the scene when Rob Ford arrived at an event in her ward. "As soon as he came in, these Italian seniors were jumping up and down like a bunch of kids at a concert—grabbing him, kissing him, wanting to take pictures with him. He was like a rock star. Every place he went, they were all around him. People just love him. Because he comes across as being down to earth. They don't feel intimidated talking to him. He talks *to* people, not above them."

Ford returned calls late into the night, seemingly unaware that others might be sleeping while he was awake. The next day they'd call the office to ask if that was really the mayor who'd woken them up. "I love that the mayor called me back. But next time, can you tell him not to call me at midnight?"

Cam Weldon, the city's CFO, remembers rolling into Rob Ford's office at the end of a discussion with Doug Ford about the mayor's power.

"You guys are part of the team," Doug had tried to tell him.

"The mayor has a lot of influence, and you can make suggestions, but you can't order us," Weldon explained. Startled by this news, Doug wanted to bring it immediately to the mayor's attention.

"Yeah, I know," said Rob, not wanting to interrupt his calls to constituents. "That's how it works."

"And there he was behind his desk," said Weldon. "He had that *long* list of phone numbers, and he had a pencil with the eraser on the end and he's punching in those numbers, leaving messages. He was like a machine."

—

"Rob's a campaigner," Tom Beyer said. "I think governing bores him. It's boring to go to the office every day. It's boring to read reports. It's boring to sign your name over and over and over again on these scrolls. After a while the excitement of being mayor wears off. 'Oh man, is this all there is to it?'"

I suggested that Rob only enjoys or understands politics as a sport. Like football. My team against your team.

"Absolutely. Without question," responded Beyer. "Either you're with us or you're not. There's no grey middle ground. It became more and more black and white as things went on. And then people were *enemies*. If a certain councillor went against him or said something, immediately that person was branded as an enemy of the state."

"One thing I've learned about the Fords is they are a day-to-day-operation kind of family," said Nick Kouvalis. "One day at a time. I've never seen anything strategic, long-term, visionary, in anything they do. They can't even figure out, 'If I do this, this will happen, and if that happens, then this will happen.' They can't even think two steps ahead in anything that they do. They're bulls, for sure. Once you teach them a trick, you can't teach them another one. You just can't."

Is that how bulls are?

"No, I don't know about bulls," he said. "When I say they're like bulls, I mean they stand their ground. They're stubborn. They're strong, right? They don't move easy. If you tell them something they don't want to hear, they don't want to hear it. They can't bend and look at it like, 'If I were in his shoes, how would I feel?'"

Casual observers think Ford's mayoralty came undone only after the crack scandal, in 2013. That's correct if you're talking about the collapse of his popular support. But by early 2012, Ford had already lost control of council. The decline was set in motion even as the honeymoon was in full bloom.

Kouvalis was barely in the job a month before he knew he couldn't stay. Rob wasn't listening, and Doug was interfering. "I wanted to leave at Christmas 2010. They wouldn't let me quit. Doug asked me to come down to Florida over the holidays, with my family. I did. Had a great time. Doug wanted to patch things up. We had a breakfast meeting on the beach, just Doug and I. I said, 'I'll stay with your brother one more year, but you need to let me run the office. If you're not willing to stop interfering and just be a councillor, then I have to go.'" Doug Ford refused to meet his ultimatum, Kouvalis told me. A month later, Kouvalis was gone.

His departure, in February 2011, left Rob Ford without anyone truly in his corner. Although he lacked the resumé to be chief of staff, Kouvalis had brought a stormy stability to the Ford tempest. He didn't know city hall, but he understood political cravings and machinations. Most importantly, he'd compiled a year's worth of observations on the Fordian brain. Kouvalis monitored Rob's demons and curbed the bully-boy behaviour of his senior staff.

"I had all that shit under control—for a while," Kouvalis told me. "Then it became too much for *me* to handle. Once I left, Doug was off the leash."

—

"'If he's not with us, kill him.' It was that kind of mentality," said Councillor Josh Colle.

At first, Councillor Denzil Minnan-Wong had been an enthusiastic supporter of Ford's tax-cutting approach to government. "The whole thing started going south when Rob and his administration and Doug started to go after members of council," he said. "They thought they could actually bully people into supporting them. Rob and Doug both. They'd just go in and threaten that they were going to run people against them in their wards. 'Better support us, or we'll get Ford Nation to work against you.'

"The mayor and his office needs to *exude* power. And power is a self-fulfilling thing. If people know you have power, they'll give you even more power. But if you lose it, if people think you're weak, you won't be able to get their votes. They pissed off so many people that they weren't winning the votes. And once the left on council smelt blood in the water, you know that was it."

"It didn't take very long to realize these guys were off track and were really *heavy-handed* in their approach," said Councillor Jaye Robinson, an early member of Ford's executive committee. "They really were whipping the vote. So every executive meeting, and every council meeting, you felt *uncomfortable*." Robinson says the mayor's staff visited her before each council session, returning multiple times if they didn't like her answers. "Earl Provost was assigned to me, and he was very heavy-handed. 'This is important to the mayor. You have to be part of the team.'"

At council meetings, Provost stationed himself directly behind Robinson, who sat in the back row. This continued until other councillors complained about it.

"It was trench warfare for the first year and a half," said Colle. He is an independent-minded centrist who was offended by the Ford bully tactics. "They would just use every leverage point possible." At first, Colle often voted with Ford. But often wasn't good enough. When he didn't knuckle under on *every* vote, the Fords threatened to go after his father—extremely aggressive behaviour coming from sons who understood family loyalty. Josh's father, Michael Colle, was a Liberal MPP and was coming up for re-election.

Colle told me that after he voted against the mayor on one issue, Rob Ford said, "I guess we have to go after the old man now."

"Doug would go out to fundraisers or events for my father's opponent—it was so childish," Colle said. "Talk about rubbing somebody the wrong way! As they realized it wasn't working, they'd remind me how good they were being by *not* getting involved in my father's campaign—like I owed them for *not* getting involved."

Soon Ford supporters started to bristle at the "cheat sheets" handed out by Provost, then in charge of councillor relations, and policy adviser Mark Towhey. Before each meeting, the mayor's staff gave Ford-friendly councillors detailed instructions on how to vote on a long list of agenda items. "It wasn't like it was thoughtful analysis," said Colle, who refused the sheets after a few meetings.

—

Kouvalis's exit and Rob Ford's complete inattention to complex policy and financial matters left an open playing field that both Doug Ford and Mark Towhey would attempt to exploit. When not butting heads with each other, the two led individual initiatives that often hadn't been worked out with one another or with the mayor. Doug was instinctive and out front: the very public wannabe mayor. Towhey was logical and covert, a former military man who still thought and acted like one. The secret mayor.

A proponent of small government, Towhey tried to roll Ford's tax-cutting obsession into his own mission to reduce the size and scope of government. In February 2010—before he'd joined Rob Ford's election campaign—Towhey previewed his ideology with a blog proposing to sell Toronto's public transit system.

> How will people get to and from work, shopping, school, etc? Good question. I imagine more people may drive. . . . Others will be forced to use bicycles, hire more taxis, join car pools, etc. . . . Some bright entrepreneurs will smell an opportunity. Someone will approach the city to buy pieces of the TTC with a view to continue operating them for a profit. . . . Someone would buy the subway system. There would also be buyers for some parts of the street car and busing networks. Some of these could be profitable—either those that feed into the subway, or those that operate in high traffic areas where the subway doesn't exist.
>
> Many bus routes, however, would be abandoned. They're not profitable. But what about the people who need them? Well, life's tough. Instead of being the only three people on a 60 passenger bus, these people will have to introduce themselves, get to know their neighbours and share a taxi.

Towhey's militaristic style became the dominant factor in the mayor's office, even before he was appointed chief of staff in August 2012.

"He's a former officer of Princess Patricia's Canadian Light Infantry," commented former deputy mayor Norm Kelly. "He had that approach. And he was very definite in what he wanted to do, very precise. 'This is so obviously the right thing to do, you should be doing it.'" Kelly banged a fist on the table to illustrate Towhey's style. Ford's administration didn't understand the nature of city politics, Kelly said. "You don't force members of council. You attract them. What you're doing on a continual basis is forming one alliance after another."

"Their message to councillors was, 'You're either with us or against us,'" said Michelle Berardinetti, a moderate who at first supported Ford's cost-cutting. "They were flexing their muscles. It wasn't just the key issues. It was every single small vote, and sometimes even just petty historical fights." Berardinetti refused to go along with a vote solely intended to punish a left-wing female colleague. "It wasn't about the work we were doing, but about one team winning against another."

Peter Milczyn blamed both Towhey and Doug Ford for trying to force their own unpopular policies on councillors as if they were coming from the mayor. Milczyn twigged to this when he set up a meeting between Ford and Karen Stintz, who were battling over what Stintz assumed was a Ford-inspired plan to fire the TTC's general manager, Gary Webster.

"And Rob said—I'm paraphrasing—'So what's going on? What's this I hear about getting rid of Gary Webster?'

"And Karen goes, 'Well, I hear that's what *you* want!'

"And Rob says, 'Well, I never said that.'"

As with other presumed directives, this one assumed a life of its own. The politically motivated firing of Webster, for refusing to support subways over Light Rail Transit, cost the city half a million dollars in severance and sent a chill through the bureaucracy. Disagree with the mayor and you're next.

But Milczyn figured the greatest harm to Rob's mayoralty came at the hands of his brother, whose freelance initiatives created division within the Ford camp and gave the enemy something to shoot at. In the summer of 2011, while Rob still easily controlled a majority of votes on the 45-member council, Doug announced his plan to build a giant mall, with an enormous Ferris wheel, on the city-owned waterfront property known as the Port Lands. The proposal came out of nowhere, and was an attempt to bypass the decision-making process on a valuable public asset.

"If you look at the first twelve to eighteen months of this term, pretty well all of the initial messes were Doug related," Milczyn observed. When Rob wouldn't publicly criticize Doug's mall and Ferris wheel scheme, Milczyn went to the mayor, one-on-one. "I said, 'I'm going to help you fix this. But one of the things that we need to do is distance you from Doug. Do I have your permission to go to the media and really criticize Doug for screwing up? Will you be upset if I do it?'"

"No, go ahead. Do it," the mayor answered. Avoiding what would have been his administration's first major defeat, Rob Ford sanctioned a compromise motion that cut his brother off at the knees. Doug was livid. "I've got tire marks all over my back after I got thrown under the bus," he said.

—

My own tussle with Mark Towhey involved a decision, made by Towhey but voiced by the mayor, to turn down a provincial government offer of funding for two additional public health nurses to help reduce rates of chronic disease among newcomers to the city. As chair of the Toronto Board of Health, I tried to convince Towhey that it made no sense to reject two nurses when their salaries wouldn't affect the city budget.

"It's a good issue for us—size of government," he told me, stating his belief that Public Health already had too many nurses. When I said I'd take the matter up with Doug Ford, Towhey offered a lesson on power and influence in the mayor's office. "He's the mayor's brother, and the mayor listens to him. But he's not the person in the office with the most influence." I didn't need to ask Towhey who he thought that person was. Then Towhey told me about an upcoming report that would propose such a wave of cuts that "nobody is going to give a shit about your two nurses."

At council, I tried discussing the nurses directly with the mayor. He seemed to know little about the issue. "Wait a minute," he said to me, then walked over to Towhey, where he spoke no more than three sentences. Towhey shook his head. The mayor returned to me. "Nope," he said.

Public Health soon asked for approval to hire three more provincially funded nurses, this time to fight bedbugs, a growing problem that required immediate attention. Ford's vote caved. Council approved those three nurses plus the original two it had earlier rejected. Afterwards, I pointed out to Towhey that he'd lost a battle by picking an unnecessary fight. "Oh, no," he said. "We won that one."

Towhey's understanding of policy greatly surpassed that of the Fords, but he shared their stubborn certainty that there was only one correct way to proceed and, like them, he habitually overplayed his hand. The sword he would have the Fords die on was the blandly named "Core Services Review" carried out by consultant KPMG. Released in July 2011, it disappointed some Ford followers in that it found very little gravy, but otherwise it was a blunt attack on city government. It separated what was "core"—required as part of the city's basic mandate—from what decades of local politicians and citizens had seen as desirable, whether essential or not. The report was quickly turned into a long list of proposed service cuts, program elimination and the selling off of the city's facilities, such as its homes for the aged and its theatres. Even the zoo.

The fight over these cuts and sell-offs lasted months—the most epic moment being an end of July 2011 executive committee meeting that lasted twenty-two consecutive hours. A total of 164 citizens spoke, only three of them supporting the cuts. The feeling in the room, as day turned to night, was both electric and frightening. Ford moved with detachment from one impassioned speaker to the next, while his henchman, Councillor Giorgio Mammoliti, attacked them. Such swagger from the Fords and their hangers-on disturbed the more politically moderate members of Ford's executive, but not enough for them to risk stepping out of line during his first year as mayor, when the public in many parts of the city was still decidedly pro-Ford.

But that same summer, the anti-Ford forces got a boost

from an unexpected source: Doug Ford, who mounted an attack against the city's cherished libraries. Toronto is a city of readers, boasting the most active library system in North America. Doug said he would close libraries "in a heartbeat," declaring, incorrectly, that he had "more libraries in my area than I've got Tim Hortons."

Doug's comments prompted much-loved author Margaret Atwood to re-tweet an online petition supporting libraries to her 250,000 followers. The response crashed the petition's website. The next day Atwood tweeted again: "TwinFordmayors seem to think those who eat Timbits (like me) don't read."

That made Doug Ford mad. Margaret Atwood—whoever the hell *she* was—had picked a fight. "Well good luck to Margaret Atwood," he said. "I don't even know her. If she walked by me, I wouldn't have a clue who she is." Doug spoke as if that reflected badly on Margaret Atwood. "Tell her to go run in the next election." It didn't help Ford's anti-library cause that both he and Rob called them "liberries." People who'd been using liberries since they were young enough to call them that gave city-wide life to what had been a downtown-centred protest.

By the end of August, the Ford brothers had polarized council to such an extreme that only two groups existed: Ford supporters on the right and opponents on the left. When I complained to one reporter that he put the words "left-leaning" in front of my name every time he mentioned me, he explained that this was how the paper described any councillor who generally voted against Ford. I considered myself a centrist on most issues, but in the highly polarized environment of Ford's city hall, the mayor and his allies had portrayed opponents of the cuts as union-loving downtown lefties. I decided it was time for a covert action plan to loosen up enough votes to help solidify a centre group that councillors like Josh Colle were hoping to form.

Opposition to the cuts had been organized mostly by the city's unions. Their public protests made fellow-travellers feel good but did nothing to reduce the number of votes Ford controlled on council. Every time a union leader or downtown councillor attacked Ford, it strengthened him in the former suburbs. The potential defectors who represented these areas didn't want to appear to be joining the left. The more either side positioned it as a left–right contest, the more likely it was that Ford would hold his vote.

Because the unions were the only ones with the financial resources to help organize the opposition forces, I set out to change their approach. Over a beer in my living room with a union leader I hadn't met before, I presented a strategy aimed solely at getting Ford below twenty-three votes. The plan was to remove the left–right equation and focus the conversation on the programs and services residents valued and wanted to preserve—everything from snow clearing to school crossing guards. The union leader agreed to fund my ideas, the only condition being that I had to coordinate them with a union adviser and pollster named Bill Reno. Most union leaders knew little about me, other than that I was an independent councillor who didn't always vote their way. Several of them wondered what I was doing in this role.

"I know that some other union people did not consider you a reliable ally," Reno told me in 2015. "But there was respect for your independence and your *savvy*—that was most important. We were relying on you to give us advice on where to apply any resources."

To begin, I asked for an expensive city-wide poll, large enough to provide an accurate opinion sample in each of the city's forty-four wards. I wanted to show what residents actually thought about the cuts, not what either side claimed they did. To ensure the poll's credibility, Reno hired a mainstream pollster, Forum Research, who conducted one of the largest public opinion surveys ever carried out in the city. The results showed that an astonishing 77 percent of respondents thought their councillor should oppose Ford's package of cuts. Public opinion was against the cuts in every part of the city, including Ford's native Etobicoke.

I took the poll to the *Toronto Star*, with the understanding that the city editor could look at it but only keep it if he deemed it newsworthy enough for prominent coverage. In particular, I wanted individual ward results to be highlighted, as this would be critical to moving councillors away from Ford. Without making any promises, the editor outlined his intended approach, and I handed the poll to reporter Robyn Doolittle. I kept my involvement to myself, even when I was chided by some colleagues for not actively fighting Ford the way they were.

On Friday, September 16, 2011, the poll was front-page news. The ward breakdown was on the front of the GTA section. Forum Research president Lorne Bozinoff observed that councillors supporting Ford's cuts were "putting their careers on the line."

Next, I asked Reno to provide a social service agency with a software program that sorted e-mails by ward. The agency would then share the program with organizations opposing the cuts. Mass e-mails were generally ignored by politicians, but every councillor paid attention to those from individual constituents with a name and address. With the program, residents needed only to type in their address to have their message delivered to the councillor representing the ward in which they lived.

Then came the "push polls," an old idea with a relatively new twist, known as the "ring-through." An automated call asked residents if they thought their councillor should oppose the Ford cuts. If the resident pushed the number signifying Yes, they'd be invited to express that view to their councillor. If they pushed Yes again, the call would "ring through" to the councillor's office. The call display showed only the resident's phone number.

"The councillors didn't know where the calls were coming from," explained Reno, who had already been using this tactic. "We would program it to vary the number of people that would ring through. So one day it might be twenty, the next day it might be ten. We could drop it down to five. We could turn it off so that nobody got through for a couple of days and the councillor would say, 'Gee, I'm glad that's over.' Two days later we'd turn it back on and they would get another twenty calls."

For a few weeks, Reno took my advice about which councillors to target. Results were mixed but generally positive. When one councillor took a big step away from the Fords, I asked Reno to do the push poll in reverse: a ring-through to prompt thank-you calls. A week later, that councillor happily told me how popular the anti-cut position was with constituents. But before long, Reno and I began to disagree over who should get which calls. Some councillors were getting ready to move on their own, I argued. Until a safe centrist haven existed, too much pressure might entrench them with Ford.

At one point Reno confided that my name was initially on one union's target list—an indication to me of how poorly they read some councillors. Not unlike the Fords, union leaders tended to divide the world into friend and foe. Early in the fall of 2011, Reno expressed concern that my voting pattern wasn't sufficiently pro-union and I ended the collaboration.

—

Around that same time, a loosely aligned collection of five or six councillors took tentative steps to the centre. As the budget debate of January 2012 approached, the administration started making small concessions, but not enough to ensure that its budget would pass.

"That's when everyone was really counting sides and votes, which camp are you in, who could break to one side or the other," Josh Colle said. Just before the January vote, Colle put together a package and led a delegation of councillors to sell it to the mayor. With Rob was Doug Ford, Mark Towhey and budget chief Mike Del Grande. Colle asked the mayor to add back another $15 million for ice rinks, pools, community grants, homeless shelters and bus routes. "These are hot button issues, and for a fraction of the budget you can fix it all and be the hero."

The mayor stayed silent. "He would never say anything in a meeting," Colle remembered. "Even in that meeting it was all Towhey and Del Grande. There was no way they were hearing it. Rob sort of shook his head and that was it. Their approach was going to be, 'Well, we'll put the heat on.'" Which they did, but by now those tactics had offended one too many councillors.

Colle's motion, which Ford could easily have made his own, passed 23–21. Even with the extra $15 million, the budget was still less than the previous year's, a post-amalgamation first. But two natural inclinations—stubbornness and a preference for intimidation over diplomacy—turned victory into a very public defeat for the mayor.

After that vote, bullying by the mayor's office was not nearly as effective. "It made a few people realize it didn't have to be like that," Colle said.

13. FEELS LIKE HOME

"I only trust the man in the mirror."
Doug Ford Sr., Doug Ford Jr., Rob Ford

Dominating Rob Ford's office, on the wall behind the mayor's desk, was a blow-up of his father posing with Mike Harris. Covering the screen on the computer Rob never turned on was another photo of his father. There were other reminders of his dad throughout the office but, oddly, no photos of him with Rob. Nothing from childhood, not a campaign shot, nor anything from the years just before his father died, in 2006.

No warm memories. No stories of happy times together.

"Was he proud that his father was a Member of Provincial Parliament? Yes," said Ford policy adviser Sheila Paxton. "Did he have any nice things to say about his dad? I've never heard him say anything personal about the man, or affectionate about the man."

Whenever I asked Doug Jr. about Rob and their dad, he changed the subject. In a 2014 *Toronto Star* interview about their father, Doug was asked what his dad would do, if he were alive, to set Rob on the straight and narrow path. "After he kicked the shit out of him?" Doug asked with a laugh.

—

The walls in this mayor's office held no secrets. Loud voices carried right through them, and the Fords were anything but soft-spoken. While Rob Ford was mayor, the office held an atmosphere none of those who worked there had ever experienced before. Except for Rob. His office was just like home, but here Rob was the "dad."

His mother chose the colours, selected the art and decided where everything would be placed, even in the small outer staff offices. "The first time I met her, she was coming through to peruse the office," Sheila Paxton said. "She had a friend with her, and they were both very pleasant."

Paxton had a favourite painting she wanted to hang on the wall above where she sat. No way, a supervisor told her. You don't touch anything Diane Ford has put in place. Following the fear-nothing approach she'd learned from *her* father, Sheila put her painting up anyway.

Although Paxton and other former staffers spoke to me on the record, some didn't want their names associated with the crazy days in Ford's office. They all described Diane Ford as charming, capable, entitled and in charge. Many said she acted as if the mayor's staff were Ford family employees. Not with a haughty manner, but more as if this was a matter of fact. "I think Diane Ford considered herself a Rose Kennedy," one commented. "I used to call them the Etobicoke Kennedys. I always got the sense that they thought their business was politics."

The former staff members I spoke with hadn't met Doug Sr. But knowing Rob, they could guess at the similarities.

—

"I only trust the man in the mirror," Rob Ford's father often said. Rob and Doug learned to say it too. With conviction.

"His father was a real taskmaster," said Ford receptionist and his one-time friend Tom Beyer. "I think he had a very complicated relationship with his father." He declined to comment on specific relationships within the Ford family. "What I *will* tell you—whether he learned this from the father or not—the challenge we faced in the mayor's office is that he would pit people against each other. You never ever knew who to trust. So he would say to me, 'Tom, everybody wants you fired.' I would say, 'Why would that be? I thought I was doing a fantastic job.' He'd say, 'Oh no. They want you fired, man. But don't worry, *I've* got your back, man. So you just trust *me*, and you let me know if *those guys* are doing anything wrong. What's Brooks doing? What's Brian doing?' Then I heard later, Rob would say, 'You know, Tom is saying this about you. What do you know about Tom?'

"We never really jelled as a team because the top man would undermine us at every turn. It was always, 'Watch your back—because somebody's trying to fire you or fuck you over.' I had never been in such a toxic work environment."

Only one voice mattered in this office. It could be harsh. Rob rarely uttered a "job well done," and when you weren't measuring up, in his eyes, he punished you. Tough love? You're damned right! That love got even tougher after he'd been drinking. How do you deal with the demanding voice whose instructions are incoherent? Even for an adult, that doesn't feel safe.

Beyer, a former drinking buddy, said when Ford drank too much, he became "very animated. *Extremely* animated. He comes across very aggressive. He becomes the Incredible Hulk. Sort of a Jekyll and Hyde character."

So booze seems to unleash his beast? I asked.

"Oh yeah, without question."

—

"They asked us to do some unbelievable things for that guy—take his kids to soccer, or buy his groceries, do his laundry. To me these things were way, way, way far out of what a special assistant to the mayor is supposedly supposed to do," Beyer told me. Both Mark Towhey and Earl Provost reminded him that his contract contained a category of "other assigned duties," Beyer said. "I'm not even going to tell you half the stuff. There was nothing illegal that they made us do. But some far-out stuff. If it was a duty assigned to you, you did it whether you liked it or not."

Buying alcohol for the mayor became an assigned duty after Ford's visits to liquor stores started showing up on Twitter. Towhey even developed some rules around it. Staff were to let Towhey know every time they left the office to buy liquor. More importantly, no staff member was to get in the car if the mayor was driving. That rule was put in place after staff said they endured some harrowing outings with an obviously inebriated Ford behind the wheel.

The mayor's drink of choice was Iceberg Vodka, usually consumed straight from mickey-sized bottles, sometimes with alternating gulps of Gatorade. One staffer told police he went to the LCBO for Ford about twice a week—more often than that after the crack story broke. He gave his boss the bottles as he was leaving the office, usually between 4 p.m. and 6 p.m. Sheila Paxton told me that during Earl Provost's tenure, a stash of mickeys was kept in the office. "The mayor would disappear into the washroom and was usually in a better mood when he came out."

Although nobody was entirely sure which substances he was taking in what combination, Paxton learned to recognize the signs of a mayor under the influence. "He speaks faster, and his eyes would be going around the room. He'd be a little more paranoid in his comments, and he couldn't focus—not that he has a good attention span at any time. I've been in meetings where he'll say, 'OK, I've had enough,' and get up and leave. He can't sit still. He's got ants in his pants."

For many staff, "other assigned duties" included taking phone calls from him in the middle of the night. "I would get a lot of calls at three-thirty or four o'clock in the morning," Beyer said. "I know most people did. Very nonsensical calls. He would ramble on and I knew he was under the influence of something. I guess I could have turned the phone off, but somebody calling you at three-thirty, you're petrified that the worst is going to happen. 'I'm in the ditch and I need a tow truck.' Or, 'The cops just pulled me over and I need a lawyer.' We were on call twenty-four hours a day, seven days a week."

They could be out for dinner with friends, attending a family get-together or in bed for the night. When the call came, whatever else they were doing had to stop. Starting with the 2010 campaign and continuing into his mayoralty, Ford had a personal assistant—a "body man." The mayor's first body man, according to several of his colleagues, quit after being roughed up when he tried to get the mayor to leave a strip club to attend to city business.

Special assistant Chris Fickel became the new body man in 2012. He helped Ford coach the Don Bosco Eagles high school football team. Among his duties, Fickel changed batteries in the mayor's children's toys, put new bulbs in his outdoor lights, and bought laundry detergent and cartons of cigarettes for Renata.

Fickel later told police that the mayor was "a tough man to read" and would be verbally abusive towards him in the office and at football practice, especially after he'd been drinking. Ford seemed to enjoy belittling him in front of others, often incorporating the type of colloquialism his father so often used: "This kid is as useless as two tits on a bull."

Fickel told police the mayor had once cocked his fist at him. Another time they were talking football in the car when the mayor pulled over, grabbed a mickey of vodka in a paper bag, drank the whole thing in less than two minutes, then drove off again.

The most inconvenient—make that most *uncomfortable*—of Fickel's surprise assignments occurred one weekend in January 2013. He was picking up his dinner date when the mayor summoned him to fix his wife's computer. Forced to choose whom he could least afford to piss off, Fickel brought his date with him to the mayor's house, asking her to wait in the car for what he hoped would be a few minutes.

Bring your date inside, the mayor insisted. Noting the extreme mess, and the stench of stale smoke and cigarette butts, Fickel demurred. But Rob Ford was insistent, saying he wanted to help Fickel make a good impression. Ford stepped outside and waved her in.

Renata came downstairs so the two couples could chat. While the women exchanged a few sentences about the school Fickel's date was attending, Rob left and returned with a marijuana cigarette. He lit it and offered her some. She declined. After finishing the joint himself, the mayor became more animated and turned the conversation to football. The couple stayed more than an hour before they were able to make a run for it.

Fickel's date was *not* impressed. When police called her in for an interview about her evening with the Fords, they referred to her as Fickel's "ex-girlfriend."

—

Out among the common folk, Rob could be friendly, engaging and generous. Office staff received very different treatment. There was no leniency for an honest mistake or a misunderstanding. Insubordination, real or imagined, was punished.

Sheila Paxton said the mayor flew into a rage once when he called her cellphone and a male voice delivered her voice mail message. A friend had set it up for her. Ford ordered Paxton suspended for a week without pay. She ignored the penalty. He suspended another staff member for taking too long getting his car repaired, and blamed two others after he read out a scroll extolling the virtues of Lithuanians at a Ukrainian event in Bloor West Village. "He didn't look at it and say, 'Oh, this is wrong,'" said Paxton. "He just read it as is."

Another time, Ford tried to suspend Paxton because he wanted a handkerchief and she didn't have one with her. When out in public, the mayor required certain things, chief of which was a handkerchief to mop his brow. Paxton bought a bundle of them at Walmart and packaged them in kits with Kleenex and bottled water. Whoever was staffing him was expected to have these kits, together with business cards and fridge magnets. On the day in question, Sheila was observing a community council meeting on her own time.

"He calls me over and says, 'I need a handkerchief to wipe my brow, I'm sweating.' Well, I didn't have a handkerchief, so I got some Kleenex and gave it to the mayor and I said, 'I've called for the handkerchief.' A few minutes later he calls me back over and says, 'I need a handkerchief, not Kleenex.'

"I said, 'Mayor, they're bringing them, I don't have one.' So he phones Earl, he wants to suspend me for five days because I didn't have a handkerchief. I said, 'I'm not going to take these stupid suspensions. You don't have the right to do that and I'm not taking it.' As long as I stayed together and had a backbone, the others weren't as afraid." The staff, she said, feared both his bark and his bite. "The mayor's a big guy and when he yells, it's frightening."

I asked what Sheila made of a boss who looked for trivial reasons to punish others when he had so many of his own flaws.

"Well, that was our big laugh," she said. "How many days do you get suspended for doing drugs and alcohol on the job?"

—

When it came to staff salaries, Rob was as tight as the skin on a grape.

"We were the next best thing to a slave," one staffer told me. Junior staff received $35,000 annually for workweeks that lasted sixty hours or more. Some went a few years without a raise. Ford figured they were lucky to have a job working for him. At first, they thought so too. Some imagined he'd teach them political strategy and offer a guiding hand, like the father figures in their own lives. He had a different model.

"As soon as you spend any time around him, you know he's not interested in being a mentor," said a former staffer. "He's not interested in being nurturing in any way. Advice consisted of the common sayings. On financial policy, for example: 'Look after the pennies and the dollars will look after themselves.'"

To test a theory, I again contacted Ted Herriott, Doug Sr.'s former business partner, to compare Rob's management style with his dad's. Ted didn't want to volunteer anything negative about the man who started Deco with him, but he readily described a work style that left a lasting impression. "With Doug's upbringing and home background, sometimes he would have a hard time expressing warmth," Ted remembered. "Doug was, 'Hey boy, it's a tough world—and you've gotta be tough if you're going to make it.' He played hardball. All the time, he played hardball. There were several instances where I would ask Doug, 'Be a little more fair, pal. Come on. Tone it down a bit.'"

Was he fixed on a certain way of doing things?

"He had his way of thinking and you couldn't change it," Ted answered. "Once his mind was made up, no matter how hard you tried, you couldn't change it."

Difficulty admitting a mistake? Check. Unable to understand any point of view other than his own? Check.

Friendly with the customers? Yes. But inconsiderate and lacking empathy?

Ted, a kind and thoughtful man who passed away suddenly, at age eighty-two, a few weeks after this interview, summed up Doug Sr.'s approach: "Business was business. That's all there is to it. There was very little empathy towards some of the people we did business with. It was, 'This is the way it is.'"

—

Christmas in the mayor's office was a time for re-gifting. Baskets, boxes of chocolates, bottles of booze—anything the public sent him—was placed on the large table in the boardroom. "You know how this works," the mayor explained as staff took their seats. "We're all going to draw a number and we'll go back and forth, like a football pool." And they selected gifts from strangers, in priority sequence, until the table was cleared.

Next came Rob's personal gift. His first year in office, he pulled out a wad of fifty-dollar bills and handed one to each of them. "Here's fifty dollars—it's enough to buy you a Christmas dinner," he'd tell one. "Here you go," he'd say to the next.

"It was an easy way for a rich man to try to show his appreciation, and it came off flat," said one former staff member. "There was no feeling behind it. He didn't look you in the eye. There was no, 'I'm very grateful for all you've done for me all year.' I would have appreciated a handshake and a thank you."

The next year, he wrote cheques for the same amount and gave those out instead. Some people liked that better because at least it contained something personal—his signature. Many of those cheques remain uncashed, framed and hung on apartment walls.

Each year, Christmas lasted only until the mayor had rounded the boardroom table. Then it was back to work—and don't even think about leaving early to make up for unpaid overtime or "other assigned duties."

One of the younger staffers remembered standing by the front desk with two senior staff, watching the clock on Christmas Eve. Other political staff in the building had already left for family dinner or had the day off as thanks for many hours of unpaid overtime. The mayor was already in Florida.

"The concern was that he'd call at 4:59 to see if that phone was still being answered. So we stayed there until exactly five o'clock so he couldn't accuse us of cutting out early."

—

At one of the mayor's New Year's levees, a young staff member waited until the lineup to meet his boss was almost finished. Then he went to the end of the line so he too could get a photo with Rob Ford, at the time a man he still admired.

"I was the last one in line and I said, 'Would you mind if I get a picture?' And he said, 'Sure, as long as there's nobody else.'" The photo got taken and was later inscribed, "Thanks for your support. Rob Ford"—the same message the mayor wrote on everyone's photo. Prodded by his chief of staff, the mayor added a line: "Thanks for being on the team."

14. "IT'S A DEMOCRACY, HONEY"

*"It's not a political story. It's a personal story.
It's a family story."*
Chris Caple, founder of Rob Ford Must Go

O n Day 6 of their 258-day sit-in outside the mayor's office,
the small group of protesters were about to gather up their
signs to end that day's shift when the elevator doors opened. Out
stepped Rob Ford with his seven-year-old daughter, Stephanie.

The mayor went straight for his office, but Stephanie wanted
to see the signs. Walking closer, she sounded them out.

"Rob. Ford. Must," she began, pausing to comprehend the
full sentence before saying the last word. "Go.

"What does that mean?" she asked her father.

"It's a democracy, honey," he replied.

"They should take it down," Stephanie complained.

"No. No," Rob Ford told his daughter. "They have a right to
have it there."

Democracy, Rob Ford–style. Anyone can play and—clearly—
anyone can win. Rob loves that about politics, a game in per-
petual motion, interrupted only by periodic elections that
freeze the action for a day, so a score can be tallied. His game

is usually some variation of right versus left. But his brand of politics attracts people from all over, who want to play for him and only him.

Rob's big brother, who loves this game too, is so competitive he makes a sore winner. Able to sense when someone is even thinking about taking him on, Doug often retaliates by throwing the first punch. Once everyone understands who's in charge, he figures, they'll just stay down.

—

On city hall's second floor, the offices of Toronto's forty-four councillors line four interconnected "streets" labelled A, B, C and D. The city's political leaders manoeuvre these corridors, trading stories, swapping ideas, devising strategies. When Rob Ford was mayor, the action never stopped. Conversations moved up one street, down the next and back around the circle. Hallway encounters led to deeper conversations inside the offices. Opposition councillors talked about ways to increase their strength. Ford's allies were visited frequently by the mayor's staff, checking the temperature on the floor and turning up the heat when the reception wasn't warm enough.

The mayor's office sits at the strategic centre of the circular floor. Its front doors face the elevator, which stops here frequently as it travels between the councillors' basement parking area and the private back entrance to the third-floor council chamber. When its doors opened outside Ford's office, you never knew who would walk out.

Wrestler Hulk Hogan came out of that elevator and was welcomed by the mayor; Brutus "The Barber" Beefcake was not. When The Iron Sheik headed for the mayor's office to challenge Ford to an arm wrestle, Tom Beyer hit the emergency button to lock the doors. Former heavyweight boxing champion and convicted rapist Mike Tyson dropped by to declare his support, as did former sprinter Ben Johnson, who had been stripped of his Olympic gold medal for taking banned substances. On a more typical day, the elevator would unload tourists, school kids or a man in a yellow banana suit, proclaiming that the mayor needed to eat more fruit.

———

Two flagpoles stand in front of Toronto city hall.

As you face the building, the city's 99-foot official flagpole is on the left. The Canadian flag always flies there. To the right is the 18.5-foot "courtesy" flagpole. This pole flies the flags of other nations, non-profit organizations or the City of Toronto.

On the morning of February 7, 2014, the Toronto flag came down so that a rainbow-coloured Pride flag could be raised, as requested by a local organization, to show solidarity with the LGBT community in Russia during the Sochi Olympics. Other Canadian cities were already flying this flag. But news that this had happened in *his* city triggered Rob Ford's homophobic and patriotic fervour.

Ford left an angry voice mail for Joe Pennachetti *demanding* the Pride flag be taken down. Pennachetti called back to say that wasn't going to happen.

"No, I want it down," Ford ordered.

"Mr. Mayor, I've double-checked with the protocol office," Pennachetti told him. "We're following the approved policy of council and it's staying up. I'm not changing my mind. It's not coming down." It was the only time Ford tried giving the top bureaucrat a direct order, but not the first time the mayor swore because he didn't like an answer.

"I sent him the policy and then he called back," Pennachetti told me. Ford continued to complain angrily that the Pride flag should be replaced with the Canadian flag. Pennachetti pointed out that the Canadian flag was flying where it always did—on the *other* flagpole. Ford's next move was to duct-tape a Canadian flag to his office window, overlooking the square.

"This is about being patriotic to our country," Ford said. "This is not about your sexual preference." A few days later, in case the wedge he was driving between gay rights and Canadian patriotism wasn't sharp enough, he publicly asserted that the Pride flag had *replaced* the Canadian flag. "I've done everything I can to get a Canadian flag back up where it should be, to represent all Canadians, whether they're gay or straight," he told reporters.

That same day, six mothers and three of their adolescent children staged a quiet protest outside the mayor's office, questioning his fitness to lead the city, for multiple reasons. "I'm glad they brought their children down here, even though they should be in school," Doug Ford commented. "That's their democratic right. If we wanted to, we could have a thousand mothers down here in support of Rob."

Following the events on social media, Chris Caple, a 39-year-old website designer, was inspired by the protest. "Yes!" he thought. "I want to see that there all the time."

———

With Rob Ford's election as mayor, Toronto municipal politics became very *personal*. The mayor wasn't just right or wrong, according to your political perspective. He was good or bad. Reactions to him were emotional. He made some people feel good inside because, for the first time, they'd found a government leader who cared about them. Others got angry just looking at him, as if he headed an occupying power intent on imposing its values and culture.

At city hall, supporters and opponents came and went. But one group sat looking into the glass walls of the mayor's outer office for almost nine months, beginning in February 2014. The Rob Ford Must Go protest was started by Caple, who hadn't previously been involved in political movements of any kind. Now he felt compelled to start his own.

"What finally pushed me personally over the edge was the Pride flag situation," Caple told me. "This is the mayor of Toronto openly promoting homophobia. In *Toronto*, the most gay-friendly city in Canada. I'm not gay, but that *hurt*. It hurt physically."

Homophobia had been a factor in Ford's 2010 win. Now, what seemed like the deliberate stirring of intolerance over the rainbow flag struck many in the city as intolerable.

"It's a lie to say the Canadian flag was taken down," said Caple. "To demand that the Canadian flag be put back up—appalling—and he repeated it over and over. Several people pointed out that this was not the case, and he kept saying it. They lie constantly, both Fords. It's their modus operandi. When they're caught in the lie, they double down on it. If it's propagandistic, if they can claim it and create confusion, they'll repeat it until they die."

Caple registered the domain name RobFordMustGo.com, created a Twitter account and set up a simple website. Then he tweeted out the launch of a sit-in, to begin outside the mayor's office at 1:00 p.m. the following day, February 12. On Day 1, more than fifteen people showed up. They quickly created a schedule—8:30 a.m. till 9:00 p.m. weekdays, 10:00 to 6:00 on weekends—and began slotting themselves into shifts. Their protest was so civil it went largely unnoticed amid the daily melee outside Ford's office.

Katherine Carleton, one of the first to sign up, was fifty-one, worked in the arts, lived in a condo not far from downtown, travelled by public transit and bicycle, and owned two cats. The protesters had a lot in common. Most were self-employed or had flexible work schedules. They followed social media but also loved books. They tended to be introspective but intensely curious. As with their polar opposites in Ford Nation, the Fords provoked them in ways they couldn't ignore.

"Do you see the attraction of sitting here?" Carleton asked when I stopped to talk one day. "So many of us had been *alone* with our deep, deep concern about what's going on in the governing of our city. Social media is amazing, but it is fundamentally anti-social: me alone with the glowing screen of my phone, *yelling* at my phone. This was an opportunity to break out from my Facebook friends and the people I'm following on Twitter to actually have *face-to-face* conversations."

The sit-in provided opportunities for observation and insight, as well as moments of wry humour—all of which the protesters tweeted and re-tweeted. Rob wasn't much bothered by political opposition; without another team, there'd be no game. But Doug took their presence as a personal affront and periodically tried to assert Ford supremacy over their space. "You know, we could get a thousand Ford Nation volunteers over here—just cover up all your signs," he told the sit-in one day. "But we're not gonna. We're going to *let* you stay here until October 27."

The protest was initially focused entirely on Rob, but Doug soon bothered the protesters in ways that were the same but different—like the brothers themselves. Rob seemed to be constantly trying to find his way out of whatever trouble he'd just got into. "I said to him, 'You'd be up in the Arctic Circle and you'd get in trouble with the Eskimos,'" Doug told me one day, after Rob got himself in another tub of hot water. Rob's lies were mostly defensive, a denial of whatever it was he'd just done. Doug was more aggressive, wielding his version of the truth to match whatever point he was arguing. Caple prepared himself for the next time Doug came out to address the media. "I stood up behind him, eight or nine feet away, and held up the sign: *Doug, That's Not True*." As Doug spoke, Caple took note of each claim. "Okay, that's not true. And that one's not true either. It was just obviously not true stuff. Don Peat from the *Sun* was motioning for me to get into position so he could take a picture.

He tweeted it out so that the sign is very clearly readable behind Doug. That photo got tweeted out all over the place."

Doug went into the mayor's office then quickly returned. "We could get fifteen members of Ford Nation out here and cover you guys right up," he told Caple and company. "But they're all working." Then he stormed off.

Katherine Carleton remembers her delight at the *Doug, That's Not True* tweet. She wanted to take it further. "I would like to engage with Cirque du Soleil and, when Doug is speaking, I would like to have people do *backflips* through the air and *cartwheels* and walking around on stilts—just some way of expressing it's a circus, it's not reality, we are somewhere else entirely."

Not that the absurdity in front of the mayor's office didn't speak for itself.

"Yesterday was bobble-head day," Carleton told me in one of our chats, referring to the unveiling of the third edition of tiny Rob Fords in April 2014. "I was here in the afternoon and the CP24 reporter was asking questions about the bobble-heads. So Graeme, who works in the mayor's office, brought out the two bobble-head models and put them on a table. And the bobble-heads had what I can only describe as a scrum. I actually took a picture of a cameraman doing a close-up of the two bobble-heads standing side by side.

"The Fords," she concluded, "have occupied our brains and they have hollowed them out."

———

Rob Ford Must Go's fascination with all things Ford extended to Diane, the enigmatic force at this family's core. The sit-in encountered her only once. After attending the funeral of family friend and former federal finance minister Jim Flaherty, Diane went with Rob back to his office. Spotting the protesters, she asked her son about them. "Oh, they're here all the time," they heard him answer. Katherine Carleton picked up the story. "A little bit later they came back. She looked at me and I smiled at her, and then she went back into his office."

When mayor and mother came out again to wait for the elevator, Diane eyed the signs carefully. Some were plain, others ornate. Some listed questions the mayor wouldn't answer. One sign totalled the number of days since the start of the protest, another the days left until the election.

"She spent a solid fifteen seconds looking at that day's array of signs. Her face didn't move," Carleton said. "I was trying my very best to detect any sign that any of this had any impact, and I was not able to see that it did. She strikes me as a very fierce and a tough woman, and it was important to her to see what our signs said. That would be more information she could apply to whatever support she was providing to her sons."

This fleeting encounter held significance for Carleton. "She's someone that I have thought about a lot, wondering how she feels about how her family is doing right now. Does she really truly believe that Rob's a wonderful mayor and Doug's a great campaign manager, and the Fords are like the Kennedys? Or is she someone who is putting on a brave front and recognizing that the things that she and Doug Sr. hoped for their children have all kind of blown up and gone terribly sour?"

The brief moment of eye contact between Diane and Katherine was an unusually intimate level of interaction between the protesters and any member of the Ford family. "I have not *sought* eye contact with the Fords," Carleton said. "Rob doesn't look over. He's very unidirectional. Even watching him walk through the media, if he stops to talk, he doesn't make direct eye contact." Up close, she witnessed "the profound physical discomfort of the man. I get the sense that he's this bizarre combination of bluster and extremely shy, and I also get the sense that he's a very unhappy person.

"One of the great puzzles is, 'Why would you do it if you don't want the job?' The mayor seems to me like someone who had some bizarre family event. Something happened that cut him off from the possibility of self-awareness, gave him a profound sense of entitlement, failed to instill a sense of shame—so many things that he may not be questioning himself about. But he still seems to be quite unhappy. He seems just hunted and unhappy." Carleton consciously avoided observing Rob too directly, "not wanting to enhance his sense of being like an animal in the zoo, behind the glass."

Doug evoked no such compassion. "Doug terrifies me," Carleton said. "He is incredible at not answering the question. I mean, the man has got terrifying focus. It's like he knows where all the Easter eggs are hidden and nobody else does, and he likes it that way. I'm afraid of Doug. He is a large angry man. I don't think I would actually want to start a conversation with him. I don't think it would go well."

—

Even after the mayor admitted smoking crack, a surprising amount of everyday life continued at city hall, as if nothing could disrupt the daily routine. Many school groups still ended their tour of the building with a visit to the mayor's office.

In the early days of the sit-in, Toby the button-maker sat outside Rob Ford's office, cranking out more than 1,500 Rob Ford Must Go buttons to give to visitors. "Around the second or third week of the sit-in, a group of young kids—ten or eleven years old—came by on a tour," Chris Caple recalled. "Toby was there with the button machine. Their teacher was showing them the picture of the councillors and the mayor and showing them the city seal and the motto. The kids kept looking around and one of them said, 'You guys have buttons!'

"They all swarmed over, and every single kid took a Rob

Ford Must Go button. Then they all went into his office." It was the day of a council meeting and the mayor was upstairs in the chamber. "So I tweeted, 'Wouldn't it be weird if Ford walked into his office right now.' And then the elevator door opened and Rob walked out and into his office."

When the students emerged twenty minutes later, their teacher gave the protesters two thumbs-up.

—

"Here's a weird little vignette," Chris Caple offered. "I think we're starting to get a bit of a grasp on how Rob Ford actually perceives the world. He seems to fundamentally lack the capacity for abstract thought, for any sustained high-level conceptual thinking. He experiences the world in terms of physical objects that are in front of him.

"Last Wednesday, Jude MacDonald brought in these rainbow Pride matryoshka dolls, Russian nesting dolls, as an aspect of the protest against Russia. Ford came out and sat in one of the visitor's chairs in front of his office, silently watching, semi-transfixed as they were taking these dolls out and picking them up and talking about them. It's the only time he's actually come out and focused on the sit-in for an extended period of time. So we're thinking, 'Maybe the signs aren't the way to go. Maybe we need some physical objects.'"

Later, Ford walked by and spotted some bright green shoes on one of the protesters. "Like the shoes, man," he said.

"So his attention was pulled by these bright shoes. I feel like I'm getting this weirdly accurate sense of how both Fords see themselves and the world, and how their supporters largely experience the world. It is in these very concrete terms. But there's a complete lack of any awareness beyond that.

"So it's this wildly simplistic, locked-in, hermetically sealed world view, where they're genuinely not aware of anything else.

This is what I've become aware of in the last few days after sitting here for weeks and weeks and weeks. And Whoa. Whoa! Wow!"

—

At first, when I asked Chris Caple if anything in his life, apart from the sit-in, links him to Rob Ford, he answered, "I hope not." I tried again, asking him to explain why, after years of being politically uninvolved, he dove into Rob Ford Must Go as if he had no choice. The person who usually strings sentences together effortlessly is suddenly full of uhs and ums. "There is an explanation. It's somewhat complex. Related to childhood issues. This actually speaks to me a lot on that level."

Chris told me he grew up in an extended family where there was abuse, bullying, lying and—perhaps worst of all in his eyes—an inability to take responsibility for bad behaviour. The Fords, he said, set off triggers in many people with similar experiences. "My therapist has had multiple clients who've just been triggered *like crazy* by all of the stuff Ford does and gets away with. What he says. How he acts. It just brings up their own family issues. It brings up their problems with alcoholism, with drug abuse, or just growing up in families that were straight-out abusive, emotionally abusive, physically abusive.

"It's like the city is stuck in an abusive relationship with a guy who *won't leave* and who won't recognize that he's being wildly abusive and destructive. I feel that really personally. The political layer is like this," Caple said, holding his fingers a centimetre apart. "The psycho-emotional layer is like 95 percent of it. I think that's why people respond to this with such fascination around the world. Because it's not a political story, it's a personal story. It's a family story. It's this emotional story. People see aspects of themselves or their own families in him, things they were trying to repress or don't want to acknowledge. So he forces a reaction from people. It's difficult, perhaps impossible, to be neutral towards him."

—

Many in Toronto revere Rob Ford as fervently as others revile him. He touched something in them too.

Sandra Pavan was a Rob Ford zealot long before Ford Nation had a name. Disappointed by a long line of politicians before him, Pavan saw something different in Ford. "Rob came into the buildings. He didn't hesitate. You tell him to go over and crawl under a car to find something, he'll do it. He's not afraid to get himself dirty. He's there to help the people, especially tenants, because tenants are the neglected ones. . . . So Rob, he came and he did what he said he was going to do. And he never gave any indication he was anything but our saviour."

Now well into her sixties, Pavan had been a Ford volunteer for fourteen years, delivering election flyers, helping out at FordFests, generally being at the family's beck and call. Several times, Pavan made a point of telling me that most of the men in her life, from her father on down, have been police officers. Rob Ford showed that he cared about her, and others like her, by upholding the law, whether it be property standards bylaws or anti-drug statutes.

When Ford admitted he smoked crack, Pavan at first couldn't believe it, thinking he must be covering for somebody. When the truth sank in, she felt crushed, unable to explain her disillusionment without breaking down. Sitting in Perkin's Restaurant with me for an interview, she regained her composure enough to speak. I was the only one with her when she started talking, but she was addressing Rob Ford as if he was with us at the table.

"If you were bored or wanted something to do, you could have phoned up any of your volunteers and gone to their place and had a great time. There would have been no drinking or drugs. But you chose to hang out with this group. And people think, 'You people in Ward 2, how crazy you are to still cling to hope for this man.'"

Pavan then spoke to me for a few minutes, became emotional once more, and turned again to imaginary Rob. "You let everybody down. You led a different life. You talked about the kids, keeping them off the street. Giving them something to do. You started these football leagues. You put out $20,000 the first year for uniforms to keep the kids off the street. But then were you doing drugs? How can this be? It's contradictory. I don't understand. How can you say one thing and do totally the opposite?"

Soon after this conversation, Pavan stopped talking to me. Perhaps she found a way to resolve the contradiction.

—

For months, I searched for a Ford Nation equivalent of Chris Caple, someone with a pro-Ford point of view who could tell me how their life had led them to Rob Ford. When I asked Doug Ford to suggest people, he invited me to Rob's 2014 campaign launch, where he said I'd find plenty of them. But when I chose a few to interview, Doug privately told them not to speak to me.

Neil Flagg is the founder and administrator of the "I Hate the War on Mayor Rob Ford" Facebook page. In one online comment he described page followers as "a highly intelligent group of like-minded individuals committed to truth, kindness and rational discussion."

I phoned Flagg to ask for an interview. He declined. I asked if he could suggest someone else. In the summer of 2014, I texted him: "Hi Neil, I'm really having difficulty getting a pro-Ford perspective. Any suggestions? Feel free to call." He texted back: "Maybe it's because a hate-Ford ringleader is doing the asking."

A few weeks later, Flagg wrote this online: "One afternoon in August I got a call on my home phone from Councillor John

Filion, the angry old leftist and chief Ford-tormenter from Willowdale." After a relatively accurate account of our brief conversation, Flagg outlined the conspiracy he had uncovered. "Then a few weeks later out comes the big endorsement of John Tory." I had indeed endorsed Tory for mayor, against Rob Ford. "Now who better is there in Toronto to get someone a book contract than John Tory, former CEO and current director of Rogers, which owns countless properties in the publishing industry." My book, Flagg announced, was to be released in October 2014, just before the election. "John Tory will proclaim it as the reason why you can't vote Ford. Filion will claim it to be the honest gospel truth. So-called 'journalists' will take it seriously.

"And you will know the truth about how the whole scam came together."

Neil Flagg, I'm guessing, supposed all of this to be true. At some point, would he realize he'd manufactured it to match his Ford-like view of the world? Not likely.

—

Among the Ford supporters who did speak with me, taxes and government spending were common themes in a "Get your hand out of my pocket" sort of way. They saw Rob Ford as the *only* politician who could deal with that issue.

"We want someone in there to represent our *money*—and he's the only guy who can do it. Okay?" John Anga pulled a money clip from his pocket and raised it high to make his point. A hundred-dollar bill was wrapped around other bills. "The rest of them are full of crap, okay? They talk the big talk, and they do *nothing*. All right? John Tory with the white shirt. Fine, you get him in there, guaranteed you'll be sharing your paycheque with the city. With Rob, you're not going to. He's going to stop the spending. He's going to do *whatever he can* to minimize this money from going to the city. Bottom line. People understand that.

"Okay, he's screwed up personally—but he didn't screw *me*. Not like the Liberals who took my money. They screwed *me*."

Anga spoke with me at Rob Ford's 2014 campaign launch, before Doug had time to shut anyone down. He was accompanied by Bob, another Ford supporter. "Those guys should be in jail," chimed in Bob, referring to the Liberals.

I asked John and Bob to explain the importance of lower taxes. "You don't have money, you're living in the street," said Anga. Bob added, "Money is important because that's how the city runs. Okay? You've got so many taxpayers who are paying money to the city. It's just like any kind of a business, you need to manage that money properly. What we see—and have seen—is councillors down there who don't understand the business aspect of things. He does. He gets it."

"Rob, he goes out, gets drunk, he comes back and makes you a fortune!" Anga said. "When everything's said and done, it's all about money."

—

"Rob is like a Robin Hood for the suburbs," said Andrew, who described himself as "pretty much the biggest Ford supporter there ever was." The 30-year-old Etobicoke resident asked that his real name not be used, fearing his pro-Ford sentiments would be unpopular at his workplace—Toronto city hall. "He's an average person, despite being wealthy. He doesn't live in a palace. He lives in a normal house on a regular suburban street. He made himself just an average person."

Shouldn't a mayor be above average?

"The majority of the city is average people," Andrew responded. "They're people who drive hatchbacks and live in Agincourt. Rob was able to connect on a basic level with people. He doesn't need that job. He's a millionaire. But Rob isn't doing it for himself. He's doing it for other people."

For a short time, just after Ford admitted smoking crack, Andrew's faith was challenged. "But it was all fleeting. I came back around to Rob pretty quickly. He always did things with a good intention. He was always well-meaning. I'd say he's selfless."

Andrew sounded intelligent and normal. Average, he might prefer. He'd known Rob Ford since he phoned him, in 2008, and Rob called right back. When he asked to chat about politics, Ford obliged, many times. Andrew considered him a mentor.

"He makes politics simple. A lot of people try to make it complicated. He explained it to me. 'It's just returning phone calls, returning e-mails.' He's amazing. He works magic."

At the two Ford gatherings I attended, event-goers often recognized me as a councillor who didn't support Rob politically. Some were instantly hostile. "Fuck you!" one man shouted at me, then returned every few minutes to shout it again as I tried to carry on a conversation with friendlier folks. Some wanted the non-believer in their midst to explain himself, truly puzzled that everyone didn't think like the Fords.

People who did believe in Rob Ford often got themselves all tangled up trying to explain the basis of their faith, as if you could get there with facts and logic. "He got rid of the unions," said a fifty-something hockey coach who liked Ford's everyman persona. I agreed Ford had saved money by privatizing garbage collection in half the city, but he hadn't eliminated the unions. "That's not true," the man said, getting angry, as if I had challenged his belief in Rob Ford.

Another man said he supported Ford because he was the only candidate who would build subways. I pointed out that opponents Olivia Chow and John Tory had subway plans too. Tory's subway didn't count, he said, because it wasn't underground. When I observed that subway cars sometimes travelled on surface rail, he figured I was using some smarty-pants trickery against him.

As I left one Ford event, I overheard two young men in an animated discussion. "No way," said one. "No, really, Rob Ford's a millionaire," said the other. "There's no way that's true," replied the first.

—

"I would not be able to take that person seriously," Richard Ferin said when I related Andrew's description of Rob Ford as selfless. "They see a mythical Rob Ford. Because there's *nothing* selfless about him. He's *totally* self-absorbed." Two people looking at the same picture and seeing something completely different: there'd be nothing alarming about that if it wasn't replicated across the city.

Ferin channelled his anger at Rob Ford into humour, something I told him I hadn't encountered among Ford Nation. That's because Ford used anger to attract followers, Ferin observed. "There's a tribal quality to his appeal, and the reason he was able to keep that appeal, despite all of the terrible things people would gradually learn about him, was it was still their guy against the enemy."

Ferin had set up a MayorFrod Twitter account, which he used to parody the tweets issued by the mayor's office, as if someone on Ford's staff had slipped up and accidentally revealed the truth.

"I know it's a bit anticlimactic," MayorFrod tweeted on the day Ford admitted smoking crack cocaine, "but I was lying about LRTs too. They're not so bad really."

"Folks, I have nothing more to hide," he tweeted the same day, before the release of more incriminating police documents. "And some of that nothing will be released on Friday."

"Occasionally someone would reply as if I was really Rob," Ferin told me. "I would respond to them in character until they realized what the gag was." When the first batch of bobble-heads was released, Ferin stood in line to get Rob Ford's personalized signature. The bobble-head he came away with is made out to MayorFrod and signed by Mayor Rob Ford.

Ferin stayed anonymous for six months. Then, just after Ford's crack confession, he came out from behind the Twitter account to reveal that he had once been a heavy crack user. Ferin wanted to contrast his story with Ford's "denial and blaming everyone else for it." This was more than six months before Ford would admit he needed help. "He had no empathy for other people, but he demanded unlimited empathy for himself and his struggles. I didn't want him to get off the hook for that," Ferin said.

Ferin understood much of Ford Nation's alienation, but not its choice of leader. "What you can't explain to me is, why this guy? Why you would have faith in this guy in particular. That's the mystery to me."

—

When the 2014 election was over and no Ford was mayor, Rob Ford Must Go—which temporarily became Doug Ford Must Go—packed up their signs for the last time. "I did not in my wildest dreams imagine it going on this long," Chris Caple told me. The sit-in didn't bring the results he'd hoped for: an epiphany in Rob Ford's own soul that would inspire him to remove himself from office.

"People had lots of personal reasons for wanting to participate in the sit-in. My own motivation was to see if it was possible to reach this guy directly, through approaching him non-confrontationally with a completely different form of energy than he was used to. We were trying to create a very compassionate space, a space that was non-judgmental and was just very open and loving and accepting and *kind* and honest."

But how could Rob Ford see a group called Rob Ford Must Go as caring and loving?

"Well, by seeing how we were behaving. We were just going to sit here and express something that is the opposite of what he's doing, and see if he will come over." Not only did that not happen, but Rob Ford, post–cancer diagnosis and treatment, came back to city hall as a councillor.

"The guy just staggers me. He still staggers me. If there was a Rob Ford out there working in a car wash, okay, fine, whatever. But for a person like that to ascend to a high level of political power—it's *mind-blowing*. How the *hell* did that happen!? How *did* that happen? There are countless lessons to be learned here. I'm going to be grappling with that for years, because I'm horribly fascinated."

—

In one of our phone conversations in the winter of 2015, Fabio Basso warmed to the topic of political polarization in the city. Rob's high school buddy acknowledged the problem but figured it would go away if everybody just thought like Rob Ford. (To be fair, the anti-Ford folks think much the same, moving in the opposite direction.) "Like, if you like subways, you're for Rob. And if you like streetcars, you're not. Stupid things like that," said Basso. "What, did the guy invent the fuckin' subway, you're so against it? They don't want to admit that he was right. They'll go to their grave and not say, 'The guy's right!' Too much pride in people, I guess."

Despite the grief Rob caused him by choosing *his* basement to smoke crack in, Basso had nothing but political praise for Rob.

I asked if he thinks Rob was a good mayor.

"Oh fuck yeah! He's the best."

What would he consider Ford's greatest achievements?

Basso paused to think. "More or less just doing what he said. Straight-up. He returns a phone call. Straight from the horse. He calls straight back—and it means a lot."

I asked him for a story about a kind-hearted Rob, maybe

something from their high school days. I'd been told such stories existed, but nobody, including Basso, was willing to share one, perhaps because they didn't trust me to retell it accurately.

"These people don't know him," Basso said of Rob Ford's critics in general. "How can you have a hate for a person you don't even fucking know? That's what I don't understand. Where did this hatred come from?"

It was important to me that Rob not see me as one of the haters. I'd seen his extreme reactions—at times angry, at others sad—when he felt he had been portrayed unfairly. He was especially sensitive around subjects that went to the heart of how he wanted to see himself: a good father and husband, a hard worker, loyal, a caring football coach, an honourable man who honours his debts and pays his bills.

In July 2015, he became very upset with me over a misunderstanding about a friendly sports bet. He thought I was accusing him of not paying a debt and said he could have nothing more to do with somebody who thought that about him or, worse, might repeat it to others. He wanted me to accept a cheque, as proof of payment, for the small amount I thought we had wagered, even though he had no recollection of any such bet. I told him there was clearly a misunderstanding and, if he didn't remember the bet, I'd agree that it never existed. Rob remained upset for at least ten minutes.

"I don't question your integrity," I said, meaning that I believed he would always intend to honour a commitment that matched his core values.

"I hope not," he replied in a firm voice.

If he was that upset over what seemed like a small issue, I wondered how Rob was going to react to this book. I offered to read him portions of it, so he could respond to anything he thought was inaccurate or unfair. I told him there would be parts he certainly wouldn't like, but that I hoped he could see it as an attempt to portray him fairly.

"I appreciate that," he said. "But it can't be fair, because you're writing it." What he meant was that nobody other than Rob could possibly tell Rob Ford's story fairly. He wasn't going to read the book, he told me, but there would be no hard feelings between us because of it.

"I wish you success with your publication," he said.

15. THE OTHER SIDE OF THE FENCE

*"We will not rest until being a gang member
is a miserable, undesirable life."*
Mayor Rob Ford

R ob Ford often acts as if he thinks he's invisible. If he doesn't
see you, you can't see him.

Rob began the Family Day weekend in 2013 with good
wishes to everyone on his e-mail list. "Have a fantastic long
weekend. Drive safe and take caution in the winter conditions."
On Sunday evening, Rob was with members of the Basso family:
Fabio, Rob's friend since grade ten, his sister Elena, another
brother, and their aging, widowed mother, Lina. They lived at
15 Windsor Road in a house that, from the outside, looked like
others on a street of 1950s-style bungalows.

Other big-city mayors might choose more important
people to hang around with. That's not Rob. He's just trying
to relax in the comfortable surroundings of the basement of
an old stoner buddy. Dressed in a white T-shirt, Rob holds a
glass cylinder in one hand, a lighter in the other. Applying the
flame to the tip of the cylinder in a circular motion, he inhales
and exhales.

Off to the side, Elena Basso is talking politics. She'd like to put her foot up Justin Trudeau's ass "so far it comes out the other end." It's the sort of political discourse Rob enjoys—right to the point, not too philosophical, an exchange of opinions among like-minded friends. The mayor tries to join in, muttering something about the federal Liberal leader.

Elena's criminal record, dating back to 1993, includes cocaine trafficking and prostitution. Police also know her as "Princess." (Now past fifty, she later tells investigators that Princess "died a long time ago.")

There are other visitors in the room, younger guys from the nearby apartments. Police say they're part of a gang, the Dixon City Bloods. At 15 Windsor, they're known simply as the guys who come right over when Rob needs a release from the stress of everyday life—you know, the job, the family. Not so different from anyone else when you think of it that way.

It's just past 7 p.m., already dark outside. A light shines from a top corner of the room, like sunlight peeking in the window. A phone rings. Ford opens half-closed eyes, becoming dimly aware that one of the young visitors, Mohamed Siad, has been standing opposite him with an iPhone. He drops the cylinder and lighter onto the table in front of him. "That phone better not be on," Ford warns him, the last words on a recording millions of people will soon be talking about.

When news of this recording goes public, Siad will first go into hiding and then to jail, where he'll be knifed in the back. Another man who tried to peddle the video will be found with a bullet wound in an apartment stairwell. Others will go into hiding. Fabio Basso will lose his job and be beaten with a metal pipe. Sandro Lisi, the mayor's best friend, will be charged with extortion.

Rob Ford's punishment will be drawn out. Eventually he'll check into rehab, his mayoralty overcome by personal tragedy.

At first, Mohamed Siad is pleased with himself for having

caught the mayor in the act. He thinks the recording on his phone will provide protection in a dangerous world, maybe even a fresh start somewhere far from Dixon. Back in his car, Siad makes a second recording, in which he reflects on the first. "That's how you catch a person slipping, or even catch a mayor smoking crack," he says to his phone.

—

The summer of 2012 now seemed far away. Back then, the mayor had stood solemn and resolute, armed with moral authority and a prepared statement, spouting law and order. Camera crews followed as he toured a northeast Scarborough housing complex, the scene hours earlier of Toronto's worst-ever mass shooting. Gunfire from rival gangs killed two and wounded twenty-three others on Danzig Street, where a community had gathered for a barbecue on a warm July evening. Earlier that summer, members of different warring gangs opened fire in the food court at Toronto's Eaton Centre, killing two of their own and injuring six others at the city's most popular tourist mall.

Toronto's relatively small number of murders usually involved situations that average citizens couldn't picture themselves in: an altercation outside a late night club, an encounter in a dingy staircase. But the Eaton Centre and a neighbourhood barbecue? Those felt too close for comfort.

Rob Ford, the crime fighter, arrived at Danzig ready to chase all the low-life gang members out of town. He was glad reporters were there to record his words.

"There is no room in Toronto for violent gangs," he told an anxious city. "We will not rest until being a gang member is a miserable, undesirable life." By the following day, he'd dropped a more ambitious proposal on the table. "I want something done. I want these people out of the city. And I'm not going to stop. Not put 'em in jail, then come back and you can live in the city. Go somewhere else. I don't want 'em living in the city anymore."

The mayor said he planned to speak with Prime Minister Stephen Harper about changing federal laws so criminal gang members would be banned from Toronto. When Harper didn't play along, Ford dropped it.

This wasn't his first tough-on-crime message. An anti-drug stance helped get him elected in 2000, when he defeated a councillor offering no solutions to the rising gang problems in north Etobicoke. At the time, he told a local newspaper how he and his father had chased drug users out of Scarlettwood Court. "When people would drive through to buy drugs, we'd send the owner of the car a letter," Ford said. "It would tell them not to come back to the area."

Ford's 2012 vow to rid the city of gangs caught the attention of Mohamed Farah, who watched it on YouTube from his home in north Etobicoke's Dixon apartment complex. Farah was part of a group of community members trying to keep the area's Somali-Canadian youth out of the emerging street gangs. The mayor's comments troubled him, especially when combined with what else he knew about this man.

Years earlier, when Ford was a councillor for the area, Dixon's Somali-Canadian community leaders had asked for his help to stem the spread of drugs and gangs in the neighbourhood. They wanted to set up after-school programs to keep kids away from trouble in the hours between when school left off and parents took over. Hearing that Ford often met constituents at a plaza restaurant near Dixon and Islington, they sought him out there. Just after their arrival, they spotted Ford walking towards the restaurant.

They approached him. "Councillor Rob Ford, how are you?"

"Pretty good. How you guys doing?" he answered.

They asked for a meeting in his office. "I'm not an office guy, so talk to me now," he replied.

"He was very patient, quite frankly," says Abdi Fatah Warsame, who described the meeting to me.

"There are challenges and issues that our community faces," they told him. "We want the young people who are growing up now to be connected with success in this great nation." They asked for his help to start recreation and mentoring programs.

Ford didn't believe in taxpayer-assisted programs to keep youth out of trouble. Except for football. "I have no money for this," he told them. "You folks need to understand Canada and the Canadian way. Like anybody else, your community needs to toughen up, man up."

But Ford wasn't finished. "Don't get me wrong. I'm not an asshole. I'm willing to help." He pointed to a nearby bank machine. "If you guys can walk with me, we can go to the ATM and I can withdraw $500 for you. I hope that solves your problems."

The group was offended, explaining that they weren't asking for personal charity.

Ford didn't like their attitude. "Ciao. Ciao. Ciao," he said, walking away.

—

A chain-link fence separates the Dixon buildings from the surrounding neighbourhood. Mohamed Farah talks a lot about the fence. It's a metaphor for many things, but Farah speaks mostly about the help the community inside the fence needs from those on the other side of it. But those people turn away, try to build a bigger fence, or come to the fence's edge to buy drugs from the youth inside.

Rob Ford did all three. The same summer Mayor Ford pledged a crackdown on gangs, Farah heard stories about him buying drugs in the community. "How would you feel if you were in my shoes, and you turn on the TV and you see this guy saying there's a war on gangs?" Farah asked. "And then he goes back to the other side of the fence doing what he's doing?"

When the time came, Farah would try to expose him.

—

The unmasking of Rob Ford happened in a swirl of revelations that must have felt like a thousand hands tearing at him all at once. But the pivotal point in the drama had been set in motion years earlier, part of a string of events that started in a place Rob had likely never heard of as a rambunctious 22-year-old in Etobicoke.

By 1991, Ford had abandoned an attempt to complete his first year of university in Ottawa while struggling to earn a spot on the football team, the Carleton Ravens. No matter how adrift he may have felt, family privilege provided the security of a job at Deco, somewhere to live, and a bailout if he got himself in a jam.

That same year, in the refugee camps of Kenya and Ethiopia, remnants of families blown apart by civil war and genocide in neighbouring Somalia heard of a place called Dixon. It's all they knew of Canada—a six-building high-rise community on Etobicoke's Dixon Road. The people in those camps imagined Dixon as a place where life could begin again.

"A lot of the early people from Somalia came right there to Dixon Road," recalled Doug Holyday, who was the last mayor of Etobicoke, from 1994 to 1997. "The first ones came and they'd pass the word back. And then others came."

Built in the 1970s, Dixon's large condo units at first had been snapped up by empty-nesters and investors from central Etobicoke. Units on the higher floors had unobstructed views of downtown Toronto's new CN Tower, then the world's tallest free-standing structure. But the noise from jets flying immediately overhead to land at nearby Pearson International Airport prompted some of the original owners to move elsewhere and rent out their units.

Vince Cianfarani managed all six of the Dixon buildings, grouped into two condo corporations, between 1976 and 1997. "The government done it to us," he said. "They had a list of all the absentee owners in the six buildings. They would call them and say, 'Listen, we know that you have an apartment on Dixon Road. Are you renting it? If it becomes empty, we'd like to rent it from you to accommodate the refugees. Our rent is going to be around $1,400 or $1,500 a month, and we'll pay you directly.'

"Now, the absentee owner that was getting around $900 went to the tenant. 'Listen, my son is getting married. You'll have to move out. He's going to be living here in two months.' Within a year, they had chased out every renter and replaced them with refugees. That's where the problems started."

—

Somalis leaving the camps for a new life in Canada often knew two other words that went along with Dixon: *Emmett* and *Kingsview*. Naomi Emmett was the principal of Kingsview Village Junior School, located just behind the buildings. For refugees trying to forget the past, the school represented the future, in a land where children could grow into successful adults.

"The school was their entry point," Emmett told me. "When I got there in September 1990, there were 385 kids. By June, there were 550." By the time she left in 1997, the number was 800. Almost ten thousand people now lived in buildings designed for half that number. The area had a nickname: Little Mogadishu. A large percentage of the newcomers were young children, most with one parent and some with none. Many who had watched their mothers and fathers being murdered were brought to Dixon by surviving relatives. Here, a new neighbour arriving as a refugee might be someone responsible for the death of one of your family members back home.

"It would bring me to tears to hear what these kids had experienced," said Emmett, who was struck by how little support was provided for those whose need was so great. Most newly-arrived children spoke no English. Many had never attended any school and, arriving in a Canadian winter without boots or coats, had difficulty getting to class in their new country.

It wasn't working out the way anybody had planned—if anybody had planned anything at all.

Mohamed Farah was twelve when he arrived at Dixon in 1992. "It seemed unwelcoming when we first came here," he said. Because his family had spent a few years in Windsor before that, his English language skills and cultural assimilation were strong enough for him to mentor other newcomers. But as a newcomer himself to Dixon, Farah was startled by the racism he experienced there. At the grocery store with his mother, soon after they arrived, a woman in the checkout line shoved her cart in front of theirs. "Go back to where you come from, Paki," she snarled.

"I didn't know what 'Paki' was," Farah said. But he quickly learned that Somalis were "the other" in three ways: newcomers with a different culture, Muslim and black.

"At the very beginning, it was a mixed community," recalled property manager Cianfarani. "There were people from Europe and Asia. The new people started to arrive and they thought they were discriminated against because they were black." He told me tensions within the buildings in the early nineties precipitated "a riot" by the Somalis and "a demonstration" by the established residents.

The riot at Dixon, he said, was sparked when security guards roughed up a Somali man who parked illegally in a handicapped spot. Trying to reduce the tension, the mayor of Etobicoke and the local police superintendent gave instructions not to enforce the parking rules. But the black residents, who weren't told about this rule change, became even more incensed the next night when a white man parked in the same spot, with impunity. The demonstration at Etobicoke City Hall involved busloads of mostly white-haired folks asking local officials to do something about the deteriorating conditions in Dixon.

Cianfarani said the refugee tenants engaged in "all kinds of hanky-panky. They would sign a lease for three or four people and bring a bunch of friends in with them. The couple next door that was using one-fourth the utilities but paying the same common condo fees started to get upset about it. And on and on it went."

Cianfarani quit managing 320 Dixon and its two neighbouring buildings in 1997, when their condo boards rejected his plan to install a parking gate and surveillance cameras. But he continued to manage the three condos to the south, whose boards had approved his security measures. "Troublemakers" from those three buildings moved elsewhere, he said—sometimes to the Dixon condos that didn't have cameras.

Naomi Emmett and other advocates continued to plead for help from anyone who would listen. But the principal doesn't remember any level of government doing anything close to what was needed.

Children who arrived from the refugee camps in the 1990s became young men, as new families with more children than adults continued to move into Dixon. The Dixon buildings soon teemed with youth who started out disadvantaged, often struggled in school, had meagre legitimate prospects and saw no path out. Drugs entering through the front doors soon attracted people who came around the back. The demand from outside the fence increased the supply inside. By 2011, guns and crack were hot commodities moving in and out of the buildings.

—

As if this saga needed any more symbols of a system gone wrong, the only path out of Dixon was literally closed off in 2011, at the urging of Rob and Doug Ford. While he was still a councillor, Rob Ford had again been called upon to improve the situation, this time by the residents of the bungalows on Windsor Road. They were up in arms about criminals in their midst and wanted Ford to plug a small passageway leading from the condos to Windsor Road, so that nobody from Dixon could directly enter their street.

"We had a problem on Windsor," remembered Nijole Ardavicius, who lived a few streets over. "There was a bunch of those fellas from those buildings terrorizing the seniors in that area. What they were doing I don't actually know. I just know that the seniors said they were being terrorized. And they called Rob Ford."

Ford went to Windsor Road to meet with the residents. "There was a bunch of us who went to the meeting," Ardavicius said. "They wanted to have a fence put up. He listened to them and, next thing I know, up came the fence." Construction was initially delayed by the city's due process, which, as usual, began with a study.

"Approximately 500 pedestrians, more than two-thirds of whom are children and youths under the age of 13, use this connection on typical weekdays between 7:00 a.m. and 7:00 p.m., evidently to take access to the schools located to the north," the study reported.

But the homeowners had a petition with 121 signatures. "We the residents of Windsor Road and Kingsview Village want/demand that the passageway/gate at the end of Windsor Road be closed. In the last 6 months, there have been 3 shootings at that location," the petition said. "It is a safety concern for all the residents of the Kingsview Village area. There has also been an increase in theft, vandalism and noise at night especially on Windsor Road. We pay high taxes and the value of our homes is going down."

Municipal politicians have a term for agitated older residents who sign petitions and attend community meetings in a neighbourhood like this: voters. Shortly after the 2010 election, their new councillor, Doug Ford, got the fence formally approved. The accompanying staff report provided a technical reason to ignore the study and favour the petition.

"It is a good thing," said Ardavicius, "but they should have made it higher. It's short enough for those younger kids, around 13 years old, to jump over it. And I see them doing it. The only bad part of it is that there are a lot of us seniors that don't have vehicles, and now we have to go all the way around" to get to the bus stop on Dixon Road.

I asked about the house at 15 Windsor, on her side of the fence. Ardavicius wasn't bothered much by stories that Rob Ford smoked crack there. "That's what they were saying. I always had trouble believing it," she told me. "But when you see the picture, it's gotta be true, right? It's a shame." A shame that the media said bad things about Rob Ford, she meant. And a good thing that people around there didn't believe everything they read.

"Here in Kingsview Village," she told me in 2015, "everybody's very fond of Rob Ford."

—

Rob Ford's long-time connection to 15 Windsor Road was part of the chain of events that brought him down. The Basso home was only a few doors away from the buildings inhabited by the Dixon Bloods, who were under surveillance by a special guns and gangs unit.

On the morning of Saturday, April 20, 2013, the mayor dragged himself out of bed, sleepless and hungover after a druggy late night at the Bassos', accompanied by his ne'er-do-well sidekick Sandro Lisi. He was leading a Clean Toronto Together event at Colonel Samuel Smith Park in Etobicoke, but his mind was on his missing phone. It had a lot of *personal* stuff on it. Someone at the house last night must have stolen it.

As Ford fretted, Sandro Lisi was on the phone to Liban Siyad, *demanding* he return Rob's cellphone. *Or else!* Lisi was one of several Ford friends who still lived in their parents' basements, not far from Windsor Road. His criminal record included assault and criminal harassment. In 2011, when Lisi was being sentenced for threatening to kill an ex-girlfriend, the mayor submitted a character reference:

> Mr. Lisi has demonstrated to myself that he has a great work ethic and has always shown tact and diplomacy. I have known Mr. Lisi for several years, and he has always conducted himself in a courteous and polite manner. Yours truly, Rob Ford, Mayor of Toronto.

In October 2013, after Lisi was charged with drug trafficking but before his arrest for extortion, Ford said this about his drinking and drug-taking companion: "He's a good guy and I don't throw my friends under the bus. He's straight and narrow. Never once seen the guy drink, never seen him once do drugs."

For a while, Ford made Lisi his occasional driver, resisting Deputy Mayor Doug Holyday's suggestion that he hire a retired police officer. Ford didn't want some snitch driving him around, and Lisi could be relied upon to also perform less official duties— like getting the mayor's cellphone back after his drug dealers had stolen it.

—

Suppose you are the mayor of Toronto and your cellphone has been stolen by the *Dixon Bloods*. And your best friend phones the Bloods, *threatening* that *you'll* bring the cops down on them if they don't give your phone back *immediately*. And the Bloods say everybody should just chill because they've got a *picture* of *you* smoking *crack*. And all the Bloods' phones are being *tapped*. And the *police* have heard *everything*.

If you are Rob Ford, you have absolutely *no idea* how much *trouble* you are now in.

In the aftermath of the Danzig shootings and Ford's tough-on-crime pronouncements, although not as a direct result of either, Toronto police began a new gang investigation known as Project Traveller. The objective was to investigate and shut down a north Etobicoke gang they believed was responsible for drug smuggling, gun smuggling and murders. By March 2013, police had enough evidence for a judge to authorize wiretaps on alleged members of the Dixon Bloods. Those under surveillance included Mohamed Siad, who had shot the Ford video, and Liban Siyad, a crack dealer. Others under investigation included Anthony Smith, Mohammed Khattak and Monir Kasim, the three young men who had posed for a soon-to-be-famous photo with Ford, outside 15 Windsor Road.

These "persons of interest" led Project Traveller detectives to the Bassos' home, where the mayor of Toronto had smoked crack. By April 9, police considered 15 Windsor a "crack house," a place from which drugs were sold. On April 20, they listened in as Elena Basso ordered a special delivery from Siyad for Rob Ford.

Police chief Bill Blair had already heard about the mayor's problem with drugs. Police also knew about the crack video, having listened while gang members discussed an alleged offer by Ford to trade $5,000 and a car for it. When you are the chief of police, what do you do with information that the mayor may be smoking crack?

"It was brought to my attention," Blair told me in 2015, "but it was clear to all of us that our investigation had to continue to focus on the higher purpose, which was to make that neighbourhood safe." Investigators couldn't "go off chasing any particular individual for something less serious." When pursuing major crime, police typically overlook less serious transgressions, not wanting to jeopardize the core investigation; Blair didn't want to shift the focus of Project Traveller away from gun smuggling and violence. Also, if he played this one differently because Rob Ford was involved, it would look as though the chief had targeted the mayor. Blair had told his officers to continue the gang investigation, neither focusing on the mayor nor giving him a pass.

—

On the night that the mayor's phone went missing, Sandro Lisi started calling it at 4:23 a.m. and then called eighteen times after that, apparently getting no answer. He called Fabio Basso twice. By morning, Lisi correctly surmised that Liban Siyad, who'd been with Ford and Lisi at the Bassos' the night before, either had Ford's phone or knew who did.

Lisi's call to Siyad on the morning of April 20, 2013, prompted Blair to change his approach, turning police attention directly on Rob Ford. Descriptions of conversations involving Lisi, Siyad and others are contained in the police documents released by a court. At the time of this writing, not all of the information contained in the documents had been proven in a court of law. But here's a summary from April 20, 2013, the night the mayor's phone went missing and the day he got it back.

12:52 a.m.: A woman believed to be Elena Basso, Fabio's sister, tells Liban Siyad that Rob Ford is at her house. She asks Siyad to come over quickly.

12:54 a.m.: Another alleged gang member, Abdahulli Harun, tells Siyad to go to Basso's house because Rob Ford wants drugs. Siyad says he already knows.

2:18 a.m.: Harun tells Siyad that he had Rob Ford smoking on the "dugga" (believed to mean crack pipe). He says he has many pictures of Ford "doing the hezza" (believed to mean heroin).

5:51 a.m.: Siyad says Ford was "smoking his rocks today" (believed to be crack cocaine) at 15 Windsor and that Siyad will post pictures on Instagram.

11:37 a.m.: Lisi calls Siyad, accusing him and a friend of stealing the mayor's phone. Lisi says Ford is "freaking out" and will "put heat on Dixon" if he doesn't get the phone back.

1:01 p.m.: Siyad tells an unknown male about Lisi's call. "You want threats, I have fucking Rob Ford on a pipe, a picture of him," he says. To which the man replies, "We have Rob Ford on a lot of fucked-up situations, but yo we don't say nuttin'." They decide not to tolerate any threats from Lisi but hope to keep things friendly because "they love and respect Rob Ford."

1:22 p.m.: Siyad tells Lisi he has the phone and will give it to him at a nearby Country Style doughnuts. Lisi offers Siyad some marijuana for his trouble.

Bad enough for Ford that the cops listened in while Elena Basso phoned for a crack delivery as casually as if she were ordering him a late night pizza. Here was Lisi, seemingly on behalf of the mayor, threatening to use the police against the mayor's drug suppliers while the dealers talked about countering that with a threat to expose the mayor. Senior investigators quickly brought this new situation to Blair.

"We couldn't just leave that unresolved, unexamined," he told me. "You can't ignore that threat to the integrity of public institutions—the office of the mayor or the police service." Blair began contemplating a separate investigation of Rob Ford.

Through wiretaps and other sources, police already knew most of the details in the *Star* and Gawker crack video stories before they were published. But having these allegations out in public increased Blair's need to focus on Ford. On May 18, the chief of police officially launched Project Brazen 2 to investigate "allegations against Mayor Rob Ford, specifically to investigate the existence of a cellular phone containing a video of Ford smoking crack cocaine." He assigned a senior homicide detective to the case, one from outside Etobicoke's 23 Division, keeping it away from Superintendent Ron Tavener, who was a Ford family friend.

On June 16, three days after Project Traveller culminated in a series of pre-dawn raids that resulted in 44 arrests on 220 charges, Blair zoomed more police resources in on Ford. Officers were assigned to tail the mayor and Sandro Lisi. A week later, a Cessna airplane began watching Rob Ford from the sky.

—

"There are two kinds of drug dealers," Mohamed Farah told me. "There are the drug dealers who have to provide food for their home—this is a career for them. And then there's the person who's escaping reality." The second of these, the ones seeking an alternative to a miserable daily life, are the most common in Dixon.

"The lifestyle becomes an escape from reality. You're somebody else. You're a drug dealer, you're a coke kid, the girls all love you and you have money in your pocket. A lot of these guys would find happiness in the lifestyle—partying, drugs and drinking. You kind of invent your own reality."

Did Rob Ford take drugs for the same reason these dealers sold it: to escape the stress and unhappiness of his everyday life? I asked Fabio Basso.

"Who knows? Could be," he answered. "Everyone's got their reasons, right? Why do people beat their wives? Why do they beat their children? Why do people blow themselves up? Like who knows? As long as humans have been around, there's something they do on the side. Everyone's got their vice, pretty much. Gambling, food, whatever it is, everybody's got something. Just humans. Many people are too fast to judge other people."

"Life's complicated," I suggested.

"Sure is," he said. "Simple but not, you know what I mean?"

I said that description might fit Rob Ford.

"Could very well be," he answered.

—

"Don't write unsympathetically about that neighbourhood," police chief Bill Blair asked of me, when I was done with my questions.

Earlier in the interview, Blair explained why some Dixon residents might think police had overdramatized the situation by calling the Dixon Bloods a gang. "People sometimes don't understand the way in which street gangs are organized. It isn't based on a traditional organized crime model. They associate with each other, there is an allegiance, a network of communication. They may be involved individually or collectively in various criminal activities." Often there is no leader.

"Another thing people need to realize about gangsters is that they're not bad guys all day long and every day. They'll engage in criminal behaviour at times, and at other times they're just kids in the neighbourhood."

After the Project Traveller raids turned up large quantities of guns and drugs in June 2013, a lot of these neighbourhood kids found themselves in jail, where many were still awaiting trial a year and a half later, when I spoke with Blair. I asked the chief, who was about to step down after ten years, what needed to happen in Dixon. Blair answered with passion. "You've got to *mobilize* that community, *strengthen* its resiliency. People *shouldn't be afraid* in their own houses, they shouldn't be afraid to interact with the neighbours. They shouldn't be afraid to send their kids out to play in the park. So you've got to *restore* their sense of safety.

"Then you've got to *go into* those communities and make some investments—education and employment opportunities. *Make sure* that there is safe recreational space for the kids. You've got to have strong settlement services. You've got to *make sure* that they have access to that network of support and of *opportunity* for themselves and their kids. You can create a cohesive neighbourhood by making those types of investments.

"And then, when it's a neighbourhood where people *interact* with their neighbours and interact with *us*, and have a *strong sense* of themselves as a *community*, and their kids feel *included* and they have an opportunity to reach their *potential*—that's a *lousy* place to be a gangster, it's a *lousy* place to sell drugs, it's a lousy place to carry a gun, it's a lousy place to victimize people.

"There's other things you can do. A neighbourhood should always have a grocery store. A neighbourhood should have a bank. A neighbourhood should have good transit that comes close enough so that people can get to work. Neighbourhoods should have good recreational space and good support services, and *pride*.

"There's *a ton* of things you can do besides just locking up the gangsters."

—

Two years after Rob Ford bought crack from neighbourhood drug dealers, I asked Mohamed Farah how most Dixon residents view political leaders. Politicians aren't well regarded in Dixon, he told me. Except for one man. Despite everything, Somali-Canadians still saw Rob Ford as someone who's on their side.

But what about all the negative publicity? I asked.

In this too, Farah explained, Rob Ford is just like them. "He didn't cause it. He was the victim of it."

16. KARMA'S A BITCH

"Cash in!? For what? On my own misery?"
Fabio Basso on money, crack and misery

There are two things Fabio Basso wants you to know about him and the place he calls home. "It's not a crack house, number one. Number two, we pay our own fuckin' bills."

I had phoned Basso out of the blue in 2015, introducing myself and striking up a conversation that lasted forty-five minutes. For a guy who'd been through one helluva lot since Toronto's mayor was caught smoking crack in his basement, Basso was unexpectedly pleasant when I called asking for insights into his old friend. After speaking with him for a while, I saw how he and Rob could have become fast friends in the mid-1980s, just after Fabio switched high schools from Don Bosco to Scarlett Heights. Like Rob, Fabio didn't want to be interviewed, perhaps thinking it would be too much like an inquisition. But he was happy to chat.

The crack story, he said, had "ruined my life and is still ruining my life." He had endured everything from being kept awake by Ford's all-night partying in his basement to the home invasion and beating that followed. Fabio was most disturbed, though, by the suggestion that Rob Ford paid his utility bills.

"He's never paid a bill for us, nor has anybody ever paid a bill in our house." Other than the Basso family, he meant. The misunderstanding about the bills—I'm accepting Basso's declaration on this—occurred when police examined a notebook turned over by one of Rob Ford's former staff. In it, police discovered a list of outstanding utility bills for the Bassos' home. "One possible explanation for these entries," a detective wrote, "could be that the mayor is dealing with house maintenance and bill payment at 15 Windsor Rd." This musing was later released in court documents.

"He's Paying Their Fucking Bills!" the headlines screamed, according to Basso. His wording, while not exactly as written, did capture the impression the coverage left. The actual *Star* headline hit both of Basso's sore points in one shot: DID ROB FORD PAY UTILITY BILLS FOR A CRACK HOUSE?

"It's gotta be true because it's in the paper, right?" Basso said contemptuously. As the story took over his life, even old friends started to believe the media's portrayal of him: a guy who didn't pay his own utility bills. It made him particularly bitter towards the press and only slightly less so towards the police. He didn't just *think* they were in cahoots. "I know it for a *fact*," he told me.

"We're nobodies," he said, explaining why so much had been written about his family. The unwanted attention started as soon as the *Star* figured out that *the* photo—the one of "fat fucking Rob" with the Dixon Bloods—was taken outside the Basso residence. "Like I told the reporters, I'm not in the video and I'm not in the stupid picture. 'Send an entertainment reporter,' I told the *Star,* 'because this isn't news.'" Although the media attention had died down by the time we spoke, "they'd do it all over again in the drop of a hat," he told me. "Bang! They'd be all over it again."

Does Basso feel like an unwilling character in somebody else's story?

"Perhaps, yeah," he said. "Just to help them," he said of the story writers. "Portraying whatever helps them. You know what I mean?"

Like somebody wrote a part and put your name in it?

"Could be," he answered. "One might think that."

Basso was still offended that one journalist expressed surprise that he held down a job. "Oh, so really, you work?!" he imitated a reporter's reaction when he told her he worked in construction. "I *had* a fucking job," he told me. "After the newspapers started talking shit, I never got hired back."

People wanted nothing to do with you?

"Yup," he answered.

And Rob?

"Haven't heard from him once. He thought maybe I got some money out of this ordeal. I never got a cent. Nor do I want a penny. I don't do that. That's not me. 'Cash in!?' For what? On my own misery? If anyone should, I should. Everybody else is selling me out for whatever they can fucking get."

—

The knock on the door came at 10:56 p.m. on May 21, 2013, according to police records. Basso's elderly mother, Lina, heard it. If her husband had still been alive, maybe he would have known what to do about the man at the door. A black man dressed entirely in black, according to what witnesses told police. He asked for Fabio.

"He's not home," his mother lied. The man pushed his way through the door—knocking her aside—and turned down the hallway, to where Fabio was trying to forget the whole awful week in the presumed safety of his bedroom, in the sanctity of his bed, in the company of a girlfriend. The man in black pulled an extendable metal baton from his waistband and beat Basso and the girlfriend severely enough that they were taken to hospital.

"Get hit with a steel stick about thirty times in the head, see how you feel," Basso told me.

Basso also said he didn't know the man, or who sent him. But as we talked, it got him thinking about an incident a few weeks earlier. Basso had been in line at the gas station and convenience store near his home. Directly in front of him was the Fords' friend Dave Price, "a dirtbag," says Basso, who had badgered him about the crack video just before the home invasion.

Now, two years later, in the lineup at the store, Price said nothing to him. But after they'd both left the store and Basso had turned the corner to walk home, Price drove alongside and opened the window.

"Karma's a bitch!" he shouted.

—

By the time he'd finished reading the opening sentence of the *Toronto Star* story, Mohamed Farah knew he was in danger.

"A cellphone video that appears to show Mayor Rob Ford smoking crack cocaine is being shopped around by a group of Somali men involved in the drug trade," it read.

Approached by the video's owner at the end of March 2013 to help sell the recording, Farah had contacted the *Toronto Star*'s Robyn Doolittle. Trying to entice the newspaper to pay the $100,000 the owner wanted, Farah let Doolittle and another journalist watch it in the back seat of his car.

"The broker said he represented two Somali men who had supplied crack cocaine to the mayor in the Dixon Rd. area," the *Star* said further down. When the story was first published, the word "Somali" appeared eleven times. The newspaper later apologized and issued an edited version that reduced the Somali references to five.

Gawker, an American media website, broke the story at 8:28 p.m., May 16, 2013. The *Star* published its version online at 9:25.

Within hours, the video's broker and its seller were trying to get the hell out of Dixon. Farah told me he didn't expect the *Star* to identify the neighbourhood. The paper didn't name *him*, as promised, but it might as well have. "It narrowed it down to who it might be," Farah said, "and me and Robyn had been seen in the community a week and a half prior to the story breaking."

Farah had taken Doolittle to a youth basketball game, hoping she'd write some neighbourhood-friendly sidebar to world-breaking news about a mayor caught smoking crack. He supposed this combination of stories would provide some impetus for positive change in Dixon. Farah also thought that news from Dixon was a commodity he could broker to news outlets for a fee, and told me he would have accepted a commission from the video's owner if the sale had gone as planned. It didn't.

"When the story broke, it set in motion a lot of events," Farah said. "First, it ruined my relationship with the original video owner. He was pissed. Second of all, it put my life in danger, because anybody that was trying to suppress the video, or trying to get the video, they knew I was involved." Drug dealers and gang members were extremely displeased at the unwanted attention Siad and Farah had brought them. The much larger Somali-Canadian community, the ones *not* involved in criminal activity, felt stigmatized once again. Within the Dixon condos, some were merely angry; others were looking for someone to punish.

—

Before Farah got involved, there had already been at least two clumsy attempts to sell the video. The first was to a CTV cameraman, who took the story to the police instead of the network's crime reporter. The second potential customer, according to wiretapped information, was Rob Ford himself. In a recorded conversation, Siad asked another man if he remembered Ford's insulting offer. "Ya," said the man. "He said, 'I'll give $5,000 and a car.' What the fuck is that?"

There was no established market value for a video of a mayor smoking crack. When Siad had first approached Farah, he talked about a million dollars. Farah thought $100,000 was more realistic. For five weeks, Farah negotiated with the *Star*. But when the newspaper repeatedly refused his price, Farah told me, he contacted Gawker editor John Cook.

Cook flew up from Chicago and viewed the video with Farah and Siad, in Farah's car, parked in back of 320 Dixon. As they watched Ford on video, police watched them. Gawker didn't have $100,000 for the video either, but, according to Farah, Cook had a plan. He would run with the story of an alleged Rob Ford crack video *for sale*. The story would create a huge buzz, which would create a value, which would produce a buyer.

Cook's version of events, posted online, is that Gawker needed to go with the story because a CNN reporter called the mayor's staff asking about the video. Gawker had approached the network, confidentially, to see if it wanted to contribute to the purchase price. Now that the mayor knew the video might be exposed, Cook wrote, the story needed to get out before the mayor tried to get rid of it.

The explanations are not mutually exclusive; both may be correct. (Cook didn't respond to a request to be interviewed.) In any case, nobody fully anticipated that the Gawker and *Star* stories would set off a firestorm that would make the video no longer available for any price.

As news of Toronto's crack-smoking mayor sped around the planet, those who had the video were focused on survival. Sharing information about the video outside the Dixon Bloods' inner circle "is a violation of their code of conduct," explained someone close to the scene. "Talking about it can get you killed." Once the heat was on, he told me, "no amount of money could release that video."

Mohamed Siad was in triple trouble. He had simultaneously brought dishonour on the Somali-Canadian community and unwanted police attention to both the Dixon Bloods and Rob Ford. Just past midnight after the story broke, Siad phoned his sister and asked her to go to his pencil case, take out a phone and hold on to it for him. Then he fled town.

Upon his return, Siad was "kidnapped" by two men and held for an hour, according to police documents. "Siad was crying, saying he'd destroyed the video and his family is in trouble." One of the men told him, "If I see you in Dixon again, I will kill you." A third man told the first two they should have forced Siad into a car. "You guys are stupid. You really should have hurt him." A few weeks later, in prison following the Project Traveller raids, Siad was stabbed in the back, chest and cheek. The raids would have happened even without the crack video, but try explaining that to the guys in jail. Or to the many ardent Ford supporters among the prison population, who didn't like snitches to begin with.

Not wanting to put his friends and family in danger, Farah stayed away from Dixon for a few weeks. Even then, he didn't feel safe on Victoria Day weekend, when the pop pop pop of firecrackers was punctuated by the occasional BOOM. "You didn't know if it was fireworks or somebody shooting at you," he said. "I decided to get information on whether the threat was real or not real. Were people going to come and hurt me? And where were they going to come from?"

Fearing the Fords might send someone after him, Farah told me he approached an intermediary who knew the family, "trying to make sure they've got information that is *accurate*, letting them know that this is not a personal thing. It's not trying to bring your family down. It's not malicious." He concluded that Doug wouldn't harm him because "he was more of a politician or a businessman." Rob, he thought, might put the word out that "those guys sold me out, they snitched on me."

Concluding that his greatest threat came from unanswered rumours, Farah called upon "mediators" within the Dixon community to make it safe for him to return to explain himself. Angriest of all were the many friends of Anthony Smith, who had been photographed, along with two other alleged gang members, mugging for the camera next to a grinning Rob Ford, outside the Basso home. Smith's friends initially posted the photo online and everybody had a good laugh. But after Smith's murder, in an unrelated incident outside a nightclub the next month, the photo was taken down out of respect. Subsequently, Farah gave the photo to both Gawker and the *Toronto Star* to increase their interest in buying the crack video.

This had angered Smith's friends. Never mind what the police said, people who knew Smith thought of him as a good kid, not a gangster, and he wasn't there to defend himself. His mother's grief was magnified as her son's face was splashed across front pages everywhere. Farah told me that's what he regretted most about his involvement in the whole video debacle: causing Smith's mother more pain.

—

In the frantic days after the story broke, the video was all anybody in that community talked about. Who had taken it? Who was selling it? Where was it?

"Everybody wanted it," said Mohamed Farah. "Everybody."

The *Star* was still interested. Other media outlets were circling. And Gawker was talking about crowdfunding. Even as he went into hiding, the entrepreneurial Farah raised the price to $200,000 to reflect the increased demand. That made the video even more dangerous to own, an object valuable enough to harm somebody over.

Everyone involved in the chase enjoyed some natural advantage. The police had the resources: an arsenal of informants, wiretaps, ground surveillance teams, an airplane, the ability to bust the door down with a search warrant, and technologists who could bring a deleted computer file back to life. Gang members lacked organization, or even a common purpose, but they were on the scene and able to employ persuasive techniques if they got their hands on anyone who had the video. Anonymous buyers who reportedly showed up at Dixon with large amounts of cash might have found an instant seller if anyone had been brave or stupid enough to step forward.

Few knew where to go looking, and those who did were looking for somewhere to hide.

Rob Ford's trusted friend Sandro Lisi was threatening to have the whole place busted, apparently not realizing the absurdity of this threat on behalf of a crack-smoking mayor. Not to be outdone for sheer stupidity, Dave Price, the mayor's "Director of Operations and Logistics," caused such a commotion hunting for the video that the cops called him in to explain what the hell he was up to.

The video story was less than twenty-four hours old when Price phoned Mark Towhey, Ford's straitlaced and uncompromising chief of staff. "Hypothetically speaking . . ." Price cautiously began. An impatient Towhey ordered him to get to the point.

What would the mayor's office do, Price wondered out loud, *if it knew, for example, that the guys with the alleged crack video could be found at 320 Dixon Road, Unit 1703? Just asking.*

Price was a recent addition to the mayor's office, hired at Doug Ford's insistence, bypassing any selection process to become a highly paid staff member. Doug had answered questions about Price's qualifications this way: "You can't teach loyalty." The questions got louder after the *Globe and Mail* reported that Price had been Doug's hash-dealing partner in the 1980s.

In answer to Price's hypothetical question, Towhey knew exactly what to do with this type of information. He called the cops. Investigators immediately wanted to speak with Price.

"Ahh fuck, Dave," Doug Ford reacted when Price called him in Chicago to explain what had happened. Price didn't bother to paraphrase Doug's comment when detectives asked him about the conversation, no doubt equally unenthused about this unwelcome turn of events. How would he explain to police why he was chasing a video that wasn't supposed to exist? How did he know about the non-existent video's possible whereabouts, right down to the building address and unit number? No, no, of course he hadn't spoken with the mayor about any of this, Price told investigators. Meanwhile, Rob Ford had given the same address to his communications director, George Christopoulos, who texted it to Towhey, who just happened to be at the police station when the text arrived and immediately passed along all of *that* information.

Price told police he was given the Dixon address and unit number by an unknown caller with a blocked number, who also gave him the cell numbers of the two men selling the video. Price's information was alarmingly good. The phone numbers belonged to Mohamed Siad and Mohamed Farah, and the Dixon location he gave Towhey was, within days, the spot where another alleged gang member was shot, following a hallway argument.

On his first trip to the police station, Price didn't tell investigators that he had visited 15 Windsor Road the morning after the *Star* crack story broke. The second time he was pulled in, Price told police he recognized the house in the photo of Ford with the three young men and decided to have a chat with the homeowner. When Price left after the second interview, investigators sent a surveillance team to tail him.

—

Even as the story was breaking, at 9:25 p.m. on May 16, Sandro Lisi was on the phone with Fabio Basso, and then with Liban

Siyad. At 1:17 a.m., he tried Mohamed Siad twice but got no answer. At 1:48 a.m., he spoke with Basso again for ten minutes. Then Basso called back and they spoke for another two minutes. By the next day, Lisi was practising the tact and diplomacy the mayor had praised him for prior to his sentencing for threatening murder.

"You're fucking dead and everyone on your block is dead," Lisi warned a gang member, according to a police summary of wiretaps. "You see the heat on Dixon, bro?" Lisi said to Liban Siyad a day later. "The whole place is going to get heated up all summer. Until that fucking phone [with the video] gets back, the whole place is going to get lit up!"

Lisi also found time for a courtesy call to the Bassos' home. "Where are the guys who made the video, Fab?" Lisi said, according to the *Toronto Star*, quoting a witness who was present. "You know where they are."

"They've gone out of town," Basso reportedly told him. "Gone to Windsor."

The morning after the story came out, Price and Lisi, both wearing sunglasses, showed up on Ford's street to block reporters and cameramen. Then Price spent an unpleasant three minutes with Elena Basso at 15 Windsor. She was high, he said, and not happy to see him. Over the next few days, "two large men" visited the house several times, according to reports published by Gawker. They demanded that Fabio lure the video's owner back to the house. "Look, leave me alone," Basso finally told them, according to Gawker. "This is my mother's house. Rob got himself into this situation. It's his problem, not mine." Other reports said he was less polite, telling them to "fuck off." The home invasion and beating came soon afterwards.

Elena Basso, meanwhile, was all worked up about the impact on her small business.

"He's a big fucking idiot," she said of Mohamed Siad. "He fucked my business up, he fucked everybody up. The whole area is going down." Speaking to Liban Siyad, she complained that "Rob's people and cops are coming every day. He's the fucking mayor of Toronto. We're going to feel the heat everywhere, not just in fucking Dixon."

—

As the search for the video reached a crescendo, it seemed to vanish. As early as May 17, Mohamed Siad had either sold it privately or decided his life was worth more than the $200,000 Gawker was about to raise. Siad told Farah the video was no longer for sale.

Early the next week, Dave Price again approached Mark Towhey about the video, this time assuring Ford's chief of staff that the video's whereabouts was being dealt with as they spoke. Less than reassured, Towhey asked Price how he knew about such matters. "It's a small neighbourhood," Price answered.

Two days after this conversation, a confident-looking Rob Ford with an extremely short haircut finally addressed the public. The wording of his brief statement struck everyone as odd. "I cannot comment on a video that I have never seen, or does not exist."

Ford's communications staff, both of whom left abruptly that week, made it clear through intermediaries that they hadn't prepared this statement. It came from the family. The primary author, it was widely rumoured, was Diane Ford.

—

Five months later, in the mayor's office, red lights flashed like the top of a police car in your rear-view mirror. Skeletons moved in and out of a closet. Fog filling the room made it difficult to see anything clearly. An old Etobicoke friend of Doug Ford's had turned the office into a Halloween horror show. A laughing skull was connected to a motion sensor. "Ha ha," it mocked anyone who entered. *Help* was scrawled in fake blood outside the office door.

That Halloween morning, at police headquarters, Bill Blair was flanked by his senior officers, about to hold a press conference to announce that police had recovered the crack video. After months of coming up with nothing from the computer hard drives and cellphones seized in June's Project Traveller raids, police technology experts had retrieved an erased file from a laptop found in Mohamed Siad's apartment.

"I don't want to see any smiles," Blair told his officers, not wanting them to seem pleased that they'd uncovered what nobody else had been able to find. After overcoming his own surprise that the video still existed, Blair turned his thoughts to how this news would play out.

"I spent a lot of time thinking about it, had a few sleepless nights," he told me. "I was very concerned at how that was going to impact my city. I was aware that there was going to be a lot of people who would be deeply affected by this information, one way or the other."

Proof that the video existed provided the missing evidence prosecutors needed to lay an extortion charge against Sandro Lisi for using threats to try to obtain it. Once the charge against Lisi was made public, so would the existence of this crucial piece of evidence.

During the ensuing press conference, Blair was asked if he was shocked. "I was disappointed," he responded. It had sounded to me like something Blair was intending to say, as soon as the right question came along. He told me that wasn't the case. But even without the comment, Blair expected reprisals from one or both Ford brothers.

"We do this without fear or favour," he told me in his office, repeating a phrase he used at the press conference. "I anticipated that there would be consequences for me personally, but I don't think the police chief can be afraid to do his job. That's the 'without fear' part. You can't be afraid of the consequences."

Even as he was being booked, Lisi couldn't stop threatening, telling police that Blair should expect an attack on his integrity. "He gave us an indication of approximately when that would take place and the form it would take," Blair told me. "And by the following Tuesday, it took that course." Tuesday was the day Doug Ford attacked the chief of police, metaphorically speaking, for the premeditated political assassination of his brother, shortly before Rob Ford finally admitted smoking crack.

Those events didn't seem well coordinated, I observed to Blair.

"That crossed my mind." Blair had watched Rob Ford's admission live on the large TV screen in his office, while meeting with his staff to consider a response to Doug's comments.

Doug Ford and Bill Blair would tussle a few more times, most notably in August 2014, after Doug accused Blair of leaking news that Rob Ford would receive a subpoena to testify at Lisi's preliminary hearing. "When you have the leadership of the police department releasing a subpoena to the media, you wonder why they need a change at the top? It's a little payback," Doug said, implying that the police chief was leaking documents because the Police Services Board had not extended his contract a month earlier.

Blair's communications staff asked him how he'd like to respond.

Four words only, Blair instructed. "Doug Ford is lying."

"Do you really want to say that?" a spokesperson asked.

"Let's see if he says he's not," Blair responded. He later told me, "I knew he couldn't."

Blair's terse comment made a good headline, and the scuffle continued until Blair sent Ford a Notice of Defamation, the first stage of a lawsuit. "Insults can be ignored," Blair told me. "But lies should never go unchallenged." Doug blustered a bit longer, then tried to fix it all with a phone call.

"Can I apologize?" he asked Blair.

"No," the chief responded. "Put it in writing."

Doug Ford wrote an apology with wording pre-approved by Blair, along with a $1,000 donation to a charity chosen by Blair.

"Lies that go to the heart of your integrity cannot be tolerated," Blair told a press conference convened to announce that he had accepted the apology. "The law does not protect lies or the people who tell them. And they must be held accountable."

—

"To close the chapter out," Mohamed Farah told me early in 2015, "I would like to have a discussion with the Fords."

To say what?

"I will do *anything* to make the community better, and I'll be a willing partner if you've got any ideas." Almost two years after trying to sell the crack video, Farah estimated that his reputation was now 80 percent restored within the Dixon community. He had not lost the optimistic naivety that got him in trouble.

"I want him to really acknowledge the issues—what happened and his role in it—and that hasn't happened yet. You've got to address issues, you've got to apologize and come up with solutions."

Farah had tried to contact Rob Ford through a *Toronto Sun* columnist. "I gave him my number," he said, "but he hasn't called."

17. EXAMINING THE MOULD

"Folks, I have nothing left to hide."
Mayor Rob Ford after confessing to one-time crack use

If Rob Ford welcomed your visit—let's say you'd dropped by to talk sports—he'd move to one of two office couches, inviting you to sit on the other. The sofas faced one another as you entered the room, a coffee table in between to create a cozy setting. For visitors with less congenial topics, Ford remained behind his large wooden desk, from where he could stare straight ahead into the empty centre of the room. Ignoring the subject, avoiding eye contact.

The stream of councillors who trooped in during the early part of November 2013 found him barricaded behind the desk, his back to the wall. Some came driven by their own self-importance, believing *theirs* was the voice that could get through to him. But nobody pretended to understand what broken thoughts ran scrimmages through his brain, what half-formed images appeared behind his closed eyes.

During this time, several of the visiting councillors were coaxed in by Earl Provost, the mayor's chief of staff since May—the fourth of five men to hold that position in three years. Those days found Provost anxious, headachy, overwhelmed. He wanted to jump ship, but not without another one to board. Provost needed someone to persuade his boss to take himself away somewhere, anywhere.

The mayor assumed Provost had summoned his once-loyal allies in order to shore up their support. "You've got to stay with me, buddy," he'd say to one. "You've got to vote with me," he'd tell another. Who wouldn't be moved by the massive blank-faced human tragedy before them? "Take some time off," they told him one after another. "Look after your health."

"Yup, okay, thank you," Ford replied. "You know what? I'm not going to drink as much. I don't have a problem."

"It's important you get some help," tried Councillor Frances Nunziata. "Take some time. See a doctor."

"There's nothing wrong with me," Ford answered her.

"Yes, there is something wrong with you," Nunziata insisted. "You're a sick man."

Ford exploded.

"Swearing and threatening. Very threatening," Nunziata told me later. "He was going to get me in the election. I said, 'What are you threatening me for? I'm your friend. You need help. I'm here to help you.' Then he just threw me out of the office. He got me so upset that I was in tears."

Peter Milczyn arrived to speak his mind just as Nunziata was being dismissed. "Go away. Make this stop. Get help or don't get help, but just go away," Milczyn said he told Ford. "If you take a break, nobody's going to hold it against you. If anything, it'd be the opposite."

Rob Ford nodded, though not in agreement. Milczyn couldn't tell whether he'd heard any of it. "You know, whatever's going on with you, think about your kids, because my heart breaks when I think about your kids," he said to the mayor. "And whether it's fair or not, your kids have to listen to this at school. Your kids have to see this on TV. And one day they're going to go online and read all this stuff. Do it for your kids."

Milczyn was recalling the scene for me later.

"Then he got quiet," he said. "He was just kind of staring. I was getting frustrated, and at a certain point I said, 'Is any of this getting through that fucking cement skull of yours?'

"He jumped to his feet and said, 'Get out of my office. I'm not going to sit here and be insulted. Get out of my office!'

"I said, 'It's your office, I'll get out. But think about your kids.' And I left."

———

Two images played in my mind during those days, like freeze-frames from a nightmare. One was Rob Ford way up in the sky, on a high wire, hopelessly unable to balance, teetering and about to fall. The other was Ford holed up in his office with a gun. Both were surreal, of course, but an indication of just how otherworldly city hall felt.

The revelation that police had the crack video sent Ford stumbling and tumbling, more out of control than ever before. So much happened that month, it's hard to decide which stories to tell, in what order.

November 5 was one of those days when one Ford happening was superseded by another, which was then overtaken by something else again, until an even bigger incident washed it all away. Let's start there.

While a chorus of influential voices called on his brother to step aside, Doug Ford began his counterattack on the police chief by demanding that *he* resign. "He believes he's the judge, the jury and the executioner," Doug Ford said in a radio interview. "He wanted to go out and put a big political bullet between the mayor's eyes." Had he known what was coming later that day, Doug might have held his tongue.

Leaving the radio station for city hall, Doug repeated the

attacks from a podium in front of the mayor's office. He was still in full stride when the elevator door opened and I found myself on the edge of his scrum. I stopped to watch, so transfixed I momentarily forgot about my mission. I was carrying a plan, not yet shared with other councillors or the media, to remove most of the mayor's powers.

When Doug left to speak with some journalism students, I went to the clerk's office to submit my Notice of Motion. Its title looked innocuous: "Motion to Improve the Decision Making Environment at City Hall." It was my first in a series of motions to remove all of the mayor's special powers, eliminating his ability to take the city government down with him. Immediately after I released it, you'd have thought—for about fourteen minutes—that my last name was Ford. CNN and the *New York Times* wanted to talk. Radio stations from across the country were calling.

My motion was procedurally complicated and took too many words to explain. An hour or so later, Councillor Denzil Minnan-Wong presented another motion telling the mayor to step aside. That wasn't going to happen, of course, and council couldn't make him. But the simple *demand* that he leave appealed to those who wanted to express their outrage. *The Today Show* wasn't so interested in having me on anymore.

—

As Doug Ford declared war on the police chief, most councillors were ready to place their hands against the mayor's back in order to push him out the door. Rob Ford, meanwhile, was trying to keep his mind on other things. This morning, it was mould.

"I remember that day," former councillor Peter Leon told me. "We were up here on the East Mall. On Capri Road. We went to look at a mould problem in one of the Toronto Community Housing apartment buildings." When a tenant had called Ford for help, the mayor put the man's fungi at the top of that day's "to do" list.

"So he went to look at it," said Leon. "I have to give him some credit."

Ford arrived in the lobby shortly after 10 a.m., accompanied by two of his staff, a Community Housing area manager and the building superintendent. Leon, who joined in as the ward councillor, described the scene: "We had maybe fifty people waiting in the lobby. They all wanted their picture with him. He was their hero."

From years of making visits just like this one, Toronto's mayor was an expert on certain subjects: bedbugs, broken windows, hoarders and mould. "He knew *how* to look at it. He knew *what* to look at," said Leon. "And there was a conversation back and forth. 'You've got to open the doors. You've got to let some fresh air in. You can't close the curtains where they're long and covering over the heating vents.' We noticed that the bathroom was blocked up. He said, 'You can't do that.'"

Another resident pleaded with the mayor to examine his mould too. So he did. "He was dedicated," Leon told me. "He knew how to deal with it, and he could prioritize: 'I'm only here for this. I can't deal with that.'"

Shortly before noon, the mayor left for his office, clutching a clipboard of scribbled notes about the mould. As he got closer to city hall, without a distraction to ease the pressure, Ford got on the phone to his chief of staff.

"I can't take it anymore, buddy. I've got to get it off my chest," he told Earl Provost, according to what Provost told others in the office. Putting down the phone, Provost began pacing anxiously. Then he placed an urgent call to Tom Beyer. "Grab Rob when he comes in. Meet him downstairs and bring him in. *Make sure* he comes in the back entrance."

By the time Beyer ran downstairs, Ford had parked in the underground garage and was already heading up in the elevator to the second floor. Beyer ran back up to find the mayor standing just outside his office doors, inviting reporters to ask him a question. Provost gave Beyer new instructions:

"Get him the fuck out of there. Get him inside."

Media clips show Beyer helplessly trying to get Ford's attention amid the pandemonium that had already erupted. "Once you're in a media scrum, it's hard. There's no pole to yank somebody in," explained Beyer. "I went out there, but by that time the damage was already done. That whole thing happened so quickly."

—

It was lunchtime. The reporters waiting in a crush outside the elevator were hungry, needing a coffee, wondering why they still waited for a guy who seldom spoke to them anyway. Several had received tips that investigators wanted to speak with the mayor about the crack video and had offered to show it to him. That was the story they were ready to file, even if he didn't comment.

But today, Ford was strangely talkative. He knew what he wanted to say, even if he didn't know how to say it. Maybe Ford thought he could turn the clock back on a half year of lies by getting reporters to re-ask the question he'd been lying about all that time. Then he could claim he would have given an honest answer in the first place if they'd only asked the question properly!

"You asked me a question back in May, and you can repeat that question," the mayor instructed.

Not understanding, they continued to ask about police and the video.

"You asked me questions back in May, and you may repeat those questions," Ford tried again.

"The questions we asked you back in May?" one reporter repeated out loud. "Can you explain . . ."

"You asked me a couple of questions," said Ford. "And what were those questions?"

"Do you smoke crack cocaine?" called out Global TV's Jason Proskow.

"Exactly," Ford responded. "Yes, I *have* smoked crack cocaine. But no, *do* I?" Maybe he thought it would be easier to provide both questions and answers. "Am I an addict? No. Have I tried it? Probably in one of my drunken stupors, probably approximately about a year ago."

As if conditioned to expect the punishment to begin even as the confession is under way, Ford was defensive before anyone else said a word.

"I answered your question. You ask the question properly, I'll answer it. Yes, I've made mistakes. All I can do is apologize and move on. . . . So I wasn't lying. You didn't ask the correct questions. No, I'm not an addict, and no, I do not do drugs. I made mistakes in the past and all I can do is apologize. But it is what it is."

Ford went on about wanting to see the crack video, saying he couldn't remember anything about it. He might have rambled on a while longer, saying who knows what else, but a reporter ended the moment with a new question: "Are you on drugs now?" Ford turned and walked into his office.

"That's it. It's out there," Ford shouted to no one in particular, walking past stunned staffers who had watched the episode on the screens in their offices. The mayor went to his inner office to speak with Provost, who was reeling. This wasn't supposed to have happened.

"I think Earl thought he could keep him on the straight and narrow, and he could tone down the pressure and it would all go away," recalled Sheila Paxton. "It would be a political triumph for him. So when the mayor just blurted it out, I don't think Earl knew what to do."

"I didn't know he was going to say it. I didn't know he was going to say it," Provost said when he came out of the meeting with Ford. He didn't want anyone to think he'd played any part in this fumble.

Doug Ford, caught totally off guard, arrived to meet with his brother and Provost. The timing of the admission, right after Doug had launched an offensive in defence of Rob, added to his distress. They agreed that Rob would hold a press conference later that day, this time with a script exonerating his brother.

"I had to go look after Doug so he wouldn't go and talk to the media," Paxton remembered. Doug had gone to be by himself in a small office. "And he was just sitting there stunned, not moving, not knowing what to do. Just stunned." Paxton had never seen him like that: rambling, flustered, shaken. "I really honestly believe that Doug did not know until that moment. He was totally in shock." Doug told Sheila his brother needed to take a month off. The family had reportedly spoken about it the weekend before. But when Rob refused, his mother had backed him up, as she would on television later that week.

At the press conference he held four hours after his initial admission, the mayor was visibly emotional and embarrassed. His brother stood behind him, but farther back and more to the side than usual. Doug was stone silent, grim, arms hanging limply by his side.

"I know what I did was wrong, and admitting it was the most difficult, embarrassing thing I've ever had to do," the mayor said. "Folks, I have nothing left to hide. I would do anything—absolutely anything—to change the past. But the past is the past and we must move forward. These mistakes will *never, ever, ever* happen again.

"I kept this from my family—especially my brother, Doug—my staff, my council colleagues, because I was embarrassed and ashamed. . . . I love my job. I love this city. I love saving taxpayers money. And I love being your mayor. For the sake of the taxpayers of this great city—for the sake of the taxpayers—we must get back to work immediately.

"Again, I *sincerely, sincerely, sincerely* apologize. God bless the people of Toronto."

—

In the boardroom, the mayor's staff were assembled for an obligatory display of solidarity. They waited more than thirty minutes, listening to Rob and Doug argue in the next room. The words were hard to make out, but they could imagine what Doug was feeling. Some of them wanted to yell at Rob too. He had lied to them and, even worse, got *them* to lie for him. They worried that their careers would be compromised. All had at one point been excited to work for a mayor with a new approach, dreaming they could be part of something new, big, important and good. Nothing was left of that now. Paxton tried to ease the tension by cracking a few jokes. Nobody felt much like laughing.

When Rob Ford finally arrived, "he comes in and sits down, and he looks like shit," recalled a former staffer who asked not to be identified. "He says, 'I'm not perfect—and none of you are perfect either.' He does the whole non-apology apology. 'We need to keep doing what we're doing. We don't stop. And I'm going to go after these cocksuckers. I'm going to go after these fucking cocksuckers.'"

"There were some tears," remembered Sheila Paxton. "He was very emotional having to admit a failure to his staff. He apologized, but he was very adamant: he was *not* going to go to rehab, he was *not* going to take time off, and it was business as usual."

Sitting up near the front, Paxton was the first to speak. "The emotion in the room was very high and I wanted to diffuse it by saying, 'We're with you, mayor,' to placate him. It's kind of embarrassing when you're in the room, and you're his senior staff, and he's crying and admitting this stuff. It's an embarrassment to *you*, and you just want it to be over."

Earl Provost chimed in, professing loyalty on behalf of them all.

"Earl was 'Yes, yes, we're going to do our job, Mr. Mayor. It was very brave of you to have confessed to all of this.' I remember Earl saying how brave it was," Paxton recalled.

"'It takes a big man to admit when he's wrong,'" the other staff member remembered Provost saying. "'And I speak for everybody in the room when I say I'm going to stay on and fight it out and keep doing what we're doing.' And then the entire staff started clapping. It was so alarming to me that one minute you have people who are hurt and angry and as betrayed as I am, and an hour later they're applauding this guy."

Paxton told me she started the applause, preferring it to the awkward, humiliating silence. "You had to save face for him. He's the mayor. And you had to make the staff feel there was something they could do. So that's why there was applause. That's what he was looking for when he came in. He was looking for that confirmation of loyalty. The applause gave it to him."

—

"We were inundated," said Tom Beyer, stuck in the mayor's fishbowl-like outer office. "It was terrible. And part of the challenge was that for *all* the previous six months we had vehemently toed the party line: 'This is a smear campaign, the *Star* has it out for him.' We all had our talking points. 'This is not true. It's people who want the mayor out who are casting these lies about him.'

"And then, in a matter of seconds, he goes and admits it without even being prompted. He *completely* tipped everything over. So I had a lot of people calling and saying, '*You told me* that he had nothing to do with this, so *you're* a fucking liar.' We got lots of calls like that. They cast aspersions on us *personally*. That totally sent our world topsy-turvy."

Life in the fishbowl became untenable. "After that, I was finished. Mentally and physically, I just couldn't do it anymore."
Within a week, Beyer went on medical leave, never to return.
When I spoke with him a year and a half later, he was still job-
hunting. "I've been to lots of interviews. But I think what happens is they go on Google and they see these innuendoes, and the
fact that I was in his office for as long as I was."

As for Ford's office, post-confession, "it was complete and
utter chaos," Beyer said. "Like it always was. Pandemonium.
Disturbed."

18. FEEDING THE MONSTER

"They're like bullies. If you don't feed them, they will track you down. You've got to feed the monster."
Doug Ford on the media

The sound assaults him the moment the elevator doors open. Rob Ford steps quickly into the gauntlet. In a few paces—twenty feet exactly—he'll reach the sanctuary of his office. Reporters jam in tight, shouting from all directions, their questions lost in the commotion. A large, muscular man, the mayor's driver, clears his path. The noise chases Ford until the office doors close behind him.

As the mayor brushes past a crowd of unanswered questions, a journalist might get knocked out of the way. One time Ford himself got a camera in the face. That made a lot of people laugh.

Once inside the office, Ford stays there as long as he can, making the crowd wait. They want to go home—a place he's in no hurry to get to—and they can't leave before he does. It's a game he likes playing with the enemy, knowing they have no choice but to play along. In November 2013, he'd stopped twice in that space and said things you'd never imagine coming from the mouth of a mayor, not even this one. Since then, journalists follow him everywhere he goes. Nobody, it seems—not even Rob Ford—knows what he might do next.

One pursuit was so chaotic that *it* became the story. Ford decided to take a London *Times* food critic outside for a hot dog. A pack of media followed, out through city hall's impressive wooden doors, back and forth across the crowded public square, and in through the building again. Reporters shouted questions. The mayor ignored them.

Back inside, with some still following and others trying to head him off, Ford paused below a curved staircase, getting into a football formation. "Let's go! Let's go!" he shouted, leading a dash up the stairs, security guard blockers out front and behind. A photographer for the *Globe and Mail* was knocked down by the charging mass. Everyone else scrambled for safety. Watching the television clips that night, you'd have thought Ford was being pursued by a pack of wild reporters, hounding him, persecuting him, putting innocent bystanders at risk.

Normally, a politician would head off such scenes by stopping to answer questions. Since Rob Ford took office, though, nothing had been normal.

—

This was a mayor like none before him—perhaps anywhere, at any time, in any major city. Even without the crack smoking and drunkenness, the mayor was 350 pounds of gaffe-prone antagonism, honing in on trouble like a heat-seeking missile. And that was only half the spectacle. At city hall, brother Doug was both competitor and colour commentator, an extraordinary one-man show that he wrote, produced and performed.

Doug instinctively understood schoolyards, where power was seized by those who knew how to assert it. City hall was like that too. With officially no more authority than any of his forty-three councillor colleagues, Doug granted himself an unspecified special status, a role without precedent that was accepted without question. Especially by the media, who recognized immediately that either Ford brother could rescue an otherwise slow news day. Doug sometimes stood beside Rob, but mostly he was out front, confidently commanding attention, welcoming the outstretched microphones to come closer, shining in the cameras' bright lights.

Doug gave extraordinary performances day in and day out. He could deliver a message with devastating simplicity and a full range of emotions. As the role demanded, he could be hot, cold, angry, tearful, charming, mean, funny, vengeful, direct or manipulative. He could move from one of these to another or combine them for multiple impact. Boom!

"Doug can say things with this crazy evangelical enthusiasm that is pretty much irresistible, even when it's complete crap—especially when it's complete crap," said journalist Dave Nickle. "Lying is simple. The truth is always nuanced." Nuance was not part of the Ford vocabulary.

Only when he did something wrong did the mayor get as much attention as his brother. Was that part of the reason he kept doing crazy stuff? When the media thought they had caught the mayor being bad, they would follow him everywhere, trying to provoke a confession. Even a denial or flawed defence made news. If he refused to say anything, that too could be a story. A false claim was even better.

Unfriendly questions made both Rob and Doug angry, but for different reasons. I think Doug's anger is rooted in anger, and Rob's in hurt. When challenged, both would counterattack, Doug with a heightened sense of superiority, Rob feigning the same as if to protect a wound.

After Rob was photographed partying at a glitzy nightclub, the CBC's Lorenda Reddekopp asked him if he'd been drinking that weekend.

"'Cause I got some attention at the club," an angry mayor responded, "is that what you're jealous about?"

—

Between 2010 and 2014, the news from city hall was all Ford all the time. Reality TV, featuring a powerful, polarizing family whose actions, reactions and interactions were constantly fascinating. *House of Cards* meets the UFC.

David Rider recalls the day, right after the crack story broke, when Ford learned his communications staff had quit. "The mayor's on the move!" a reporter alerted him. Most of the press gallery ran upstairs to watch. Security guards in tow, the mayor barrelled over to where his spokesmen had been stationed, as if investigating their disappearance. TV cameras and journalists set up outside the large glass walls.

"We were watching the mayor trying to figure out why his two trusted deputies have deserted him and left empty desks with a note. He's storming around, looking, and trying to figure out what's going on. It was like watching a polar bear at the zoo. It's just a bizarre, fascinating thing. The Fords are watchable, and everywhere they go, every eye is on them."

Dozens of journalists watched the brothers intensely for many hundreds of days, but their focus was always on what the Fords said and how they behaved, not on what motivated them. Why did they want to be in charge of a city they neither liked nor understood? Why were they so obsessed with getting a firm grip on power they didn't know how to use?

Everyone was watching. But what did they see?

Natalie Alcoba answered my question one day at city hall. "Everybody in this building, we're all playing roles. We're all playing parts here—the media, the politicians, the bureaucrats. It's all theatre." Like others who covered city hall for four Ford years, the *National Post* reporter acknowledged the lack of character development in the stories coming from the press gallery.

"I've always wanted a better understanding of why he wanted this job," she said of Rob Ford. "But I don't think I could have ever asked him that question in a way that would get to something real. How will I ever get that? I'm always a reporter."

So all you see is Rob Ford playing his part from the vantage point of . . .

"Me playing mine. Exactly," she finished my sentence.

David Rider arrived at an event ahead of schedule, the same time as the mayor. They found themselves standing together, waiting for the show to begin. "He kind of nodded and said, 'Hey Dave.' I said, 'Hey Mayor.' He said, 'How's it goin'?' I said, 'It's going okay. How are you?' He said, 'It's going okay.'"

Then the event started and they assumed combat positions. "For ten or fifteen seconds, I stepped out of the role and he stepped out of the role and we just said 'Hey' as people. And then I went back to being a reporter and he went back to being the mayor who hates the *Toronto Star* and won't answer any questions. And on we go."

—

As the doors opened to let me onto the elevator going up to the council chamber, Doug Ford was already inside. "Councillor Ford! Councillor Ford!" voices called out to him. "Can we talk to you?"

"I've already spoken to you," he said dispassionately.

"But you haven't spoken to *us*," one reporter pleaded sweetly, pressing up close as the door shut.

Doug was silent until the elevator was in motion. Then he thrust an arm in the air, a response to the collective media. "Fuck you!"

Later, I asked Doug about this love-hate relationship.

"More hate than love," he replied. "Because they're biased. Everyone sees it. There's more bias than I've ever seen before— ever. They're supposed to be objective. They've just thrown that out the window. It's all-out war. When the common folk come out and tell you, 'CP24's as biased as they come.' CBC—they try to attack you every which way possible. Newstalk 1010— they just attack us from *morning* all the way through the whole show to nighttime. Non-stop trash.

"They're like bullies," Doug said of the media. "*Every day* I'm driving down they'll *meet me* out at the car. I have that Elizabeth Street parking. They'll run up there and meet me, or they'll wait inside the doors. Then I get upstairs, they come after me. If I don't feed them, they will track you down. You've *got* to feed the monster. You've *got to*! If you don't, you're toast."

But don't you often go in search of the monster, offering tender morsels?

"Oh yeah, I've got to," he replied. "The bully mentality. Totally out of control. They're like ravenous piranhas."

I observed that the Fords were getting so much coverage that there was little room left for other mayoral candidates.

"Yeah, well, that's all right," he said. "Probably not a bad thing."

—

Symbiotic is a term one might use if attempting to ascribe some normalcy to the relationship between the Fords and the media. David Hains, who left a banking career to report on Toronto politics online, offered something better. "It's like that snake that eats itself," he said. "So there are a lot of people fed up with that relationship."

Stationed at his Rob Ford Must Go post, across from the mayor's office, Chris Caple had seen that snake up close. "In all the time we've been here, I've never seen any media turn down

Doug Ford. If he ever wants to talk, they're *right there*. And they'll just turn the recorders on, turn the cameras on, and they start tweeting. And whatever he says just goes *right out* to this massive audience."

Doug saw the relationship as a series of battles, with him usually coming out on top.

"There was a notice sent around to all the media, 'Don't cover Ford Nation. Don't cover Ford Nation,'" Doug told me, feeling no need to identify the supernatural media entity that could possibly produce such a missive. "So they were blacking us out. But we wedged them so they had no choice but to cover Ford Nation." Doug laughed. "If I say something, they have no choice." He laughed again.

"So if all I do every day is sit down and talk about the great job and the great finances and everything—it even gets boring, right? It's not television. So they want to talk about Hollywood. I call them out and all of a sudden, bang! The Ford Nation e-mails are coming in like crazy."

Does Doug think this stuff through or simply act on impulse?

"It's hard to know how much they know what they're doing," said *Now* magazines's Jonathan Goldsbie. "How much of it is them—especially Doug—having the tendency to say things that are so outrageous that they're inherently newsworthy? Is he doing that deliberately, or is that just what he thinks and the way he talks? I don't know. He often opens his mouth and whatever he says is so wild or spectacularly wrong—easily proved to be wrong—that it's newsworthy. I feel that a politician caught in a lie should always be newsworthy."

—

In Fordlandia, lies and misperceptions form a single, simple truth. Everyone else has it wrong or is making it up.

"If somebody believes differently," said David Rider, "they immediately look for a self-serving motive. You can't come down and protest the Ford cuts without them saying, 'Well, you're a union member.' There is a record of them believing that people can't be against them on principle, because they believe that they are absolutely right. They're very keen to divide the world into us and them, and if you're not with us, you're against us."

Journalist Dave Nickle remembered a call from Doug Ford he received early in the 2010 campaign.

"Oh, you're that Dave Nickle fella who hates my brother," Doug began, referring to some unfavourable columns. Nickle offered to meet about it. Ford agreed but arrived late, then glad-handed for half an hour while the reporter waited. "He finally sat down to tell me how it was going to be. It was a genial conversation but intended to intimidate me, it's fair to say. There was a real effort made to peg me as an enemy on some partisan level. I must be a New Democrat, or I must be a Liberal. I must be something other than the good Conservatives that the Fords were. Otherwise, why would I be so critical of his brother?"

City TV's Cynthia Mulligan was about to go live on air outside the mayor's office when Doug Ford walked by. "Are you finished with your jihadist attacks?" he asked. Later, he apologized to Mulligan. "Next time," he said, "I'll use a different term."

"He intimidated people. That was his modus operandi," the *Globe and Mail*'s Liz Church said of Doug Ford. "He would single you out. If you had written something that he didn't like and you were in a scrum, he'd name you. He would try to *shame* you in front of other people. He called me the most biased person in the city of Toronto once, on live TV."

"Doug Ford will say things to me like, 'We like you. We know you're doing your best,'" David Rider told me. "'But we know you get orders from your bosses every day to attack Rob however you can. We understand that.' I'd say, 'You seem to think there's a Rob Ford meeting every day at the *Star* where senior editors sharpen their knives and figure out what part of his body they're going to stab that day. And then I get a big memo saying, "This is exactly how we're going to do it." Nothing like that ever happens.'"

But the Fords believe it does. That's what they would do if they ran a newspaper, the *Daily Ford*.

—

The relationship between the *Toronto Star* and Rob Ford reached its high-water mark in 2000, when the newspaper endorsed his election to Toronto council. Relations quickly deteriorated afterwards, as the paper chronicled his many misdeeds. In July 2010, the *Star* ran a story stating that Rob Ford had been fired as football coach at a North York high school following a fracas with a player.

"Witnesses interviewed by the *Star* disagree on whether there was a physical confrontation between Ford and the student player," the article read, providing both versions of events. If you read the story carefully, said David Rider, the *Star* never said Ford hit the player. True. But if you read it the way an average reader would, you're left with the impression that he did.

There may be nothing more offensive to Rob Ford than to call him a bad football coach. Ford cut off communication with Canada's largest newspaper. His campaign spun the incident into a story about a biased media targeting Ford with false allegations. "I'm first in the mayor's race," said Ford, channelling Nick Kouvalis. "They're going to do anything to stop me from becoming mayor of the city, because they know when I become mayor, the party's over. The gravy train is going to come to an end and the wasteful spending will stop immediately."

"That football story—the one the *Star* got wrong—certainly helped us," said Kouvalis. "The kid that Rob allegedly hit came out and said there was an altercation but it wasn't physical. Once they got that story wrong, and it was proven, then it was, 'They're telling lies about everything.'"

Ford supporters were told to expect more attacks from an elitist media, especially the *Star*. "We said, 'All the downtown elitists are on the gravy train,' and the media were lumped in with them," Kouvalis recounted. "Every time they told people not to vote for him, they helped us." The Ford campaign portrayed it as part of their vendetta against him. This tactic helped recruit supporters and raise money. The truth-talking little guy needed their help to fight back against the big lying newspaper.

"And that's part of what kept going during the crack scandal," continued Rider. "People said, 'Oh, this is just another attempt by the *Toronto Star*.' He'll say it's our crusade against him, but I would say it's the other way around. His treatment of the *Star* worked for him for quite a while—for the campaign certainly, and through the early part of his term, when he still seemed politically quite muscular and a lot of councillors were afraid to cross him."

Rider said it was well into 2014 before the anti-*Star* spin stopped working. "During a scrum, Doug Ford started to say, 'Well, you know the *Toronto Star*.' And there was a collective groan from the reporters there and it was kind of like, 'Forget that, Doug, address the question.' And the old magic wasn't working anymore. But for a long time it did."

Rider recalled a brief moment of potential thaw in Rob Ford's freeze-out of the paper. "We had run a photo of the mayor involving a football kickoff. The first thing most people who saw it noticed is that the mayor has a very large gut. It seemed to be an unflattering, almost comical photo." That day, at a council meeting, Rider expected an unpleasant confrontation when he saw Rob Ford coming towards him holding a copy of the newspaper. "This is great," Ford told him instead. "If you keep running more football photos, maybe we can warm up to the *Star*."

Observed Rider, "It was just another example of what he

thought, and what the rest of us thought, being completely different."

———

During most big interviews with Rob, brother Doug was there too.

"There's a little sense of security there," Doug told me. "I think that's with anyone. You feel like you've got a little bit of backup. We're going to get Jimmy Kimmel on next week on Ford Nation. I'm going to be with Rob, just in case he gets out of hand. I'm going to fix him up good."

In March 2014, Rob Ford had appeared on *Jimmy Kimmel Live!* "He personally called me on my cell and invited me down," Ford told a reporter. "So, when people do that, I'm all about customer service. And it's not costing the taxpayers a dime. I said, 'You know, it's a great opportunity to come down and promote the city.'"

Ford was in Hollywood, land of the stars, basking in attention.

"You really have become a celebrity," a reporter commented.

"I don't look at it that way," Ford answered. "I'm just an average, hard-working guy. I'm a family man. And I do my job well. I respect taxpayers' money, create jobs and hold people accountable."

In Los Angeles, everyone wanted a picture with him. While the euphoria lasted, it was easy for Rob to forget he was there to be famously skewered by a man practised in the art of mocking him for laughs.

"He *loves* the idea of celebrity," observed former friend and staffer Tom Beyer. "He's a massive celebrity on purpose. He *adores* that stuff. Bad news. Good news. It doesn't matter."

"He loves seeing his mug on TV," said Nick Kouvalis. "I have watched a video with him, when he laughs after he's shown doing something stupid. But he laughs to make me think it's not bothering him. I know it bothers him, right? I know it bothers him."

Watching Ford on Kimmel's show, it felt to me like the host was pulling Ford's limbs off, one at a time, to cheers and laughter.

"Oh, he was very mean. He was vicious," agreed Doug Ford. "But, to be fair, we knew that's his shtick. He goes after everyone. Rob took the high road. Now let me tell you, if Rob had gotten nasty with him, he would have been dead."

If Doug had been onstage instead of in the green room, would he have intervened?

"Oh absolutely," he said. "I couldn't have helped myself. He's my brother."

—

"If you operate under the impression that local politics are boring, you probably don't live in Toronto," Kimmel introduced Ford to his audience.

"How ya doing?" he began.

"I'm doing amazing. How are you?" Ford answered.

"I'm doing well," said Kimmel. "Why are you dressed like a magician?"

Doug Ford gave me the full story later.

"It was Kimmel's wardrobe guys who gave Rob the stuff to wear. They were the ones who picked the tie. They were the ones who picked the handkerchief. Rob did stick with the black shirt, which I said, 'No, do a white shirt.' They didn't put the gun to his head. But they did come with a red tie, a red hankie, and did him all up." Doug laughed. "He could have said, 'I want a blue tie, a white shirt.' But they knew what Rob was coming out looking like. And boom! Kimmel said he looked like a magician. As far as I'm concerned, he looked like Pee-wee Herman, with his little pencil necktie and everything else."

Before picking Ford apart, Kimmel questioned his judgment in agreeing to come on the show. "Now don't get me wrong. I am very, very happy that you're here. But *why* are you here? What good could come of this? Have you ever seen this show?" Next, Kimmel read out comments from anti-Ford Torontonians. Such as this one: "I hope you remember that that clown you're about to trot out is a very sick, very bad man. You know about Rob Ford's domestic abuse, drunk driving, racism, homophobia and inability to tell the truth too, right?"

"I guess they don't talk about all the money I've saved—how we straightened out the city," said Ford, curling into a familiar defensive ball.

Noticing that Ford is sweating, Kimmel draws attention to it by reaching over to mop his brow. After dismantling any remnants of Ford's self-esteem by showing a greatest hits of his most embarrassing moments, Kimmel urged him to get help.

"I'm just a normal, average, hard-working guy that's real," Ford attempted.

Kimmel cut off his escape. "You are *not* the average politician, my friend. . . ."

"I'm an average, hard-working family man and I have a wife and two kids," Ford tried again.

"You are the most wonderful mayor I have ever witnessed in my many years on this job," Kimmel mocked him with false praise.

"Appreciate it," said Rob Ford.

—

When the show ended, a furious Ford stormed out of the studio. But by the time he and Doug were back in Toronto, they had decided to declare the trip a success. Kimmel even rubbed that in. "It seemed like we were having fun," he told his audience the next night. "We went over much of his remarkable life. We reviewed some of his home videos. But then, after the show, apparently he was upset—why, I'm not exactly sure," he said to laughter. "I asked him about drinking and smoking crack. What were we supposed to talk about, his other hobbies? Anyway, Rob was surprised, I guess. He left right away—mad. But then maybe he watched it again, or he thought it over on the flight, but he reflected on it today at city hall."

"I like Jimmy and I love the people of LA," Ford was telling the folks back home.

"Did Jimmy Kimmel make a fool out of you?" a reporter asked.

"I knew I was going into the lion's den," said Ford. "I held my own. And I got my message out that I was saving taxpayers' dollars."

"I gotta say that Jimmy Kimmel was very hospitable," Doug Ford claimed in a separate interview.

"He hammered him," a broadcaster countered.

"He apologized later on," said Doug, a statement Kimmel would deny on Twitter later in the day. "He's a classy guy. They treated us like royalty. He's a nice guy. He loves Rob. We're okay with it. Rob took it in stride. He was laughing. We had a good time."

—

Getting too close to the Fords, even as a journalist, you risk being drawn into their virtual unreality.

Ford called the cops on satirical comedian Mary Walsh, who invaded his driveway as Princess Warrior Marg Delahunty, dressed in a Viking outfit and carrying a plastic sword. "One good thing about being stubborn, Mayor Ford, is that you always know what you'll be thinking the next day," she called after him as he ran back into the house to dial 911. When police didn't arrive quickly enough to defend him, Ford reportedly cursed an emergency operator. "Don't you fucking know? I'm Rob fucking Ford, the mayor of this city."

After CBC anchor Peter Mansbridge lobbed softballs to Ford in an exclusive chat with the mayor the day council removed his powers, the interviewer's questions received as much attention as Ford's answers. Another respected journalist, TVO's Steve Paikin, issued "The Interview I Wish I'd Done with Doug Ford" after Doug spun Paikin's own interview into a Ford infomercial.

The *Star*'s Robyn Doolittle fared better, extending her newspaper's uncovering of Ford's substance abuse into a bestselling book.

Daniel Dale, also of the *Star*, wasn't looking to become part of any story when an enraged Ford confronted him, fist in the air.

Journalists who tried to follow the Fords too closely were branded "stalkers" by Doug, or worse by Rob. Dale declined to be interviewed for this book but has documented his encounter elsewhere. Researching a story on the mayor's attempt to buy a parcel of city-owned parkland next to his Etobicoke home, Dale visited the site. Alerted to his presence by a neighbour, Ford came towards him from the only way in or out of the property.

"Hey buddy," he yelled, according to Dale's published account in the *Toronto Star*. "What are you doing? Are you spying on me? Are you spying on me? Are you spying on me?" A few seconds later, said Dale,

he cocked his fist near his head and began charging at me at a full run. I began pleading with him, as loud as I could, with my hands up, for him to stop. . . . At some point, perhaps two metres away from me, the mayor did stop moving toward me, but his face remained menacing, and he continued to cock his fist and shake it. "Drop your phone!" he demanded, shouting louder than I had ever heard him. "Drop your phone! Drop your phone now!" Every time I tried to sidestep him to escape, he moved with me and yelled at me again to drop my phone. I became more frightened than I can remember; after two or three attempts to dart away, I threw my phone and my recorder down on the grass, yelled that he could take them, and ran.

Ford's account had Dale peering over his fence, taking pictures of his children, like a "sicko."

MAYOR NABS REPORTER: FORD FURIOUS AFTER CATCHING STAR CORRESPONDENT TAKING PICTURES OF HIS HOUSE FROM BACKYARD, read the *Toronto Sun* headline.

Dale had neither looked into Ford's yard nor taken pictures of it. When Ford continued to repeat the allegations about Dale spying on his children, the journalist took legal action. Only then did Ford retract his story.

"It was awful all around," recalled David Rider. "I felt terrible for Daniel. When I read some of my colleagues—who I considered friends—and they were giving equal weight to the mayor's story, I was angry and disbelieving. They knew as well as I did that the mayor often said things that weren't true.

"When it became clear that Daniel's great crime was doing his job and being a diligent reporter, I think some of them felt embarrassed about it."

—

Toronto Sun photo editor Michael Peake had trained his lens on eight mayors before Rob Ford became the ninth. "Your job is to cover unique moments and events, and typically there is one or two. But with Ford, you could have four or five. You'd have something great and then something even wackier happens. So that means you always have to be there, you know. It's stressful, for sure. I mean, it's tough."

Peake told me he'd need a multiple exposure to capture the essential Rob Ford. I asked about Doug. Could a single photo do him justice?

"Yeah," he said. "Angry. The look he gives you. That simmering look."

As Rob Ford's term as mayor was coming to a close, Peake told me, "I always say to those city hall press gallery folks, 'Guys, know these are very rare times right now. As bizarre as they are, you will look back on this as an incredibly rich buffet of photo opportunities, quotes and unlikely improv.'"

Will the Ford years provide any lessons on how to cover a political scandal that is hiding in plain view? Everybody in the press gallery must have heard the stories. Why did only a few try to dig them out?

"I don't know if it was this fear of the Fords, or fear of screwing up a good story, or what it was," said David Rider. "But I think there should be some soul-searching. I don't think there will be. I think people will just go on and cover the next guy and wistfully remember the crazy days of Ford."

19. BUSINESS AS USUAL

"Councillor, finish it."
Earl Provost, chief of staff to Mayor Rob Ford

D ucking through the back hallways of city hall's political
wing, dodging reporters' questions, heading for another
showdown he wouldn't win, Rob Ford turned to a young staff
assistant. "Buddy, have you ever picked up a lit firecracker before?"

"Can't say that I have," replied the staffer.

"I was setting them off on the weekend and I thought they
were out. So I picked one up and it blew up in my hand."

The mayor opened his palm to reveal a large wound con-
cealed by a thin layer of bandages.

"You've got to see a doctor," the aide thought to himself. But
there was no point telling Rob Ford to stand back from explo-
sives. Or to pay attention to an open, festering wound.

—

Even in the early days, when polls showed that more than two-
thirds of Torontonians were impressed with his performance,
the burden of failure weighed heavily on Rob Ford. By Ford's

second month as mayor, Nick Kouvalis had started finding empty booze bottles when he arrived first thing in the morning, before anyone had cleaned up. "Usually there was a direct correlation between the empty bottles and the mayor not showing up until afternoon," he told me.

When he was in the office, Ford dealt with the stress of high public expectations by watching sports on the wall screen or by taking sports-related meetings. "That's where his comfort zone was," Kouvalis said. Life outside the office was no bowl of cherries either.

"I don't think he has anyone who will just be his friend, anywhere in the whole world," Kouvalis had told me during our first interview, late in 2013. "He calls his brother, he's told to stop getting in trouble. He calls his mother, he's told not to let the family down. He goes home to his wife, she's telling him what *not* to do. At work, everyone's got advice he doesn't want to hear. Anybody who wants their photo with him just wants their photo with him; they don't really want him. He goes out to dinner with people, it's someone lobbying him to change some rule at the city so they can make money, or 'My son needs a job.'

"*Everybody wants something from the guy.* I think he's just overwhelmed by it all, and the only way he gets away from it is the booze, and once he's got a few drinks in him, it's the drugs. Then it starts all over again the next day. A terrible life."

After Ford lost some big votes at council early in 2012, his descent quickened. Still, it took another two years for him to hit rock bottom. During the latter days of his fall, Kouvalis and I spoke frequently about the shy, awkward, lonely man with the low opinion of himself, trapped in a totally unhappy place. We both wanted to help Rob but knew he had no way out until something forced him to decide to take that first step.

His drug use had become more serious than he ever admitted. Extreme alcohol consumption turned him one minute into a monster and the next into a hurt child. After one all-nighter, he told bystanders outside a nightclub that his mother and father hadn't given him what he needed. His wife and children hated him, he told others, according to a *Toronto Star* report. "I am in over my head," Ford said.

—

During the first half of November 2013, watching the mayor implode became a spectator sport. Some were excited, others tried to throw him a line. Even the *Dr. Phil* show wanted in on the action. But Rob Ford brushed them all aside and steadied himself for a last stand. His office staff would soldier on alongside him, he imagined, not realizing that they too desperately needed to escape.

As each day brought new twists to an already crazed series of misadventures without end, Ford's staff fretted over the unmanageable workload. Earl Provost was the voice of reassurance. "It's business as usual," the chief of staff told them each morning.

Sheila Paxton exploded with laughter while telling me this. "How can it be business as usual when you can't step outside your door without somebody taking your picture, and you can't go to the washroom without somebody following you with a camera to see what you're up to? Everybody was trying to find out what was going on in the mayor's office. Councillors' staff were just *roaring* at you, 'Quit, quit, quit, quit!' Councillors were asking, 'Why are you still working for him?' When you went home, people wanted to know, 'What's it like? It must be difficult.'

"Difficult?" Paxton exclaimed. "You couldn't get away from it. Whenever anybody asked Earl what we were going to do, he just kept screaming that same comment: 'Business as usual.'

"Really? What was usual? *There was no normal* in that office."

—

The collapse within the mayor's office had begun in the after-math of the May crack video story, when several respected staff members quit. Then Ford fired Mark Towhey for football-related insubordination. Although Towhey knew the art of war better than he understood the skill of political compromise , his order-liness had provided a sense of security amid the panic. "I'd go into a foxhole with that guy," said one former staffer. Others told me that Towhey kept alive the notion that Ford's office still had some purpose. But after a year of coaxing the mayor to go for treatment, even Towhey had had enough. "Get help," he'd told Ford.

What got him fired, though, was his order to staff *not* to organize a big farewell bash for Ford's football team, the Don Bosco Eagles. On May 22, after months of unsuccessful attempts at a diplomatic solution, Toronto's Catholic school board had fired Rob Ford as coach. On a deeply emotional level, Ford depended on the relationship with his players. That loss, sparking the familiar sting of rejection, churned a furious pain. Perhaps imagining that a tearful goodbye could soothe his heartbreak, Ford instructed his staff to arrange a party for the players at his house that night. Towhey knew how *that* scene would go down. He couldn't let Ford pull his young staff and teenage football players into his off-kilter orbit. After squelching the plan, Towhey issued his final order.

> May 22, 2013 5:18 PM
> Subject: Direct Order
> Do not answer calls from the mayor tonight. Take the night off. Will explain in the A.M.

When Towhey arrived the next day, Ford had him marched out through the "Wall of Shame," the term his staff used for the media gauntlet between the office doors and the elevator. Those who left on better terms were allowed to exit by the back stairs.

Promoted to fill the vacancy, Provost was once seen shoving a young assistant after Ford lost a vote. "He would transfer a lot of upset feelings onto us," one staffer told me. "The pressure was getting to everyone. The scandal seemed insurmountable, all day every day."

—

"Oh my God! It was like people falling apart all over the place!" Sheila Paxton described the office in November 2013. "People were stressed to the point where they would burst into tears—and not the junior staff, the senior staff. Nobody knew what to do."

Another staffer who attended morning meetings remembered another phrase frequently used by Provost, lest anyone question his judgment. "He'd put his hands on the boardroom table and spread out his fingers and say, 'This isn't my first rodeo, okay?'"

"I can remember Earl going into his office and putting his head down on his desk. He was crying," Paxton recalled. "Earl couldn't cope. He had headaches. He just sat in his office for a lot of it. He couldn't deal with things. He'd just walk out of the building."

Provost's deputy, Sunny Petrujkic, was also struggling, Paxton told me. "The phone calls were non-stop and he had nothing to give the press. We had no plan. His phone rang and I said, 'You better answer it.' He couldn't. He just handed me the phone. 'This is ABC News,' he said. 'I can't speak to them again.'"

When Tom Beyer went on sick leave a few days after the mayor admitted smoking crack, senior staff member Amin Masoudi was already off with a serious illness. Doug Ford's pal David Price, earning triple some staffers' salaries, wasn't improving matters any, according to several staff members. "He was always on edge when you were talking to him," recalled one staffer. "You'd see him in the hallway and you'd try to get away from him."

As Ford tumbled end over end, nobody was standing by to catch him. Expecting a crash, many at city hall closed their eyes until it felt safe to open them again.

—

With the mayor facing political annihilation, his staff should have been roaming the halls, gathering intelligence, using the considerable weight of his office to lean on wayward councillors. But as the cataclysmic November 2013 council meeting approached, his once-menacing minions were barely visible, preoccupied with their own survival. Entering B Street from a private door off the mayor's office, Petrujkic asked me what was on the petition I was getting councillors to sign. He appeared unconcerned when I didn't answer.

I was collecting signatures to call a Special Meeting of Council to remove the mayor's power to hire and fire committee chairs and the deputy mayor. This ability is the mayor's most effective tool for controlling council. Remove it and his remaining support would dissolve. I wondered why Ford's office wasn't desperately trying to stop me from locking up the votes I needed.

Confirmation that the crack video was real had removed all my doubts that the situation urgently needed to be stabilized. There was no mechanism to remove a mayor who'd lost the confidence of his elected colleagues, nor could council touch the formal and ceremonial powers conferred upon him by provincial statute. But the mayor's more practical political powers had been granted in 2006 by council in an attempt to create a "stronger mayor" system that included an executive committee composed mostly of committee chairs appointed by the mayor. By late 2013, Ford no longer controlled the votes to implement his agenda, but he still had the power to make it difficult for anybody else to do anything. There was a real risk that members of Ford's executive would resign or be fired by the mayor, leaving the city with no cabinet-like structure. Council could function through the chaos only as long as bureaucrats could feed reports to council through committees.

Because the mayor's extra powers were bestowed by council, I supposed that the same body could take them away. But how? This change needed to be approved by two-thirds of council, and I couldn't corral thirty votes without the support of many members of the executive committee itself. No matter how concerned these councillors now were about Ford's behaviour, most would not voluntarily relinquish the powerful positions he had given them.

The *how* to remove Ford's powers came to me on November 1, a Friday, as my office was deluged with calls from constituents wanting him gone. "There must be *something* you can do," a staff member said. That afternoon, in a matter completely unrelated to Ford, I'd cancelled a telephone line, a task complicated by the need to retain the phone number. That's when I understood what to do. Like the phone number, the committee chairs could stay the same even if the source of their power—the mayor—was disconnected.

Conceptual solution in hand, I sought procedural advice from the city clerk's department, then presented a five-part Notice of Motion to suspend the mayor's powers to appoint and dismiss the deputy mayor and committee chairs while freezing in place the people Ford had appointed to those positions for the balance of the term.

—

Meanwhile, Rob Ford's danger zone kept expanding. In the first week of November 2013, Toronto witnessed the mayor's unrehearsed crack confession, followed by a new video of Ford delivering a drunken, murderous rant, and then a remarkable television appearance by his mother and sister. When Ford's recent allies looked into their political futures and no longer saw Rob Ford there, they left without saying goodbye.

"I'll be running the ship, even if it's by myself," the mayor declared.

Few were surprised when the next week got even worse. On Wednesday, November 13, council would hold its first meeting since the non-stop drama began. Of the options being considered, the most immediate was a motion to censure the mayor and formally ask him to step aside. Lacking teeth, this might have caused minimal new damage if Ford hadn't declared it "the Mayor's key item" for the meeting. His bravado was catastrophically unwise; his action placed the issue first on the agenda and required him to answer questions about its subject matter: his suitability to hold office. Behind closed doors, were the mayor and his advisers devising some brilliant strategy to match his bluster?

Inside Ford's office, an entirely different problem was facing his staff: one thousand Rob Fords in miniature. Two months earlier, with the May crack scandal waning and the mayor looking as though he'd inexplicably survived it, Provost had proposed that the office order Rob Ford bobble-head dolls. The plan was to bolster Ford's image by selling his likeness, with the profits going to the United Way. "Buddy, bad idea," was Ford's first reaction.

There were complications from the start. "The designer didn't want to insult anyone, so he would keep sending these models of a very skinny mayor, and it looked like Doug," recalled Brendan Croskerry, the mayor's special assistant with responsibility for the bobble-head order. "I'd say, 'No, that's not what the mayor looks like. You've got to make them more plump.'

"So he kept making them a little bit bigger and a little bit bigger," but never plump enough. This continued for several cycles until time ran out. "Finally, there was this looming deadline, so we signed off on a model and it still looked like Doug."

Even so, the manufacturing equipment wasn't quite ready for Rob Ford. "A bobble-head has a large head and a small body," explained Croskerry. "The fact that the mayor had a small head and a big body was a bit of a challenge."

While the office waited for the dolls to be shipped from China, the announcement that police had found the crack video removed any benefit of the doubt that Ford had enjoyed. As each day brought new blows to Ford's reputation, Provost became increasingly concerned. He had paid for the dolls with his personal credit card, leaving him with an $8,000 bobble-head balance. "We'll never sell these bobble-heads," Sheila Paxton said he fretted out loud. "I'll be stuck with the eight thousand dollars."

The arrival of the bobble-heads brought with it the logistical problem of preparing them to meet the public. The dolls were placed in the boardroom, entirely filling the table, as the mayor's staff gathered around them. "They unpacked every one, numbered them, repacked them, then they unpacked them all so the mayor could sign them, and then they packed them all again," said Paxton. "The world was falling apart and you have a room full of people numbering bobble-heads. I thought I was in a Monty Python movie!"

The packaging told the mayor's story. "Born in Etobicoke, May 28, 1969, Mayor Rob Ford learned the importance of community service and political involvement from his father, the late Doug Ford Sr., who served as an MPP for Etobicoke–Humber from 1995–1999." Each doll came with a warning: "This is not a toy."

While opponents busily plotted his demise, Rob Ford couldn't have been more pleased with the bobble-heads. Neither the councillors aligned against him nor the crush of reporters waiting in the hallway to question him had any idea he was spending the day happily signing the one thousand dolls his staff had painstakingly numbered.

The press got their bobble-heads a day early, so they could boost sales by writing about them. "Do you think he'll sign mine?" Paxton remembered Robyn Doolittle asking. "I said,

'Do you want it personalized, Robyn?' And she says, 'Do you think he would?'" Doolittle was the *Toronto Star* reporter leading the investigative coverage of Rob Ford, including the crack cocaine video.

"So I walked in and said, 'Oh, Mayor, would you personalize this for Robyn Doolittle?' He said, 'There isn't room on this for everything I want to say to her.' I said, 'Maybe just her name.' So he personalized it. Because it was more important that Robyn had a bobble-head with his name on it than the fact that the woman was trashing him. He loved the bobble-heads."

It turned out that almost everybody wanted a Rob Ford bobble-head.

"It got crazy in the office that morning because city staff and councillors' offices—everybody—was coming to me trying to get a bobble-head," Croskerry remembered. "Even the mayor's staff were like, 'How many bobble-heads can *we* have?'"

The next day, buyers started lining up by 6 a.m., Ford's detractors mixing with his supporters. By the time the mayor arrived at ten-thirty, more than five hundred people were waiting. Pursuing his unique brand of retail politics, the mayor handed out his own caricatures until there were none left, sold out at $20 each. Within hours, they were selling online for more than ten times that much.

"It warms my heart," said Doug Ford, surveying the scene. "I don't think there's a politician in the country, including the prime minister, who could have bobble-heads and have them lined up around the corner."

Others were less kind. "This freak show has a gift shop!" tweeted one Ford critic.

—

My plan to take away the mayor's powers initially struck some councillors as extreme. Just ten days later, they thought it didn't go far enough. During that time, Ford had confessed to smoking crack and then admitted buying illegal drugs while he was mayor—though still denying he needed help. When I accepted Councillor Josh Matlow's suggestion that we also transfer away Ford's ability to be in charge during a city emergency, we required a second special meeting. As I travelled among councillors gathering the required signatures, several told me that the mayor's staff needed to be rescued.

A week earlier, I had bumped into Earl Provost walking the second-floor streets, speaking with councillors. Stopping to talk, I asked him to tell Rob I wished there was a better way to deal with the situation. Not to worry, Provost said, after the crack admission "everyone gets a pass." Was Provost thinking that I deserved a pass—or that *he* did? The answer arrived eight days later when I bumped into Provost again, and this time told him about the second special meeting to remove more of his boss's power.

"Naah. Naaah," Provost responded, making a noise I'd never before heard. It sounded like pain mixed with exasperation. If I was reducing the mayor's responsibilities, he suggested, I should also take away his large staff and office budget. "Councillor," he said, his voice now clear. "Finish it."

—

By then, Sheila Paxton told me later, Provost was determined that the big guy needed to go, one way or another. "I remember Earl saying, 'We either push him to the point where he does what we want—or we get rid of him.' He said it more than once."

When I asked whether Provost considered quitting himself, Paxton laughed loudly. "Oh, he never thought of himself going. We had to come up with a scheme where we stayed and the mayor was gone."

Ford, meanwhile, was doing everything imaginable and unimaginable to lose any remaining support. After the mayor had scrummed blithely about his appetite for oral sex, almost all of council was too embarrassed to be seen with him. It took me less than an hour to get enough signatures for a third special meeting, so we could "finish it" the way Provost had suggested.

20. DEMONS IN THE MIRROR

*"There was one guy I was fighting day in and day out,
and that was the guy in the mirror."*
Rob Ford

The spontaneous shunning of Rob Ford came from an unexpected source. As Ford rose on the second day of the November 2013 council meeting to defend his public comments about his sex life, Mike Del Grande turned his seat around.

"I wanted to send him a message: 'You let us all down. You betrayed us.' So I turned my back to him," the conservative Scarborough councillor and former Ford ally told me later. Unscripted, other councillors followed suit. "I think different people turned their backs for different reasons. But the common reason was him, and his conduct, and his denials."

A deeply religious man who prides himself on doing his version of what's right, Del Grande felt personally betrayed by Ford. "John, I didn't know he had demons," he said, explaining his earlier support for the man who harboured them. "I had *no idea.*"

By now, Ford's demons were so accustomed to the constant hoopla that they no longer hid from his council colleagues or photographers. Rob Ford looked like a man who no longer controlled his own behaviour.

Before the November meeting had even started, the mayor planted himself directly in front of Councillor Denzil Minnan-Wong, standing chest to chest, blocking his path in the middle of the council chamber. "Why don't you sit down?" Ford said, more an instruction than a question.

"He was in my personal space, really close, like a schoolyard bully," Minnan-Wong told me later. "It felt really uncomfortable."

Ford claimed he was only urging the councillor to observe proper protocol by taking his seat.

When the meeting got under way, Ford faced a predictable interrogation for which he hadn't prepared. This was no media scrum from which he could walk away when he didn't like the questions.

"Do you still have zero tolerance for drugs, guns and gangs?" Minnan-Wong began.

"Absolutely," Ford replied.

"Have you purchased illegal drugs in the last two years?" the councillor asked.

Rob Ford rolled his eyes up and pursed his lips. For a full eight seconds there wasn't a sound. "Yes I have," Ford broke the silence, like a quiz show contestant who'd found the answer just before time ran out.

For years, Ford had attacked Toronto Board of Health programs to assist drug addicts and homeless alcoholics. I asked whether his recent experience had taught him anything about understanding and compassion. Ford interpreted the question the only way he knew how. "This has definitely been the most humiliating experience in my life," he said, describing his empathy for his own problems. "It has been the worst week in my life."

The next day, as we debated the first of my three sets of motions, it seemed for a brief moment that Ford was capable of self-examination.

"If I would have had a mayor acting the way I've conducted myself, I would have done the exact same thing. I'm not mad at anybody. I take full responsibility."

———

After losing the vote 39–3, Ford returned to his office, where 11-year-old Colin Brennan had been waiting to brighten his day with a song. For months, Colin had seen Ford on the news. "I noticed he wasn't doing that good. My dad came in and said, 'I think we should go and sing to him.'" (Graham Brennan, Colin's father, doubled as manager for his precocious son, whose singing transcended his autism.) Arriving at city hall without an appointment on one of Rob Ford's darkest days, the Brennans took the elevator to the second floor and stepped into a wall of clicks, flashes and shouting voices. "Where are you going? Where are you going!??"

"I'm going to sing for the mayor," Colin told them.

"It's not going to happen. It's not going to happen," chief of staff Earl Provost told the Brennans. They waited anyway, trusting that Rob Ford would make time for a kid with his father. Travelling between the plotters inside his own office and those in the council chamber, Ford spotted them waiting for him. "Stick around," he said. "I'll fit you in."

That afternoon, his mayoralty collapsing, Ford opened the door to his inner office. "Come on in," he said to Colin. The boy set up a boom box in front of the mayor's desk and belted out a tune from *You're a Good Man, Charlie Brown*: "Happiness is morning and evening/ Daytime and night time too/ For happiness is everyone and anything at all/ That's loved by you."

"Feel better?" Colin asked afterwards.

"I feel amazing," the mayor answered, giving the kid a big sweaty hug. "You want a T-shirt? It says *Ford Nation* on it."

"Oh, that's so cool," Colin replied.

"Okay, buddy, I'm going to sign it for you."

Colin's visit was captured on video by Brendan Croskerry. In it, the mayor exuberantly pumps a fist, then two fists. Taking the boy on an office tour, the mayor passed on the lessons he'd learned from an unhappy life. "You are the greatest singer in the world," he told Colin. "Anybody ever says that to you, you say, '*I know* I'm the greatest singer in the world.'"

Colin spotted a framed cartoon of a fat Rob Ford. "What the heck?!" he exclaimed.

"Oh yeah, they make fun of me all the time," Ford told him. "When you get popular, trust me, you're going to be a celebrity one day, and you know what? Whatever you do, they'll make fun of you. They'll *find something* to make fun of. Because there's always jealous people out there, and the higher you go up in life, the more jealous they get."

—

As I prepared the final motion to turn Rob Ford into a figure-head mayor, I imagined the personal impact this would have on a man who would comprehend it on the most basic level: some-one he sometimes considered a friend had spearheaded a politi-cally motivated attack designed to humiliate him. For days I thought of nothing else, and worried that Rob couldn't emotion-ally withstand much more.

Seeking a way out, I'd approached him and offered *not* to submit the motion in return for a public promise from him to take a leave and seek help. He told me he was already in a pro-gram and that he'd been advised to keep working. He suggested I speak with his doctor. Although skeptical, I agreed to sign a confidentiality agreement so that I could hear what the doctor had to say. A short time later, Rob told me the doctor was unavailable. When there was no follow-up by the deadline for submitting the motion, I handed in the papers to trigger the special meeting. Ford did nothing to discourage my action, as if he presumed we were meant to play out our roles. Later, I learned that the professional help he'd talked to me about was a fitness trainer who'd been convicted for dealing steroids.

I presented the motion on a Friday for a meeting to be held the following Monday, November 18, at 12:30. By Saturday, I realized I'd moved too fast. Ford had hired a municipal law expert who pointed out that council was required to provide the mayor with enough staff and a budget to carry out his statutory obligations, the ones we *weren't* able to take away. The city's legal staff agreed with Ford's expert, as did a prominent independent lawyer I checked with. They advised me to leave the mayor with a sufficiently large staff and budget to avoid a successful court challenge.

I submitted a revised motion and, as the mover, spoke first.

"For the past six months, faced with many allegations of serious misconduct, Mayor Ford has had many choices. Would he keep the faith with the public and with council by addressing all allegations fully, truthfully and directly? Would he protect the integrity and reputation of the city of Toronto and the office of the mayor? Would he change his behaviour? Would he step aside and seek help?

"The mayor has, unfortunately, chosen the path of denial, ignoring all pleas to follow a different route. . . . And each new day brings the same question: what's next? If any Torontonians were initially fascinated with the drama, they are now fed up with it. They want it to end."

I tried not to be distracted by Rob Ford's menacing looks. Later, I watched a four-screen video that simultaneously showed everything that had happened in the room. As Doug Ford rose angrily to ask me accusatory questions, Rob watched with an eerily satisfied smile, as if his big brother was teaching me a lesson about messing with the Fords. Rob had moved to a lectern near the front of the room, either to get a better angle or to make sure I saw his smile, but I hadn't looked over.

The Fords reacted to this new danger as they had to many before it: acting on instinct, they tried to gain control of the room by finding someone—anyone—to intimidate. Since their threats against the other politicians were no longer working, the brothers got belligerent with the spectators in the packed public gallery. Rob wandered over to his driver/bodyguard and told him to video the audience. It was an implied, "We know who you are and we'll find out where you live." As his driver took pictures, Ford swaggered alongside him, sporting a grin with a snarl inside it, like a movie villain who had his victims cornered.

"Shame, shame," the crowd shouted at him.

"We're saving millions," Ford said back. "You don't like that. Is it affecting your grants?"

The scene created such a commotion that the Speaker called a ten-minute recess. By now Doug Ford was alongside his brother, inciting the public, pointing a finger at people in the crowd, angry and threatening. "You're a punk," he told someone. "Bring it on. Bring it on, tough guy," he shouted at somebody else.

Mark Grimes, a large, gregarious councillor and Ford friend, stepped into the fray to cajole Doug back to his seat. Then Grimes went back to get the mayor. "Bully! Bully!" people in the crowd called after the Fords as Grimes escorted them from the ring. But as Rob got to his seat, he turned around to see Doug already back confronting the crowd, ready to rumble. With eyes fixed only on his brother, Rob set himself in motion, racing along the narrow passageway. Councillor Pam McConnell, sixty-something and small, was slowly walking the opposite way.

McConnell can't recall the moment of impact, and remembers the seconds afterwards only in slow motion. She felt a large white surface pressing against her face. Falling backwards, she noticed a tie attached to it. At the end of the tie was the face of Rob Ford.

"He didn't seem to see me, or to be aware that I was even there. At that point his legs and feet got all entangled in mine and he started to stumble. And then I realized it was going to be really dangerous if I fell underneath this load."

Ford was easily three times McConnell's size. As she went down, he half lifted her back up, without stopping or taking his eyes off Doug.

"I was just something in his way," she told me. "I could have been a chair or a bookshelf or a person. I don't think he was in any way seeing me."

By now, Grimes was guiding Doug Ford back to his seat again. Rob turned and rushed back the way he'd come, past McConnell, who was still trying to regain her balance, to place a brotherly arm on Doug's shoulder. When he was asked to apologize for bowling McConnell over, Ford seemed only dimly aware of the collision. "I ran around because I thought my brother was getting into an altercation," he explained.

—

After more than four hours of questions and debate before the vote, the mayor had the final word. Only a last-minute act of contrition, together with a promise to enter rehab, might have affected the outcome. How would he choose to start his speech?

"I want to congratulate the Hamilton Tiger-Cats, and I want to wish them the best in the Grey Cup," he began, referring to the Canadian football championship. "I was at the game yesterday. It was a great game . . . so congratulations everybody in Hamilton."

Switching to the matter at hand, Ford continued. "Folks, this is nothing more than a *coup d'état*. . . . I didn't think it would get to this point, but it has. And I've apologized enough. But you guys just won't give up.

"I think a lot of you don't know my dad, or remember my dad, but he was a Bible school teacher. And he said, 'He who has never sinned shall cast the first stone, son.' And prayer, in our family, is very important. And he says you help people when they're down and out. And I've done that for thousands of people, before I even got into politics. And so has my family. In this world, there are more poor people than rich people. I side with the poor people. . . .

"This, folks," he continued, "reminds me of when—and I was watching it with my brother—Saddam attacked Kuwait. And President Bush said, 'I warn you. I warn you. I warn you. Do not.' Well, folks, if you think American-style politics is *nasty,* you guys have just attacked Kuwait. Mark my words, friends. This is going to be war in the next election. And I am going to do everything in my power to beat you guys. . . . What goes around comes around, friends. Remember what I am saying."

—

The mayor's staff had watched anxiously, some up in the council chamber, others on their desk screens. A few of the younger ones felt sad for him. The veterans would have to conceal their relief for a few hours more. Ford summoned them for one last meeting, before half would go to work for Norm Kelly, the politically adaptable councillor Ford had appointed the deputy mayor only four months earlier. They congregated around the boardroom table, with the mayor at its head.

"Well, I guess you know what they did to me," he began. "The bastards got me. They've been out to get me from the beginning." He talked about his staff. "This is the best team I've ever had. You guys have hung in with me, so I'm going to give you all a $5,000 raise."

Then he put his head on the table and cried. Great, heaving sobs. It was the only sound in the room for what seemed an unbearably long time.

"Nobody else cried," Sheila Paxton said. "Usually, if somebody cries, at least one other person cries too. But nobody did. I was thinking, 'I've got to do something to get us out of this room in one piece.' You had to give him his dignity back. So I said to him, 'Mayor, speaking on behalf of the group, we appreciate the opportunity you've given us all.'

"That seemed to pull him together. He seemed to think, *'Yes, I have done something for you!'* Then he sat up and said a few things and that was the end of it. Everybody just wanted to get out of the room. We were thinking, 'Thank God, it's over. We only have a day to go and we're free.'"

On the other side of the boardroom wall, CBC television news anchor Peter Mansbridge was waiting for an exclusive interview with Rob Ford. Doug joined them. Both brothers struggled to accept that their threats had been ignored and, worse, that few believed they had any power to carry them out. What would Dad have said about that!?

Rob looked red-faced and defeated, like a huge, dazed child who'd just experienced a traumatic incident he couldn't comprehend. Doug was missing the customary zip but retained his seething intensity. For all eighteen minutes of the interview, he leaned forward and stared directly at Mansbridge, seldom blinking, looking ready to eat the interviewer if he dared make one wrong move.

Later, I asked Doug if he thought his presence affected Mansbridge.

"He knows," Doug replied. "A little backup."

In that interview, Rob was all victim. "I got caught. I admitted it. And now I'm being punished for telling the truth. I'm not a very religious guy. But my dad did teach Bible school, and prayer is important to me." His voice, previously flat, became authoritative. "He who shall cast the first stone has never sinned," he declared.

Did Dad really teach Bible school? Rob was telling the story for the second time that day, in each case finding a new way to mangle the scriptural passage. What had the god of his father taught the Fords? Was it (a) Nobody should throw stones at any-body; (b) Nobody should throw stones at the Fords; or (c) The Fords are the *only* people entitled to throw stones? I'd guess (c).

"Everyone has sinned," continued Rob Ford. "I let my mom down. I let my brothers down. I let my wife down, my kids down. And I let my dad down," he said, turning towards the picture on his office wall. "I know he's upstairs watching us."

Ford declared that he'd never driven drunk, hadn't con-sumed alcohol in weeks and didn't take drugs. "Talk is cheap," he added. "If you don't see a difference in me in five months, I'll eat my words."

"We'll see you in five months," Mansbridge concluded.

———

Elsewhere in the mayor's office, Provost was fretting that he might not be able to escape Rob Ford after all. "Earl just about shit himself when the motion was changed so that some of the staff would have to stay with the mayor," Paxton recalled. "He was just beside himself. 'Oh my God, the mayor's going to keep some staff.' He thought *he* would have to stay with the mayor. He went home that night and he was a mess."

Paxton had already spoken with the office staff to find out who wanted to do what. Several of the newer staff wanted to stay; the longer-serving ones were running for the exits. Paxton took home a list of names and salaries and put together a spread-sheet that matched preferences with available funds. She listed Provost and the other veterans as moving to work with Deputy Mayor Norm Kelly. When she presented her spreadsheet to Provost the next morning, Paxton said, he immediately carried it to Kelly and city manager Joe Pennachetti.

By the time the mayor arrived at city hall, new staff con-tracts had already been prepared. But nobody had spoken to him about it. "He didn't know we'd divided the staff," Paxton said.

"Earl and I went in to talk with him, but the mayor was in the washroom. He always went into the washroom when he was making himself feel better. Earl just chickened out and ran. I thought, '*I'm* not doing this.' So I left. Then the mayor heard it on the news. He called all the staff together and said, 'I want to keep all of you.' He started talking to Winnie Lee [from the clerk's department] in front of them. 'Can I pay it out of my own bank account? I'm not bragging, but I've got $1.5 million in my chequing account, and I'm willing to pay for everybody.'" He said he was in a war and needed an army of special assistants.

"I kept saying to him, 'Mayor, can we speak to you for a moment, *by yourself?*'" Paxton recalled. After they'd left the group, Paxton told Ford that some staff had wanted to leave so they could work on policy rather than constituency work. But Ford had a question.

"I just want to know," he asked, "is there anybody who's refused to work with me?"

"No, mayor," replied Provost, "*everybody* wants to work with you."

Then Ford started going down the list of staff members who were staying with him. On it was Amin Masoudi, a Ford loyalist recovering from surgery, and Tom Beyer, who was on leave to deal with his Ford-induced stress. "Why do I have to keep these two?" Paxton recalled the mayor saying. "They're sick. I don't even know if they're going to be here. Why can't we just get rid of them?" Then he came to Dave Price and his $130,000 salary, enough for at least three junior staffers. "I don't want him. He can go," Ford said, according to Paxton. She explained that there was no spot for him on the deputy mayor's team. "Well, just get rid of him," Ford replied.

Back at the larger staff meeting, Ford started reciting the names of the higher-priced staff who *weren't* staying with him. "He says, 'Earl's gone, Sunny's gone, Sheila's gone and Dave's gone,'" remembered Paxton. Three of them knew they had jobs with the deputy mayor. The fourth knew he didn't. "Dave was sitting there. That's how he was told."

—

After Provost happily moved to the deputy mayor's office, the mayor needed a new chief of staff. He offered the job first to Brendan Croskerry, who had already decided he was leaving but took the opportunity to attempt an honest conversation with the mayor.

"I said, 'Really, you think I can be chief of staff? I only have seven months' experience here.' He basically said, 'It's not that hard, buddy. You can do it. It's not that tough.'"

Croskerry followed up with a condition: "I'll be your chief of staff if you stop hanging around with questionable people and stop drinking and doing drugs, and go to a rehab clinic."

"Oh, I can't believe what I'm hearing," Ford replied, adding that he had no serious drug or alcohol problems.

"If you can't do it, I can't accept your offer," Croskerry responded, noting that Ford slurred his words on overnight recordings left on staffers' voice mails.

"Well, okay, buddy, I wish you all the best," Ford ended the conversation. "And I hope you will still vote for me."

A few months later, when Rob Ford was talking to me again, he told me that I'd done him a favour. "Christmas came early," he said. "I got the staff I wanted. I got rid of the deadwood."

—

It took only a few weeks for Doug Ford to resume his congenial ways with the group of us who sat behind him. During the December council meeting, he joined us for lunch. Doug told us how important weight loss was to Rob's political comeback. "He's got to show people that he's changed." He talked about his own ambitions and the difficulty of always having to stick up for Rob. "I have to defend my brother," he said, as if no other option existed.

As the meeting resumed after lunch, Rob admonished Doug for consorting with the enemy. Not realizing how angry Rob was that we'd all gone out together, Joe Mihevc approached him wanting to buy a bobble-head from the new edition that was about to go on sale. Ford gave Joe a blast that left him shaken. When Doug returned, we told him what had happened.

How many bobble-heads would we like? And did we want them personalized? Doug asked. We handed over $20 each. A few minutes later, Doug returned with two bobble-heads, one personally signed for "Joe" and the other for "John." I asked Doug how he had convinced his brother to sign them for us. "I told him I had a couple of buddies waiting outside named Joe and John," he replied with a chuckle.

—

At Christmas that year, the Fords were like other dysfunctional families, carrying on their traditions as if everything in their world was holiday bright. Rob offered advice on what to give that special woman in your life. "Women love money," he told a sports radio show. "You give 'em a couple thousand bucks and they're happy." Diane Ford hosted a Christmas gathering at the family home, and the Fords sent invitations to everyone you'd have thought wouldn't be on that year's list: the city hall press gallery and all the members of council and their staffs.

Rob took the journalists on a house tour, past the living room filled with artifacts from Doug Sr.'s travels and along the basement walls that were covered with tributes to him: photos from his days as a football player and politician; framed eulogies, obituaries and testimonials; a photo of the Ford children carrying their father's casket.

Most of the city hall crowd stayed away that year. But a few political staffers attended, including a young man named Shaun who worked in my office. He'd come to Toronto that year to learn about politics. Nobody answered the door, so Shaun let himself in. When no hosts introduced themselves or asked who he was, Shaun followed their lead. For several hours, he travelled incognito among the Fords, doing as they did.

He arrived just in time to join the group singing "Happy Birthday" to Renata. He shared Randy's puzzlement over the malfunctioning beer keg. He sang along as Doug cheerfully led the Christmas carols. He watched the hockey game with Rob, sharing his excitement with each brawl. "Tiff! Tiff!" Rob would summon the others. Then he would stand to punch the air, grunting encouragement to whichever Maple Leaf was engaged in battle. As the evening drew to a close, Shaun introduced himself to Rob and thanked him for the invitation. Rob thanked him for coming.

An awful year was over. The Fords looked to the future, not knowing what waited in the blackness beyond their horizon. Whatever came up, they intended to stare it down.

—

Rob Ford's search for attention and acceptance led him to all sorts of places where it took only one person with a smart phone to catch him in the lie that he didn't have a problem with drugs or alcohol. In January 2014, Ford was recorded drunk and swearing, with Sandro Lisi, at a fast-food restaurant in Etobicoke. Ford spoke in a Jamaican patois, something he said he did with Jamaican friends. This was a man who'd go to great lengths to fit in.

At the start of any day, even Rob Ford had no idea where his quest for acceptance would lead. If you travelled with him, even to some place that seemed safe, you'd better buckle yourself in. Frank Di Giorgio, a good-natured councillor who, like other political allies, hadn't spent any personal time with Rob, accepted Ford's invitation to join him at an April 5 hockey game at the Air Canada Centre. "I thought we were just going to be sitting and watching the game," he told me. "Perhaps I should have known better." When the game ended, Di Giorgio couldn't tell you who the Leafs played or which team won.

Frank's first inkling that there was trouble ahead came during the cab ride to the arena when the mayor passed him his phone. Rob's wife, Renata, was on the line. "She wanted me to get him home at a reasonable hour," the councillor recalled. "She impressed on me that I needed to get him home safe. At the time, I didn't really understand what she was saying."

At the game, before they could take their seats, Ford was mobbed. Everybody wanted a photo with him. He obliged, non-stop. At the first intermission, he set off for the Directors' Lounge but was turned away because a private event was on. Ford figured the wealthy elites who ran Maple Leaf Sports and Entertainment were snubbing him.

"He started to freak out," said Di Giorgio. "I spent the rest of the night trying to calm him down." The crowd wasn't helping. "People could see he was in an irritable state and took advantage of the opportunity to irritate him further." Private-box holders invited him in. "We circulated from one box to another. If I turned my back, he continued to drink."

At the end of the game, the mayor was scheduled to accompany Di Giorgio to a community event where an adoring group of Italian seniors were excitedly awaiting his arrival. "I said, 'C'mon, Rob, we'll take a cab.' He said, 'It's okay, buddy, I'll find my own way.' Then he just *bolted* to the other side of the street. For a big guy, he can move quickly. He jumped into a cab and a couple more people jumped in the back seat with him. Zoom! He's gone!"

Discombobulated, Di Giorgio went straight home.

Back at city hall that night, security footage captured Ford entering the building with his two new pals from the hockey game. Jonathan Goldsbie of *Now* magazine received a tweet that Ford had taken a cab to his office. Presuming correctly that the mayor's car was parked at city hall and that he hadn't gone to his office to read agendas, Goldsbie cycled over. For more than an hour, he hid in a basement alcove watching the mayor's parking spot.

"The process of hunting Rob Ford—trying to keep up with him and his extracurricular activities—drives you nuts," he told me later. "It becomes an obsession. It's like living his life without the benefit of drugs." Goldsbie soon texted two journalist friends, *Toronto Star* reporters Robyn Doolittle and Daniel Dale, who joined the mission to catch the mayor driving drunk.

"You start to worry you're enjoying it too much," said Goldsbie. "The idea that there is this perfect truth at the centre, if only I could just get there. It plays into what journalists love, which is to dig and dig at the truth of something. But in this case, you are trying to pin down a human being, who has managed to elude accountability in so many ways for so long. You're just hoping that finally you can get that incontrovertible evidence that will make a difference."

What truth did you hope to find? I asked.

Catching him on video drunk-driving would be important, Goldsbie answered. "But that's not the giant truth. Whatever the giant truth is, no one really knows. But what is the largest truth? What is his life, really? How does he go about his day? What is it like for him at home? You get little bits and pieces all the time."

Alerted to the journalists' presence by a security guard, Ford left by cab. He ended up at the Muzik nightclub, where he reportedly snorted lines of cocaine and drank until he was babbling in front of anyone who would listen. "No one knows what I'm going through," he told them.

—

By late April of 2014, Ford's jig was up. The *Globe and Mail* obtained photos of him smoking crack with his sister, Kathy, in her basement, on the night of Saturday, April 26. The story broke the following Wednesday, April 30. That same night, the *Toronto Sun* obtained a two-day-old audio recording of Ford, drunk in a bar in Royal York Plaza, making a string of offensive remarks.

Ford is heard denouncing provincial Conservative leader Tim Hudak for voting in favour of a motion to fly the rainbow Pride flag outside Queen's Park. "Hudak comes out and says, 'Yeah, I agree with all the gays,'" Ford says in the recording. "Right there, he lost my vote." Several times, he uses derogatory terms for Italians. About mayoral rival Karen Stintz, he says, "I'd like to fucking jam her." If he doesn't get re-elected, Ford says, he's moving to California.

Within hours, the mayor issued a brief statement that he would be taking a leave from his duties as mayor to seek treatment at an undisclosed rehab facility.

"I have a problem with alcohol and the choices I have made while under the influence. I have struggled with this for some time," Ford said, making no mention of a drug addiction. "I have tried to deal with these issues by myself over the past year. I know that I need professional help, and I am now 100 percent committed to getting myself right."

Diane Ford, who had avoided all media since the previous November's declaration that her son needed only to lose weight, was caught by a reporter in a plaza parking lot. "You thought it was just the weight problem. It seems to be much more complex. Do you acknowledge that now?"

Diane responded, "I guess I have to. You know, I had no idea it was as serious as it was. But he doesn't live with me. I don't know what he does every minute every day."

—

Early in September 2014, while still in the race for mayor, Rob Ford again talked about the man in the mirror. Earlier, he'd said that this was the only guy he could trust. Now he was saying the opposite.

"There was one guy I was fighting day in and day out, and that was the guy in the mirror," Ford told a reporter. "I've been in a lot of fights, and I've won a lot of fights. But there was one guy I couldn't beat. And it was the guy in the mirror. And one day I got up and told my brother, 'That's it.' It's the best thing I ever could have done, fighting that guy."

Doug Ford went before the cameras to read a family statement about Rob's entry into rehab. "As an older brother, I'm relieved that Rob has decided to face his problems," he said, sounding shaken. "Many people believe you can handle any problem by yourself. But sometimes you need the help of your family, your friends and the professionals."

Notwithstanding the lack of acknowledgement that family and friends may be at the root of Rob's problems, and that professionals can only accomplish so much without a change in environment, Doug seemed entirely genuine. The familiar spin was absent. An extremely controlled man had difficulty containing his emotions. "I love my brother," Doug started, and then stopped, unable to speak for several seconds. "I'll continue to stand by my brother and his family during this difficult journey," he continued haltingly. "Please join me. Keep Rob and his family in your prayers."

When any of the Fords speak about almost anything, every word is dissected—not just *what* is said, but *how*, and *why*. "What's up with Doug?" people were asking. "Can this emotion be real?"

I asked Nick Kouvalis for his take. "I think it was real. It wasn't acting. I don't think it was planned. I think he lost control of his emotions at that point. The way he was breathing—I think it was real. I think the whole family's sad. But what are they sad about?

"I think Doug really cares about his brother, and I think Doug is really choked up," Kouvalis continued. "But, you know, he should have been crying two years ago, when this really started to get out of control. I think he's genuinely sad at the situation. But is he sad because Rob's on his path to death? Or is he sad because they are going to lose the mayoralty? Is he sad because the family name is going to suffer? That's what I question.

"Doug's normally a kind person," Kouvalis added. "He has money and he has a business, he has a nice family, he has love in his family. He wants everyone to be happy and successful. He's not jealous of people, other than Rob."

21. MY BROTHER'S KEEPER

Then the Lord said to Cain, "Where is your brother Abel?"
"I don't know," he replied. "Am I my brother's keeper?"
Genesis 4:9

F ace blank, eyes unblinking, gaze fixed straight ahead but detecting motion on either side: the part of his brain that separates "Us" from "Them" is on fire, igniting an instinct he would not want to suppress even if he could.

Rob and Doug were constantly on high alert for an enemy presence. When they detected danger, they would lock eyes from their seats at either end of council's second row. Then one would rise to join the other. But on this day, one brother is gone, freeing an impulse the other has stifled for four years. Rob Ford is in rehab, for two months, maybe more. Doug Ford waits and he watches.

He's restless, sitting down and then getting up again, moving around the chamber. It's May 7, 2014, the first day of a three-day council session. Doug stops roaming long enough to lean against the wall of the chamber, facing the councillors' seats. I walk over to stand beside him.

"How's Rob?" I ask. "I know this is a difficult time for him."

Rob has been gone for a week, finally taking the step that became unavoidable after the release of new audio and video tapes.

"He's doing good," Doug replies, offering nothing more. I'm standing next to him, but Doug stares straight ahead as we talk, as if passing on classified information. "You may need to write a new part to your book," he tells me, declining to elaborate.

On the move again, he approaches another councillor with a different hint. "We may need to switch horses." Doug is dropping clues everywhere. By early morning, city hall is alive with speculation that Doug will lead the Ford ticket in that fall's election. All versions of the story have Rob stepping aside willingly. Some speculate the mayor will return to his old Ward 2 council seat, which Doug has held since 2010.

Earlier that morning, with Rob absent, the area outside the council elevator had been strangely devoid of journalists. A few rumours later, the space starts to fill. This time it's Doug—and only Doug—the media wants. "Are you running for mayor?" they shout after him.

"No comment," responds the man who loves to comment on *everything*. The "no comment" comment fuels the story even more. Back in council, Doug nonchalantly wanders over to where the mayor sits. He ponders the empty seat. Then he tries it out.

After lunch, he does it again. This time, Councillor Giorgio Mammoliti disappears into a back room and returns with a piece of paper. On it he's hand-written a single word: *Doug*. Mammoliti approaches the nameplate in front of the mayor's chair, where Doug is comfortably seated, and places the name *Doug* over *Rob*. It now reads: *Doug Ford Mayor*.

The moment is captured by Michael Peake, photo editor of the *Toronto Sun*.

"I'm looking at Doug and then I go, 'Wait a minute. Holy shit! Doug Ford Mayor! That's when he looked right at me. But it only lasted a few seconds. I went to tweet it out and the sign was gone."

Doug's expression in the photo is an unusual mix of provocation and satisfaction. I asked Peake what the look said to him. "It was a smug or impish look, perhaps. It was sort of like, 'Hmmm, maybe I like the sound of that.' That's what kind of made the picture."

—

Rob Ford, in rehab, wasn't about to have a pillow placed over his face. His call display showed the *Toronto Sun* trying to connect on his cellphone. Rob answered. "Of course I am coming back, and I am going to kick butt," he told a columnist. "I will be on the ballot for mayor in October—guaranteed!"

"Rehab is awesome," he added, comparing the experience to his time at a football summer camp.

"I tore a strip off him," Doug told me the next day in council. "I told him he shouldn't be doing any interviews."

Unlike other councillors on the right, who tended to be a dreary lot, Doug is a social animal, always on the lookout for an appreciative audience for his wild anecdotes, opinionated commentary and up-to-the-minute news. At council, he needed only to turn around to engage with an animated group of "progressive" councillors: Adam Vaughan, Joe Mihevc, Mary Fragedakis and me. "Doug, Doug!" one of us would call out to him when we wanted information or entertainment. Often, he'd come looking for us.

I pointed out to Doug that he seemed to prefer commiserating with the progressives on council. "Yeah," he said. "Because I know where you're coming from. These other ones smile at you while they're . . ." He made a motion of a knife being twisted in. "That's why I hate this place."

Doug likes his fights clean and direct, mano-a-mano. When aiming a threat at a political adversary, Doug would spin in his seat and fire. But more often he was looking for friendly banter.

Then he would stand and turn our way, grabbing our attention with a bold statement. On day two of the May 2014 meeting, Doug was out of his chair, jovial and animated. "Ninety-eight percent of my stress here is caused by Rob," he told us. "I'm through defending him." Realizing that sounded a bit harsh, Doug immediately softened the statement. "Unless he stays straight. Then I still will."

—

On day three of the meeting, Joe Mihevc asked Doug whether it was a fifty-fifty proposition that he would run for mayor. "Even I don't know at this point," Doug answered. "Rob's the mayor." It's a phrase Doug used often, generally with an implied blank you could fill in yourself. As in, "Rob's the mayor—*but we all know I'd make a better one!*"

Mihevc tried to engage Doug in a conversation about the obligations of older brothers towards younger ones. Doug ignored the theme. "You'll need a family gathering soon," Mihevc tried again.

"It'll happen," replied Doug. "You better believe it."

Doug sat back down, but soon he was up again, turned our way. He leaned both elbows on the ledge above our seats, as he did when he really wanted to talk. "I'd do things differently than Rob," he told the four of us, all of whom had opposed Rob Ford's agenda. "I'm not criticizing Rob."

Before the meeting ended, Doug stood and turned again. "What do you think my chances would be?"

"One in three," I told him, thinking that would be good news. Doug clearly had hoped for something better.

"You'll hurt Tory," Mihevc said. Doug brightened.

We then speculated that his entry would take votes from John Tory, perhaps setting up a Doug Ford versus Olivia Chow showdown. Doug turned and sat back down, happier now.

A few weeks later, Doug announced that Rob would be leaving rehab on June 30, to resume the campaign immediately. "The next four months you're going to see a different Rob Ford," Doug predicted.

"Many would argue that this is his last chance," an interviewer offered. "And should he stumble again, it's over."

"I would agree with that," Doug replied, adding that it would be pointless for him to keep close tabs on his brother once he was out of rehab. "If I have to be by his side all the time, obviously the program didn't work."

"So now that he's back running for mayor, I guess you're not," the questioner surmised.

"I never planned on running for mayor," said Doug. "I don't know who wants to start the rumours."

—

"Do you have an earliest memory of Rob?" I asked Doug during a 2014 interview over lunch in the Sheraton Hotel, across from city hall. He knew I was writing a book about Rob and had come to him for brotherly insights.

"Geez, I'd take care of him all the time. We were very close. I'd take care of him all through school. All the time. Anything he needed. I'd work at Canada Packers, go out and buy him skates—not that my parents wouldn't. I'd buy him little hockey cards all the time, you know, with the bubble gum. I'd take care of him."

Doug had an image he wanted to share. "Have you ever seen Charlie Brown and Linus, with the pillow and the blanket?

"Every time I'd come in late at night—sounds crazy, but our family had [only] one fan and it was hot upstairs. And Rob would be in his room and he had the fan. So I'd go in at one o'clock in the morning and pull the fan out of the wall and bring it into my room. . . . He would come in, put his blanket down and lie beside me. I only had a single mattress—we had that same mattress for thirty years—so he'd lie beside me on the floor and he'd share the fan.

"It's just that protective instinct," Doug explained. "Anyone ever touch Rob, I'd tear him apart." Later he added, "I'd sleep on glass for that guy."

—

A 2014 parks opening provided a Polaroid snapshot of how the young Fords might have been in the playground. Spotting a see-saw, Doug, in jeans and a red T-shirt, hopped on one end. Rob took off his suit jacket and climbed on the other, grinning imp-ishly. See-saws are controlled by the bigger kid, but now Rob was the heavier brother. He immediately used his weight advan-tage to lift Doug's end up. Then, hopping up and down, he gave his big brother the bumps.

"You're killing me!" Doug laughed. He got off quickly but immediately sought to restore the balance of power by evoking a wistful childhood memory of two brothers on a teeter-totter. "I'd sit all the way down, he'd be up in the air," he told reporters. "And I'd just jump off and let him go bang."

—

"We've got the whole gang here," Doug Ford remarked approv-ingly as journalists formed a semicircle around a very large industrial scale borrowed from the family company. Trailing Doug out of the mayor's office, Rob Ford looked irritated, glum, in no hurry to participate.

Two dozen journalists had assembled, as they now did every Monday morning, to chronicle the "Mayor Rob Ford Cut the Waist Challenge." The challenge had been Doug's idea, supposedly to raise money for charity. Some who struggled to understand the relationship between the Ford brothers pointed to the challenge as their moment of enlightenment.

The risk of failure in a very public weight-loss competition was evident to at least one of the brothers, the one with the self-discipline to stick to a diet. "When you tell three million people that you're gonna lose weight," Doug had told an interviewer at the Waist Challenge launch in January 2012, "you sure better lose weight." The younger brother, the one with the low self-esteem, obviously hadn't thought this through. Now, on May 8, with only a month left to lose the promised fifty pounds, Doug was upbeat.

First out of the office door, jacket slung across his arm, he paused to slowly fold it and lay it neatly on the ground. Then he began to remove his belt. Rob, who had already done all that, was forced to step past him and go first.

"He must have had a good week," Doug declared, pointing out Rob's eagerness to be first on the scale.

"No, not at all," muttered Rob. "I've had a bad week."

"Oh, he's done *good*," Doug continued.

"Not at all," repeated Rob.

Undeterred by his brother's agitation, Doug continued to express optimism, walking over to the scale as Rob got on. "Three hundred and fourteen!" he announced, as if this was good news.

"Gained four pounds—that's real good, isn't it?" said Rob, brushing past his brother, straight back into his office.

"Is that right?" Doug asked, examining the scale. "Three hundred and fourteen," he repeated, in case anyone missed it the first time. "Maybe he didn't do as good as I thought."

Now it was Doug's turn. He untied the laces of his dress shoes, kicked them off with a flourish and stepped up. "That's not bad, guys—two hundred and forty-seven. So that's twenty-eight pounds total loss. Twenty-eight pounds."

Rob's angry exit had left Doug holding court. "Why won't the mayor answer questions?" a reporter asked.

"I don't know," the brother answered. "I don't speak for the mayor. But if you have any questions, I'll be happy to answer them."

—

Some in the press gallery refused to cover Doug's blatant gimmick to create even more Ford press coverage. But the major media reported for duty every Monday morning, afraid to miss anything.

"It had to be covered," argued David Rider, *Toronto Star* bureau chief at the time. "It was an important episode in this whole weird saga. It was a fascinating window on the dynamic between the two brothers. Doug seemed to really enjoy it, and he seemed to have no problem losing weight. Rob just seemed humiliated. And when he started missing the weigh-ins, that raised all kinds of questions about what he was doing the day before.

"But I was fascinated to see the relationship between Rob and Doug. It seemed to me more an exercise to humiliate the little brother than anything else."

On the day of the first weigh-in, Rob had patted his brother down, checking for hidden weights that would exaggerate his subsequent weight loss. Doug checked in at 275, Rob at 330—which he initially misstated as 229.

"When you were in grade school, you were 229," Doug commented.

With trademark Ford diplomacy, the brothers extended the challenge to other big-city mayors, including the already thin Chicago mayor Rahm Emanuel, New York's fanatically health-conscious Michael Bloomberg, and the more well-rounded Calgary mayor, Naheed Nenshi. "Did they call me a fatty?" Nenshi asked when told of the challenge.

Rob Ford initially dropped eighteen pounds, then started gaining it back. Three months in, he was videotaped going into a KFC outlet and walking out with a large bag. The *Toronto Star* posted the video online and others reported on it. Doug Ford expressed outrage at such mean-spirited behaviour. "He's down twenty pounds, or eighteen, and then the big bully—you guys—come on and start kicking sand in his face on the beach. The guy's trying his hardest—well, maybe not his hardest—but he's trying."

But the whole scenario was too perfect for Doug to resist piling on himself. "The mayor's out getting KFC right now, I guess," he joked on air about Rob's absence from their weekly radio show. Later that week at city hall, I heard him advising someone who was trying to arrange an appointment with the mayor, "Just get a bag of KFC and he'll be there. I guarantee it." On the brothers' Mother's Day radio broadcast that year, Diane Ford called in to reprimand Doug for making fun of his little brother.

By the end of May, a thoroughly discouraged Rob Ford declared a premature end to the Cut the Waist Challenge. He climbed onto the scale one last time, clocked in at 313 pounds, then stumbled off, adding injury to insult by falling into his brother and twisting his ankle.

"Are you coming back to talk to the media?" Doug called after Rob as he hobbled away. Then Doug stepped onto the scale. "Down thirty-five," he announced. "And I couldn't have done it without Rob."

—

When the humiliation of Rob Ford embarrasses the family or tarnishes its brand, Doug Ford is angry, vengeful, quick to launch a counter-assault. But when Rob looks bad and Doug looks good, the older brother might call that a win-win.

"They get on the scale and Doug's losing weight and Rob isn't, Doug *enjoys* that," observed Nick Kouvalis. "If Rob does an interview and doesn't do so well, and then Doug does an interview and does better, Doug *loves* that. Just the fact that he's better than his brother at *everything*. And he loves to show off."

Both brothers speak in canned sentences about their love for one another, dismissing accounts of long-standing jealousy and animosity. "It's laughable," the mayor told *Maclean's* magazine. "Doug's my best friend. We're very tight. Some brothers don't get along. We love each other past the point of love. So when I heard that, like, we called each other up and just literally started howling on the phone."

As with many things Ford, the statement is at once misleading and fundamentally true.

"They'll call each other up after there's been a war and there's blood all over the battlefield, and they'll say, 'We've got to move forward,'" said Nick Kouvalis. "They're like *Vikings*."

—

When statements by former Ford office staff implied the brothers weren't nearly as close as they let on, Doug went on the attack. "The staffers have twisted stories and lied. I don't know how they know my relationship with my brother. I think it's a close relationship. I'd do anything for Rob. I'd jump in front of a bus for him."

I asked Doug Ford what motivated him to put his US business on hold to help Rob get elected. "And that has to do with—"

"Rotary," he said before I could finish.

"Really?" I asked.

"Rotary Club," he repeated. "I've been a Rotary Club member since I was about twenty years old. It's about service above self. That was what our dad drove into us. He was a founding member of the Rotary Club. It's about putting your needs on the back burner and putting other people's needs ahead of yours. I'm a strong believer in service above self. Yeah, I don't care if people know. It has cost me, it has cost our family, millions of dollars of potential growth income."

I told Doug I was about to finish my question with the word "family." When your brother calls for help, is there really any choice?

"Yeah. That's a *huge* part of it," Doug replied. "That's a *massive* part of it, with Rob."

In 2014, Doug wanted to run as a Progressive Conservative candidate in the June provincial election—a first step, he thought, on the road to becoming premier. Amid rumours the party hierarchy wanted to steer clear of the Fords, Doug announced he would pass up the opportunity so he could finish managing his brother's re-election campaign.

So I asked if helping Rob had come at a cost to his own political career.

"Yeah. I don't care. My father made my priority Rob. I know I can take care of everything else. I just gotta make sure I can take care of him."

—

In the time between their father's death in 2006 and Rob's call to Doug in Chicago almost four years later to say he was running for mayor, some say there was major tension between the brothers. "Doug offered immediately to put the swords down, stop fighting, and come and be his campaign manager," Kouvalis said, declining to reveal the source of their discord. "I think Doug saw an opportunity for power for himself."

In July 2010, with Rob coming on strong but by no means certain of victory, a new threat emerged. Encouraged by Toronto's political ruling class, both Liberal and Conservative, John Tory was again considering a run for mayor. Kouvalis asked for a family meeting to share his research. Tory would enter the race nine points ahead of Rob, volunteers would defect and fundraising would dry up, exposing the Fords to a huge campaign debt.

If Tory entered, Kouvalis wanted them to consider a drastic solution: Rob would drop out of the race for mayor and run for councillor again. In exchange for supporting Tory, he'd secure a position of power in Tory's administration and plan to run again for mayor in eight years. Kouvalis's advice wasn't well received by Doug Ford. The two of them got into an altercation that caused Nick to temporarily leave the campaign.

"Doug went ballistic and called me a traitor," said Kouvalis, "and I told him to go screw himself. Doug threatened me and I threatened him back."

Kouvalis went home to Windsor. According to Nick, an olive branch was extended and he soon rejoined the Fords with the title of Chief of Staff to the Candidate for Mayor, Rob Ford—because Doug wouldn't let go of the campaign manager title.

—

Meanwhile, Doug Ford was contemplating an entirely different strategy if Tory entered the race.

"In July, we weren't sure who was running in Ward 2," remembered Kouvalis. "So Doug was waiting, standing by. And at one point he said, 'If Rob can't beat Tory, Rob can run in Ward 2 and I'll put my name in for mayor, and I'll screw Tory over.' He's always talking about being mayor. *Always* talking about how he can become mayor. He was telling me there was no way he wanted to be a city councillor. It was too low of a position for him."

There was talk that Doug's wife, Karla, would run for Rob's old council seat. Or his daughter Krista. Doug kept all his options open until the end of the summer, close to the deadline for filing nomination papers. Then he entered the race himself.

By now it was clear that Tory wasn't a factor and that Rob

was the clear front-runner. Doug set his sights on a new position. "Deputy mayor, that's what he wanted," Nick Kouvalis told me. "There was a big fight about that. The optics were *impossible*, and Doug had no experience with how the place runs. He didn't care. He wanted to be deputy mayor."

After the election, Rob took a break in Florida. "Before he went," according to Kouvalis, "he told his brother, 'You're going to be the deputy mayor.' Then he went to Florida and talked to Doug Holyday and told Holyday *he* was going to be deputy mayor, without checking with any of us. Holyday showed up at our transition team meeting, and that's how Doug Ford found out. He was furious. He stormed out of the room."

What's behind Doug Ford's unquenchable thirst for political power?

"That's how you make a *mark*," observed journalist Dave Nickle. Referring to the family business, he went on, "The thing with labels is that you're always putting somebody else's name on those things. It's a very lucrative business, but there's never *Doug Ford* on those labels unless he's running for office. And there's no way he's going to be able to put a label on a statue or a building or a park that says Doug Ford [unless he becomes mayor]."

"He's got a tremendous desire to be important," Kouvalis said. "I don't know what's driving him. I just know that he really wants to be mayor, that he constantly reminded me that I worked for the Ford family—not Rob Ford—and that every decision had to be put through him, not just on the campaign but even at city hall. So, I think he just wants to show the world that the Fords *can* do this job right. He *can* be the best mayor. That his brother is an idiot. That he can fix it all."

Are Rob and Doug still competing for Dad's approval? For Mom's love? For the attention of the whole wide world? Doesn't Doug always come out on top in any competition between the brothers?

Not always, Kouvalis told me. "Diane always takes Rob's side and says Doug's trying to undermine Rob. Always."

—

On July 18, 2014, Rob Ford was out of rehab and back on the campaign trail. His nephew Michael—his last name now Ford—had entered the Ward 2 race for councillor. Doug Ford was managing Rob's campaign and telling everyone he couldn't wait to get back to the label business in Chicago. Not buying any of it, Nick Kouvalis tweeted: "Rob Ford will run & win in Ward 2—Doug Ford will run & lose the Mayor's race. You heard it here first."

Kouvalis expected the Ford family to eventually decide that this was their best option, perhaps because Rob would fall off the wagon or because Doug had the better shot at mayor and Rob needed to make sure he kept a spot on council.

Nobody imagined it would happen the way it did.

—

Two nights before the election, the familiar "Unknown" appeared on my call display. It was Rob Ford, returning my call to wish him well.

"So what's up, buddy?" he began as usual, ready to talk football and elections. What was I hearing at the doors? It's the first question all politicians ask each other at election time.

I told him the Ford Nation types weren't responding as well to Doug as they had to him. Doug had the business credentials, but he lacked Rob's personal appeal, the authenticity many people saw in him.

"They think Doug's smart," I told Rob. "But they like you better."

"People are saying that. A lot of people have been telling me that, buddy," he said. "I wanted to stay on the ballot. I didn't want to take my name off."

Rob was at his campaign office. In the background, I could hear people calling for him.

"I don't want to be rude," Rob said apologetically. "But I have to go."

22. PARTISAN BRAINS

"He's the most interesting person. He could have a psychologist running around in circles."
Doug Ford on Rob Ford

There were twenty of them, unable at first to recognize themselves in one another. All were male, each identified through a random telephone survey that pulled together only those who shared the belief that Rob Ford was a great mayor.

Describe them to me, I asked Nick Kouvalis, who had brought them together. "You already know, John," he answered. "You've seen them. You've been to Ford events."

Most were middle-aged, overweight, lower-income, blue-collar. At least half would be smokers. They wore T-shirts and running shoes. They believed the elites had been given so much that little was left for them. That sense of unfairness put a chip on their shoulders. Kouvalis was already familiar with how they thought and what their reactions might be. But he needed to test it.

He formed them into two focus groups of ten. The objective was to find out what might convince them to vote for somebody other than Rob Ford. Richard Ciano, his partner, was the moderator. Kouvalis observed from behind one-way glass, closely watching their emotional reactions. Emotion, he knew, drove their political decisions.

"It's all about their upbringing," he said of the rock-solid Ford supporters. "It's all about their fathers treating them like shit. That determines their behaviour going forward. They're not self-aware, so once they've made a decision, they have a hard time admitting they're wrong. That's Ford Nation," he said. "I can't *prove* it, but I know it intuitively."

How does he understand these people so well? I asked, remembering that Kouvalis knew every button to push to attract Ford supporters in 2010.

"*I am* Ford Nation," he said. "If you're a fat kid from Windsor with no degree, you don't speak French and you're a guy's guy, you're not going anywhere. You're cannon fodder." Kouvalis eventually realized he could create his own opportunities. But he remembers how he felt before that.

"Ford Nation inherently has been treated like shit.. That's how they feel. They didn't get their fair share in life. They were rejected. They were deprived of *love* or of something. Fundamental core stuff: love, security, food."

Ciano began each session by asking what the group thought of the mayor. "They're not self-aware enough to know that they're in a room with Ford Nation," said Kouvalis. "So one guy says, 'I kind of like the mayor.' And the next guy thinks, 'He said it, so I can say it too.' So now all of a sudden they're locking arms, they're like the first platoon on the front line. Defending everything. They're feeding off of each other. It was awesome."

Ciano led them through Ford's mistakes, his buffoonish behaviour. Not much reaction. When he got to Rob Ford being under police investigation, they got defensive, then angry, then hostile. "Once they get defensive and once they *feed* on each other, that *mob* thinking sets in," said Kouvalis.

Ciano confronted them with evidence that Rob Ford lied about his drug use.

"That's bullshit!" Ford Nation responded. These folks had so completely identified with Rob Ford that they couldn't cut him loose. They'd made him their hero and had congratulated themselves on making such a smart choice. If Ford had screwed up, Kouvalis explained, so had they. "They don't want to admit it because that means *they* fucked up in *their* life. They had an opportunity and they blew it. They don't want to admit that to themselves.

"I specifically remember one guy saying, 'I don't know if you've *got it*, but this is Ford Nation in this room! I don't want to see any more of this!' I was sitting behind the glass laughing my ass off, texting Richard, *They're going to kill you*."

The second focus group was like the first. Of the twenty participants, not one would move away from Ford. "Not the young black guy who was working on Bay Street, not the guy who was a janitor in Etobicoke. There was nothing John Tory could do to get these guys. No one was getting these guys. They were immovable."

Had Kouvalis ever encountered anything like this before?

"Never," he said.

—

The partisan brain. Diehard Ford supporters are extreme examples of how it works. "Once the partisan brain makes a decision," Kouvalis explained, "it's really hard to admit that it's the wrong decision and change your behaviour. There's a direct correlation with Ford Nationers and people who are really really really immovable once they've made a decision."

Voters with non-partisan brains are the ones who every candidate and political party knows will decide most elections. "They are built in a way that says, 'I'm always learning, so I'm supposed to make mistakes to get better. That's their genetic makeup. Those are the ones that will switch, and those are the ones we're looking for."

Partisan brains seem disproportionately drawn to the Fords, whose own brains are filled with the most partisan of thoughts. "With the Fords, everything is so *extreme*," said Kouvalis. "They will tell a lie and then they'll believe it. And then later *it is the truth and it always was the truth*. There's a segment of the population that's like that."

Among the 47 percent who voted for Rob Ford in 2010, Kouvalis figures, a sizable chunk had partisan brains. By early 2011, after Ford saved them $60 by repealing the vehicle registration tax and then scored a series of other victories that seemed to put money in their pockets, these brains were congratulating themselves. Kouvalis voiced what he was sure was the thinking: "I'm so smart to have voted for Ford. Look what he's done, he's shaken things up. I'm really glad I made that decision."

A highly partisan brain will solidify a thought like that until it becomes permanent, Kouvalis explained. When Ford was caught in a drunken stupor, Ford partisans dismissed his failings because he was such a great mayor. When the faults became more serious, involving hard drugs, they refused to believe it was true.

"Some people did peel away," said Kouvalis. "*But that one-third just stayed*."

—

Doug Ford is at once the most partisan of the Fords and the one most able to reach out to you with ingratiating charm. He makes an intriguing lunch companion, displaying a full arsenal of social skills, moving effortlessly from courteous and friendly to wackily hilarious. He'll win you over with generous words and a megawatt smile, all the while observing your every move, ready to pounce.

It was the beginning of April 2014. Doug knew I was writing a book about Rob. He didn't like that I was poking around, asking questions, and he certainly wasn't looking to help me out. But whatever I was writing, he must have thought, could only improve with a little Doug Ford commentary.

With Doug, there is no awkward silence unless you try to take the conversation over a line he won't follow you across. Then he'll fill the void with a look that says you'd better move on. But if you let him guide the conversation, he'll take you to all sorts of interesting places. He started out by asking about my family, connecting his life to mine by invoking our common experience as fathers.

Doug knew about family togetherness in its many forms. He has four blond daughters, Krista, Kayla, Kara and Kyla. Less than five years separates oldest from youngest. His wife, Karla, is a competitive adult cheerleader—perfect for the guy whose life could never have too much *sis-boom-bah!* The girls have been cheerleaders too, and bodybuilders. For a short time, Krista played a role that seemed custom-made for a first-born Ford daughter: captain of Toronto's short-lived lingerie football team. Doug understood all-consuming family ambition and the compulsory loyalty that connects you, like a tether. He'd seen the pent-up family rage that can blow the lid off a house.

But enough of the niceties. "What's up, buddy?" Doug kicks off the interview. "Let's rock 'n' roll."

I'm interviewing Doug about Rob, but I know that I'll need to get there by starting with him. I ask for his earliest political memory.

"When I was born," he answers. "When I was old enough to sense what politics are.

"Hey, how are you?" he calls out to a passerby. "Good to see you." The waitress arrives. Doug turns to me. "What are you going to have, John?" I order a deli sandwich. Doug has a diet coke and chicken noodle soup.

"Rob trusts everyone," Doug tells me when we finally touch on his little brother. "And you can't trust everyone. Everyone has a lot of motives. I only trust the person I shave in the morning. That's it. And I nick him sometimes too."

Doug trusts me as much as anyone: not at all. He's told others, especially Rob, not to talk to me for this book. But in that paradoxical Ford way, he opens up to me several times, delivering a treasure trove of quips, quotes and colourful stories. Doug is the second most complicated person I've ever met.

About the first most complicated, Doug says this: "As much as he's my brother, I can't figure the guy out. He's the most *interesting* person. He could have a psychologist running around in circles."

"*Both you guys* could have *a team* of psychologists running in circles," I say back. Doug and I share a long and hearty laugh at the image of the bewildering Ford brothers leaving a full squad of psychologists shaking their heads.

If he travelled in different waters, Doug would be King of the Crocodiles, so highly developed is the reptilian part of his brain. When survival instincts set him in motion, he is also able to instantaneously draw from the other cranial areas. The combination creates fascinating results. The *Star*'s David Rider gave me an example. When the police issued a statement that there was no evidence to support Rob Ford's claim that reporter Daniel Dale had trespassed on his property, Rider was watching Doug as he read a message on his phone then walked straight to the press gallery.

"He said Daniel had made a mistake but he was basically a good kid and the Fords were going to give him a break and not going to charge him. I thought (a) that's terribly dishonest and (b) politically incredibly smart. The dynamic that will play on a radio audience is, 'Oh, what great guys the Fords are, they're going to give the kid a break.'

"The reality is that they had no say in whether or not Daniel Dale was charged. But they have a political crocodile brain, a gut instinct for how to turn something to their advantage. I have never seen it before in twenty-five years of covering politics."

———

Doug can seem warm and entertaining one minute, cold and threatening the next. There's charm on his surface, but he is one rock you don't want to turn over. As with Rob, it was difficult to predict Doug's reactions because you never knew what portion of a picture his eyes would go to. He was upset when I contacted his mother by mail to request an interview, an approach I had thought was the one most respectful of her privacy. But Doug congratulated me for my comments to a newspaper in which I offered advice on how to beat the Fords in the upcoming election.

"You nailed it," he phoned to tell me. "You're the only one who understands it." I'd told the *Toronto Sun* that opponents underestimated the Fords at their own peril. I was warning adversaries to be vigilant so the Fords wouldn't win another election. Doug liked the "don't underestimate" part. The biggest rebuke you could give Doug would be to discount him as a force. He seemed not to notice or care about anything else in the story.

"You've never seen the vicious side of me. You watch!" Doug happily confided in that phone call. He relished the thought of taking a bite out of rival mayoralty candidate John Tory. "I'm going to latch on to his ass. He's going to take off the sheets in bed at night and find my teeth wrapped around his nuts."

Despite such enthusiasm, Doug told me he was almost through with city politics. "On October 27, when Rob wins, I'm going to be doing cartwheels down Yonge Street, because I'll be out of this place and on my way back to Chicago." He said the Fords were no longer running a slate of candidates against political backstabbers. "In the end," he said, "everyone is going to be focused on their own survival."

———

Rob Ford was first at the counter when the 2014 Toronto elections office opened at 8:30 a.m. on January 2. "I've been the best mayor the city's ever had," he said, registering to run for re-election. "My record speaks for itself." Ford was again the underdog, a rarity in Toronto politics for an incumbent mayor seeking a second term, though it was the role he was most comfortable with.

John Tory was the next of the three major candidates to enter, registering on February 24. He promised low tax increases and "a different style of government." Olivia Chow launched her campaign on March 13, in the St. James Town neighbourhood where she'd grown up, part of a poor immigrant family. "We really didn't have much. We worked hard and we struggled. And we saved every single penny." Chow, a veteran municipal and federal politician, was the instant front-runner. That position had proven disadvantageous for other early favourites, Barbara Hall in 2003 and George Smitherman in 2010. Chow started with approximately 40 percent support, compared with 25 percent each for Rob Ford and John Tory. The remainder was spread among lesser-known candidates.

As a member of the New Democratic Party and the widow of former federal NDP leader Jack Layton, Chow needed to overcome anti-left sentiment in large swaths of the former suburbs of North York, Scarborough and Etobicoke. She tried to do this by emphasizing her intention to be fiscally prudent.

Kouvalis had joined the Tory campaign early in 2014. As a first step, he polled Toronto citizens to identify what type of mayor they were looking for and how this aligned with the brand attributes of the main contenders. Brand attributes—the characteristics the public sees when it looks at a product or a candidate—are difficult to change without a large and expensive public relations effort. In a municipal election campaign with a tight spending limit, it is generally a poor use of resources to even try. For known politicians, a more strategic approach is to accept that they need to build their campaigns around who people already think they are: to highlight the positive qualities voters already see, especially where this aligns with what voters want to see in a candidate. Perceived negative attributes, or those that don't align, need to be minimized. With opponents, the approach is the opposite: enhance their weakness by placing it alongside your strength.

"Perception is reality. It's hard to change a perception," Kouvalis said. "It's better to go with your strengths and your opponents' weaknesses. Whether it's true is irrelevant. If people believe it, you use it."

Kouvalis's polling found that Ford scored highest on protecting taxpayers' money. Tory scored behind Ford on that point but still high. Chow scored lowest. When she emphasized her intention to be careful with tax dollars, early in the campaign, Kouvalis was delighted. She was trying to change a brand attribute and, even better, one that played to her opponents' strength.

In March 2014, Kouvalis told me that Tory would win by stealing votes from Chow. "Ms. Chow will go against her brand attributes. So if we stay true to ours, we'll win. No one believes she will spend their money carefully. There's only so much bandwidth in an election, only so many messages you can penetrate with, and very little money to do it with. So why spend money telling people something they are not believing to begin with?"

After the election, he said about Chow: "She didn't look authentic. She didn't sound authentic. She didn't sound like she believed what she was saying. It was like jiu-jitsu. We were using her own force against her."

Tory's strongest brand attributes were integrity, honesty, trustworthiness. "He's built that brand his whole life. So that was the foundation we built the campaign on."

—

At the beginning of May, when Ford left the campaign for two months in rehab, there was widespread speculation that he wasn't really getting treatment. He did little to squelch the rumours by telling a newspaper columnist that rehab reminded him of the high-end summer football camp he'd once attended. Eventually, it became known that he was in GreeneStone, an expensive facility in the Muskoka cottage country north of Toronto.

It's another chapter in a story with nothing but hairpin turns, as if some highly imaginative screenwriter was in charge of *The Rob Ford Story*. There are parts you never saw coming, but afterwards they seem intricately woven into the plot.

Rob Ford in rehab could have been written as some sombre affair, full of heartbreaking revelation and hopeful new beginnings. Too clichéd for the unpredictable Rob Ford. It would also miss an opportunity to insert a new female character into a narrative with much too much testosterone. An entire subplot could have been made out of the sad and stormy relationship between Rob and Renata, but writers steered clear, not wanting to involve the children or to create more problems for a woman who tried to keep her marriage and her family out of the public eye.

But a different female character could bring out Rob's vulnerable, naive, cuddly side. They would meet in rehab. She'd be thirty-something, divorced, dirty-blond hair. *Very* outgoing to overcome Rob's basic shyness, and a bit of a tomboy to reduce his discomfort around women. Make her a local country girl, with some country girl name, like LeeAnne. Her last name could be a comical play on Rob's first name. LeeAnne McRobb.

Their relationship would be foreshadowed when they first met. Rob's interest is piqued when she says she has a hunting licence. Cynical big brother Doug tries to warn him she's only interested in the size of his wallet. Might she be hunting *him*? "Go fuck yourself," Rob tells Doug. A woman has come between brothers. Rob and Doug don't speak for three weeks.

City boy Rob is taken by LeeAnne's down-home ways. He calls her his "little buddy" and, in that endearing way that kids tangle common expressions, his "country pumpkin." But their budding relationship is about to be threatened by the outside world from which they've both sought refuge.

LeeAnne's car is smashed up by another rehab patient so Rob loans her his Cadillac Escalade. Next thing we know the OPP is pulling her over for driving it on the wrong side of the road, thoroughly impaired. Ford's car is impounded. Back home, people are asking what the hell is going on up there in rehab!

While big-city journalists chase the scoop, LeeAnne is found by two reporters from Moose FM, a local radio station. One of them is at the pound photographing the Escalade when LeeAnne arrives, all chatty, to collect her things from the vehicle. Where's her watch? she wonders out loud. Must have left it in Rob's room. No, wait. She didn't mean to say that. Forget she ever said that! "I am not a homewrecker," LeeAnne declares.

LeeAnne *owns* her role, but she's taking too much attention away from the central storyline and needs to be written out. GreeneStone discharges her. Back home, in an interview with a Toronto newspaper, she remembers "an experience I will never forget" and the new-found notoriety she says also got her fired from her job. Rob's unintended casualties are piling up.

"It's affecting my life. It's ruining it," LeeAnne McRobb tells a reporter. "I am just a northern girl caught up with these big people."

—

On June 30, ready or not, Rob Ford emerged from less than two months in rehab. He went almost directly to city hall and immediately returned to the campaign trail, just in time for Canada Day.

"For a long, long time, I resisted the idea of getting help," he said from the mayor's office. "Like a lot of people dealing with substance abuse, I was in complete denial. I had convinced myself that I did not have a problem. But it soon became obvious that my alcohol and drug use was having a serious, serious impact on my family, and on my health, and on my job as mayor."

In rehab, Ford continued, "they forced me to confront my personal demons. I learned about things like triggers and what happens when you have uncontrollable cravings. I learned that my addiction is really a disease, a chronic medical condition that will require treatment for the rest of my life."

Then Ford apologized to "every single person who was hurt by my words and my actions." He said he was "blind to the dangers of some of the company I kept, and those associations have ended. My commitment to living clean is now unwavering."

Had he ended there, Ford might have attracted sympathy and forgiveness. Instead, he abruptly transitioned to a campaign speech. "When I was first elected in 2010, I promised to stop the gravy train, and that's exactly what I've done," he said, repeating the familiar list of self-proclaimed achievements. "I look forward to serving you for many, many more years."

The next day, attending a series of Canada Day events, he was greeted by as many boos as cheers. It wasn't an easy reintroduction to everyday life. As he marched in the East York Canada Day parade, with volunteers carrying *Ford for Mayor* placards, he was confronted by a jogger without a shirt. "Answer one of the million questions people have," the man shouted at Ford.

When the man with no shirt made the news, other protesters who wanted media attention took their shirts off too. At one event, a shirtless protest leader was reportedly kicked by Ford's sobriety coach. For a few days, it appeared that the shirtless horde was about to clash with Ford Nation bodyguards. Thankfully, the temperature got cooler and everybody put their shirts back on.

—

Labour Day is the date when Toronto mayoralty races traditionally kick into high gear. Ford had gained in the polls but appeared too damaged to get much more than 30 percent of the vote. Still, with Rob Ford, anything could happen. At the end of August, he gave a speech at the Empire Club to a group of teenaged business prodigies taking part in a five-day Bay Street Boot Camp. Rob told them a story about how you can't keep a good man down.

"The easy part is getting to the top. The hardest part is staying on top. Everyone wants to take a shot. You can tell me, 'Rob, go jump in the lake.' A lot of people told me that. Problem is, I keep swimming back to shore."

As if he already suspected that health would be a factor in his political comeback, Ford said this: "The only thing that can take you out of the race . . . I truly believe, is the person upstairs."

—

On Wednesday, September 10, two days before the deadline for getting a name on or off the ballot in Toronto's October 27 election, Rob Ford checked himself into hospital with extreme abdominal pain. Doug Ford said the two of them were having breakfast together when Rob, who had been noticing the pain for three months, suddenly found it unbearable. By the end of the day, Rob was told he had been walking around with a tumour that was already twelve centimetres by twelve centimetres. A week later, he learned that the tumour was malignant liposarcoma, a rare and aggressive form of cancer.

The city was stunned. Ford Nation had expected him to return from rehab to vanquish all enemies. His opponents had looked forward to Ford being turfed out by the electorate. Before rehab, some thought he might die in office from an overdose, or be killed in a drunken altercation, or that he'd end up in jail. Cancer. Nobody wanted his mayoralty to end that way.

The tumour was to be treated by chemotherapy, radiation and, hopefully, an operation. By the time the diagnosis was official, it had already been decided that Rob wouldn't be running for mayor. On September 12, after the family met with doctors, Doug Ford announced that he would be the Ford family standard-bearer, taking Rob's place on the ballot. Rob would run for councillor in his old Ward 2 seat. Rob Ford's twenty-year-old nephew Michael, who'd been on the ballot for councillor, would withdraw to run for a school board seat.

"He told me he needed me to take the torch while he focuses on getting better," Doug said, pausing to regain his composure. He spoke to the media outside his mother's home, where the family was gathered, absent the hospitalized Rob, his wife Renata and their children. "He told me that he couldn't bear the thought of city hall returning to the old days at the expense of the good, honest, everyday people."

Earlier that day, before the change was official, there had been a mad dash to submit the necessary paperwork before a 2 p.m. deadline.

Peter Leon was the only councillor at city hall at twelve-thirty that day, when Rob Ford's staff went looking for someone to notarize Rob's signature on the papers removing him as a candidate for mayor. Leon signed the document, but the city clerk refused to accept it because Leon hadn't been present to witness Rob's signature. Ford would need to sign again, in front of Leon. There was only an hour left. Doug's papers were in. If Rob's papers didn't get back in time to remove his name from the ballot, there would be two Fords running for mayor.

Though they got to the hospital in record time, Leon and Ford's staff waited more than five minutes for an elevator. When it arrived, a few elderly visitors shuffled on ahead of them. Getting off, they dashed to Rob's room. Diane Ford looked drawn and worried. Rob was pale and tired, confused about what they wanted him to sign—again.

He didn't like any of this.

"He wasn't comfortable with it," Leon told me. "He was restless, I'll put it that way. Very restless. To my mind—and I'll share this with you, John—Rob's heart was not in it. He wanted to be the next mayor and he was doing something here because of circumstances that he had very little choice about. Everybody's rushing trying to get him to sign it because we had to rush back. He was going against his grain, so to speak. That's why he was somewhat anxious.

"We were pretty close to the wire. Of course, we had to wait for the elevator again. The car was waiting at the door. The drive back was very *harrowing*, to say the least. I don't want to tell you how we got to city hall, but we certainly had a guardian angel watching out for us. I won't say how fast we went, or what we did or how we did it. I still dream of it sometimes."

Leon had a staff member waiting at the front door with his notary stamp. The papers were submitted with minutes to spare.

—

Doug Ford jumped into the race with both feet kicking John Tory. A large part of the $900,000 he spent in less than two months of campaigning was for attack ads against Tory.

"What's the story, Mr. Tory?" some began. "In 2003, John Tory ran for mayor and Torontonians said no. In 2007, John ran for premier and Ontario said no. In 2009, John Tory ran yet again for MPP, and guess what? Haliburton said no. It's the same old story, Mr. Tory. The people didn't buy it then, the people won't buy it now. Vote Doug Ford mayor. *Doug* for back-to-basics government. *Doug* for the people."

In debates, Doug painted Tory as a privileged elitist who'd never had to struggle or work hard. The approach was highly effective at drawing back some of the Ford base, especially in underprivileged areas. Tory's support dropped almost ten percentage points, to the low forties. Kouvalis, who had prepped Tory for debates against Rob, now played Doug.

"With Rob, I would be more all over the place. To play Doug, I kept it really *personal*. It wouldn't matter what Tory said, I would say, 'Yeah, well, what do you know about that? You've never had to work for a living. You don't know what the common person is going through. You're an elite downtowner. You've never really earned anything in your life.' I got under his skin pretty good." Tory wasn't accustomed to his character being attacked. It took him a few debates to adjust.

Much of Tory's campaign success was riding on his SmartTrack transit plan, which promised to build a multi-station surface subway line, using existing rail corridors, in just seven years. Chow's downtown relief line would take some ten years longer to complete. Kouvalis wanted to call Tory's plan FastTrack and still believes that one-word change would have significantly increased Tory's vote. "Because the contrast is clearer. FastTrack means Olivia's on slow track. People didn't think John was that much smarter than Olivia, but they thought his transit plan was faster, and all they wanted was relief." Kouvalis was overruled. The Tory campaign would rather be seen as smart than fast.

Another key ingredient in Tory's win was the perception that he was the candidate most likely to beat the Fords. After Rob's return to the campaign, three polls showed Tory moving past Chow into first place. That then caused many anti-Ford votes to move from Chow, their first choice, to the candidate who looked like the likeliest Ford slayer.

On election night, the Ford family gathered in the family home, as they had in 2010. Doug allowed the media in to observe him watching the results on television. Early returns made it appear Doug had a chance. But before long, Tory was clearly the winner, finishing with 40.28 percent to Doug Ford's 33.7 percent and Olivia Chow's 23.15.

Reporters watched the Fords as Nick Kouvalis appeared on the screen to analyze the Ford defeat. "You're watching the Fords watching their former chief of staff criticize their administration. It was one of those moments you feel uncomfortable watching," recalled *Globe and Mail* reporter Liz Church, who was there. "They tried to change the channel in the room, and one of them said, 'We should get going.'" They left for what would have been Doug's victory party.

Rob had easily won re-election in Ward 2. Their nephew Michael, with no political credentials other than his new last name, was elected to the school board.

Doug Ford's second-place showing, in an abbreviated campaign, demonstrated the continued strength of the Ford brand. He did remarkably well in the marginalized northeast and northwest corners of the city. Those people still saw the Fords as their champions. Chow, who'd spent an entire career effectively advocating for the disadvantaged, especially poor newcomers, got only a fraction of Ford's vote among that very demographic.

Even in defeat, the Fords still managed to turn Toronto politics upside down. Anybody who thought the city had seen the last of them hadn't been paying attention.

23. FIVE-YEAR PLANS

"I can't divulge my exact five-year plan. But I have it."
Doug Ford

As I was about to finish this book, Doug Ford told me that the indomitable Fords weren't nearly done creating chapters in this event-filled saga.

"You could write this story four years ago and give it to Hollywood—they wouldn't believe it," he told me in the spring of 2015. "They'd say, 'No, this is too unrealistic.' And it just keeps going—the story. We're only on Chapter 18 in a thirty-chapter story about Rob or our family. Or *myself*. I'm just at the beginning. I'm still young. I'm just at the *beginning* of my career. And *we've got a great future ahead of us.*"

In an earlier conversation, Doug had said he maintained a personal five-year plan that he revised often. I asked for the latest update. Doug spun me a yarn, which I recognized as soon as he applied the Dale Carnegie technique of incorporating my first name into his answer.

"The plan, I would say, John, is to continue serving the people, in whatever capacity, be it another run for the mayor, be it a run provincially, or possibly federally. It all depends."

Doug had succumbed to political ambition, I suggested.

"No, no," he corrected me. "I'm never a politician. I'm just volunteering my time. What *they* don't understand, John, is that people in our area—not unlike *your* area—they put faith in you, and we've built a relationship for thirty years. When one of our family members is down," he said, referring to Rob's upcoming cancer surgery, "it's our obligation as a family to step in."

Doug told me he would be at city hall for four months while Rob was home recovering from cancer surgery. "I'll be Rob's volunteer. I'll serve the people and I'll help Rob. But I'll tell you one thing, buddy, when I go down there for four months, I'm going to be on Tory's ass like *a pit bull*, just *gnawing* away at it. Because there's nobody down there holding this guy accountable.

"The media will come to me in about ten seconds and I'll voice my opinion. As a *citizen*. As an *individual citizen*. It'll be the worst four months of his life. The media told me, 'This is great for us and it will be John Tory's worst nightmare.' I'll be latching on to the back of his ass—*like a pit bull*. And I will *not let go*! You tell him that too. You tell him I'll be on to him like he's never seen before.

"He doesn't know how it is. He doesn't know what we all went through for four years—yourself, myself, the whole forty-four councillors. It was like World War Two down there. It was *relentless* 24/7. He has a free ride right now."

I asked Doug if he really wanted me to tell John Tory that Doug Ford will be gnawing on his ass like a pit bull.

"Tell him, by all means. I'm giving you permission. Just say, 'Doug's coming down here to hold you accountable. And he told me he's going to latch on to you like a pit bull.'"

Back to the five-year plan.

"I can't divulge my *exact* five-year plan," Doug told me. "But I have it."

—

The five-year survival rate for pleomorphic liposarcoma is 56 percent. It is an extremely rare form of cancer, unrelated to an unhealthy lifestyle or drug use. Rob Ford had very bad luck. If you were inclined to search for some positive celestial spin to put on any of this, the cancer treatments helped keep him off drugs.

On a Sunday afternoon in November 2014, I ran across Rob with his mother at city hall. Mom was deciding what to do with the office decorations and artwork before the new mayor moved in. The large photo of Doug Ford Sr. with Mike Harris would go into Rob's councillor's office around the corner. Rob had been in that space from 2000 until 2010. Doug had had it for four years while Rob was mayor. Now it was Rob's again. It was a comfortable size.

On this day, Rob wasn't doing well, physically or emotionally. He was partway through multiple rounds of chemotherapy. The tumour hadn't shrunk yet, so Rob was dispirited, in addition to being sick and tired. He was temporarily out of fight.

"You'll need to get better in time for the Super Bowl," I coaxed him, explaining our football bets to his mother.

"I let him win the games that aren't important, but I always beat him in the Super Bowl," Rob said. "One year, Ma, I just *nailed* it." They both smiled.

Then Rob told his mother about the CD I'd made for him for his birthday. That got the three of us talking music. Diane said she liked Elvis, Sinatra, Pavarotti, and the guy who sang "Sweet Caroline." She and Rob searched for the name of a song they'd liked when Rob was a kid. By Pat Boone's daughter, Diane remembered. "You Light Up My Life," 1977, Debby Boone—it's about Jesus, I said.

"John knows everything about music, Ma," Rob said.

I asked Rob to name his favourite ballad.

"The same as everyone else," he answered. "'Stairway to Heaven.'"

—

Since Rob Ford's return from rehab—but especially after his cancer treatments and surgery—his demons seem to be in remission. In the summer of 2015, I see someone who looks a lot like the authentic Rob Ford. He's more vulnerable now and less afraid to show it. He's more honest and introspective than before. Even behaving badly—when he gets thrown out of a council meeting for maligning a bureaucrat and refusing to apologize— he is so much less angry.

This Rob Ford still wouldn't make a good mayor, but he might have an enduring popularity. Those who disagreed with him before would disagree still, but with much less of that hugely personal negative emotional reaction.

Councillor Joe Mihevc, who recently lost a brother to cancer, spoke with Rob more frequently after his diagnosis. "I think it has humanized him a little. We're looking more in the eyeball. A new space has opened up in him. I think cancer does that." Has he touched the real Rob Ford? I ask. "More than before," Joe says. "But not all the way. I'm not sure he's capable of that."

I asked Doug Ford if his brother is a different guy than he was before the cancer.

"A hundred percent. *A hundred percent.* He is a totally different person," Doug said, not trying to spin this time. "He's taken a few steps back. He realizes the mistakes he's made. It humbles someone when you go through what he's done and all of a sudden you get the death sentence. We're sitting there the other day and waiting for the doctors to come in." Doug is talking about the appointment at which doctors tell Rob they'll try to save his life with a highly risky ten-hour surgery. "It was almost like a stay of execution. But they don't guarantee *anything* when it comes to cancer."

Outside the hospital, at a press scrum Doug had arranged,

Rob was subdued but optimistic. "I'm just lucky to be alive today, and I'm lucky to get another chance at life."

—

After Rob's stint in rehab, Chris Caple already felt a change in the energy coming from the mayor's office. "He just does not have the same malevolent force behind him that was so tangible before. He seems really diminished," he told me that summer. When I contacted him again in 2015, Caple told me he feared the return of either Rob or Doug as a potent political force. "It would be *fantastic*," he said, "if they would content themselves with the label-making industry for the rest of their lives."

—

"The Rob Ford story is about the man who reached the top of the mountain and then threw himself off," said former councillor Mike Del Grande.

What caused that? I asked Del Grande.

"Because he had those demons in his backpack.

"At the end of the day, I feel sorry for Rob. Sad for him. It's a tragic story. The day that he didn't have these demons, he's a fun guy to deal with. He's a magnanimous guy. A big teddy bear. Likes to joke. Likes to talk about football. A really down-to-earth kind of guy. He could have had the city in the palm of his hand—if he didn't have those demons."

—

"People always ask me, 'What's the one question you would ask Rob?'" said Robyn Doolittle, whose journalistic digging uncovered the demons and put them on the front page. "I don't know what Rob sees when he closes his eyes and thinks about Toronto.

He was mayor of the city and I don't know what he thinks about the city. Maybe he thinks it's a CFL game, or the Leafs. Does he picture a quiet Etobicoke cul-de-sac? I'm not even sure he thinks about it in that way."

We talked about how the Rob Ford story ends. "What's happened with his health is just so *upsetting* for him personally and for the city," she said. "It almost felt like Toronto was cheated out of this huge decision it had to make. He can say, 'I didn't really lose the election.' The city never got to have a strong, healthy Rob Ford running against someone else and voting yes or no."

Journalist Jonathan Goldsbie remained eternally fascinated. "There has been as much attention paid to him as is possible for any human being. Yet he still eludes us in every meaningful way. He's just an incredibly fascinating character who drives other people mad trying to understand his madness. No matter how much we scrutinize Ford, there'll never be an answer. But there are enough little bits and pieces to make us want to keep going. Maybe we can get closer to some sort of answer or explanation. I'm under no illusion that it will end."

—

In a long and complex operation on May 11, 2015, doctors removed Rob Ford's tumour. His office issued a statement saying surgeons got all the cancer and declared the procedure a success. On May 26, he was released from hospital with instructions to stay home and rest until September. Instead, Ford told his staff to take him directly to city hall, where he stayed a short time. A few weeks later, he returned for the June council meeting.

He was in obvious pain, especially when he had to sit down or stand up. But when a group of elementary school students waved at him from the public gallery, he slowly and painfully pulled himself up from his seat and made his way over to them, clutching a handful of Rob Ford fridge magnets. "When they get home, they stick them on the fridge and tell their mom and dad," he told me happily. Rob Ford was back.

But where was Doug? He hadn't latched on to John Tory's ass, like he said he would, and he wasn't around city hall during the summer when Rob should have been home recuperating. I wondered whether Rob's quick return had been aimed at freezing Doug out of whatever role he'd wanted to continue to play at city hall. After getting past drug addiction and cancer—for now and, I hope, for good—perhaps Rob was getting ready to confront his demons.

"Doug always had it in his mind that he wanted to be the mayor of Toronto, and Rob always had it in his mind that he would never let him do that," Nick Kouvalis told me in the summer of 2015, when we discussed recent comments made by David Price, the former Rob Ford staffer and old pal of Doug Ford. Price told the *National Post* that, around the time Rob entered rehab, he had agreed to let Doug run for mayor and he would take back his old councillor seat. Price said Rob reneged on the deal.

"Never happened," Doug Ford told me.

Price made it up? I asked.

"Yup. Never happened."

You and Price are buddies, aren't you? I asked Doug.

"Not any longer," he answered. "Lifetime buddies, but not any longer."

I asked him how it will be decided which brother carries the Ford flag into the 2018 election.

Doug answered skilfully. "There's no doubt. Rob's a much better politician than I am. He's the best at customer service, returning calls. That's his livelihood. He loves it. And he'll be a politician the rest of his life."

24. THE ONLY AVERAGE GUY

"Why do people hate me?" Rob Ford asked me on the day before he would learn whether he had a chance to see 2016. He wasn't angry or feeling sorry for himself at a time when self-pity would be totally understandable. He really wanted to understand.

A few minutes earlier, Rob had received the call he'd been anxiously awaiting. Come in tomorrow at two o'clock, his oncologist told him. Make sure your family is with you. "I don't like how that sounds," Rob said. Good news meant a ten-hour operation, followed by two weeks in hospital and months of recovery at home, with the *hope* that the surgery would be successful. Bad news meant the chemotherapy hadn't shrunk the tumours enough to operate and there was nothing they could do for him.

After taking the call, he walked back to his council seat and pushed the red button, voting no on a routine item. I remarked on his ability to hold up emotionally under such unimaginable stress. "What am I supposed to do?" he replied. "I can't go home and cry."

Mortality wasn't all that troubled him this April 1, 2015. At school, kids told his children that worms would soon be eating their father. The cruelty shook him, as if he hadn't examined the dark side of human nature before. "Can you imagine? They get it from their parents.

"People hate me," he said. I told him that some people hated me too. "No," he said. "They *dislike* you. They *hate me*. I don't know why."

I asked Rob if he'd ever heard of a Rorschach test. He hadn't. People look at ink blots and see different things, I explained. What they see says more about *them* than about the splotches on the paper. "You're like the ink blots."

"I see what you mean," he said.

—

After the election, Rob had taken Doug's seat directly in front of me. Unlike his brother, he rarely turned around. I thought maybe he was choosing to be unfriendly. Then, looking at the back of his head during the April 2015 meeting, I realized Rob didn't really know I was there. He was only aware of what was in his field of vision. When I sat down next to him, Rob was happy to talk. We negotiated a wager on that night's Toronto Maple Leafs game against the Tampa Bay Lightning. Rob shrewdly got the better end of the deal. Later, we talked about trying to pick up some tickets. On the eve of the cancer news, Rob saw it as possibly his last chance to take his seven-year-old son, Dougie, to his first Leafs game.

That afternoon, Ford went to a funeral home in Etobicoke to give his condolences to a friend who had lost a close relative. A casket was the last thing Rob wanted to see, but he felt obligated to go. By the time he'd left the funeral home and picked up Dougie, the council meeting was almost over. So he went straight to the hockey game, taking his seat midway through the first period. ROB FORD GOES TO LEAFS GAME, SKIPS COUNCIL DURING

WOODBINE DEBATE, read the headline on a *Toronto Star* online news story. Accompanying it was a large photo of Rob, posing with a fan. The description beneath it read: "Councillor Rob Ford, who was often criticized as mayor for missing votes at Council, was back in the old habit Tuesday night."

In fact, the vote on whether to study expansion of gambling at Woodbine took place while he was at the funeral home, long before the hockey game started. He missed only a few inconsequential minutes of the meeting in order to give his son a lasting memory, just in case. I wanted the people who thought that was the *wrong* decision to have *their* pictures in the paper.

"Well, we can now add Worst Councillor Ever to Worst Mayor Ever," wrote rosedale71 in the comments that accompanied the article. "Not at a crucial council vote? But, but I was at a funeral visitation. No, you were at a hockey game," wrote Frey@99. "All those years he's been going to sporting events . . . never with his son . . . What a selfish creep," another opined.

For the first time, I felt as though I was looking out of Rob Ford's eyes. I was angry at the unfairness of the story and the unkindness of the comments. At the game, Rob had been focused on his young son, asking if he was hungry or needing to use the washroom. When Dougie got tired during the second period, Rob left early to get him home to bed. A regular good dad.

The next day, I told him to ignore the story and the online comments. "I try to, but I can't," he said. "It hurts." Rob talked about how difficult it was that his kids were old enough to understand that he might not be with them much longer. He feared death, but the dread he spoke about that afternoon was all about his kids—that maybe he wouldn't get that second chance to be the father he wanted to be, or that he might relapse into drug addiction. He told me about that awful time in his life when all he could think about was how and when he could get more drugs. "I don't want to go back there," he said. "I don't want to end my life that way. I can't—for my kids."

—

"People either love me or they hate me," Rob said. "There's no in between."

We talked about how, really, everyone is some combination of good and bad.

"I'm just an average guy," Rob said.

I reminded him that he'd once told me there was no such thing as an average guy.

"There isn't," he said, looking around the council chamber. "Where are they? If there's an average guy, then show me one. It doesn't exist."

Before I could point out the contradiction, Rob Ford finished his thought.

"Except me. I'm the only one."

I started to laugh. Rob laughed too. After talking about cancer and death and unkind people, it helped to laugh. But he was serious. "I can relate to everybody," he explained, no longer laughing. "I consider myself a normal, regular, average guy.

"The *only* average guy."

ACKNOWLEDGEMENTS

In December 2013, when I first thought about writing a book on Rob Ford, I wasn't yet sure *how* to tell his story. As I began conducting more than a hundred interviews with seventy-seven different people, it became clear that the story was not *only* about Rob Ford and his *unusual* family—although there was enough material *there* for a book twice this size. His story was also about the reaction he drew from all directions. Each personal response, extreme or otherwise, revealed something about the person making it. As Chris Caple first observed, Rob became a Rorschach test for an entire city.

I talked to those who knew the Fords in earlier years, former members of his staff, bureaucrats, politicians, journalists, protesters, supporters and assorted others who couldn't ignore his behaviour. Most of them agreed to speak with me because they had stories they wanted to tell. The vast majority of those quoted in this book were willing to be identified; of those who asked that their identities be kept private, most had an Etobicoke connection.

One interviewee told me how growing up in a dysfunctional family provoked his aversion to the Fords; another described how the same circumstance shaped his affinity for them. I was raised in a kind and even-tempered extended family—acknowledgement here to my father, mother and aunts ("the Gribbin Girls"). It was that upbringing, I think, that prompted me to want to understand what might have gone missing in Rob's early life.

Not everything I learned found its way into the book. It was difficult to establish firm rules about what was necessary to the story and what should remain private. Generally, I tried to keep wives and children out of it, unless they'd already been pulled onto centre stage. Likewise with anything highly personal from private conversations with Rob, especially from before he knew I was writing a book. When I made exceptions, such as describing Rob being fatherly towards his son at a hockey game I attended with them, or describing him telling me how he wanted to stay straight and healthy for the sake of his kids, it was usually to depict him in a more human, positive way for which I had no other real examples. Had I seen or heard anything negative when Rob invited me along to a hockey game as a colleague rather than as an author, it would not have shown up in print.

I am extremely grateful to Nick Kouvalis and Sheila Paxton for the amount of time they spent with me sharing their insights and setting scenes in great detail. It helped that they were as intrigued by Rob as I am. Particular thanks also to Doug Ford, a sometimes reluctant contributor who, when he felt like talking, spun me captivating stories containing moments of deep truth, often accompanied by astonishing irony. Ted Herriott, one of the people to whom I'd looked forward to handing a signed copy of the book, passed away before it was finished. I only met Ted once, but we spoke many times after that on the phone, and he felt like a new friend.

I might not have embarked on this book, nor have easily finished it, without the support and encouragement of my partner, Anna Maria Tremonti, and the empathetic brilliance of my editor, Anne Collins, who understood the book I was trying to write from the first time I spoke to her about it. Thanks to my children, David and Rachel, for accepting their father's tendency to over-occupy himself with more than one thing at a time, and finally to all the highly supportive staff at Penguin Random House Canada.

INDEX

John Filion has been a member of Toronto City Council since the amalgamated city was formed in 1998. For fifteen of those years, he has known Rob Ford, who sat two seats from him during most of that time. Before entering politics, Filion worked as a journalist, writing feature stories and covering municipal politics. He has chaired many boards and committees, including the Toronto Board of Health for thirteen years. In 2015, he became Toronto's first Arts Advocate.